ADVENTURES OF IDEAS

BY
ALFRED NORTH WHITEHEAD

THE AIMS OF EDUCATION AND OTHER ESSAYS
CONCEPT OF NATURE
AN ENQUIRY CONCERNING THE PRINCIPLES OF
  NATURAL KNOWLEDGE
THE PRINCIPLE OF RELATIVITY WITH APPLICA-
  TIONS TO PHYSICAL SCIENCE
PROCESS AND REALITY. An Essay in Cosmology
RELIGION IN THE MAKING
SCIENCE AND THE MODERN WORLD
SYMBOLISM: Its Meaning and Effect
ADVENTURES OF IDEAS

In Collaboration with Bertrand Russell
PRINCIPIA MATHEMATICA

ADVENTURES OF IDEAS

BY

ALFRED NORTH WHITEHEAD

F.R.S., F.B.A., SC.D., LL.D.

FELLOW OF TRINITY COLLEGE IN THE UNIVERSITY OF CAMBRIDGE
AND PROFESSOR OF PHILOSOPHY IN HARVARD UNIVERSITY

New York
THE MACMILLAN COMPANY
1961

SET UP BY BROWN BROTHERS LINOTYPERS
PRINTED IN THE UNITED STATES OF AMERICA
BY THE FERRIS PRINTING COMPANY

TO
JULIA ISHAM TAYLOR
AND
HENRY OSBORN TAYLOR

*To whose friendship
I owe
So many happy hours*

TO
JULIA ISHAM TAYLOR
AND
HENRY OSBORN TAYLOR

To whose friendship
I owe
So many happy hours

PREFACE

THE title of this book, *Adventures of Ideas,* bears two meanings, both applicable to the subject-matter. One meaning is the effect of certain ideas in promoting the slow drift of mankind towards civilization. This is the Adventure of Ideas in the history of mankind. The other meaning is the author's adventure in framing a speculative scheme of ideas which shall be explanatory of the historical adventure.

The book is in fact a study of the concept of civilization, and an endeavour to understand how it is that civilized beings arise. One point, emphasized throughout, is the importance of Adventure for the promotion and preservation of civilization.

The three books—*Science and The Modern World, Process and Reality, Adventures of Ideas*—are an endeavour to express a way of understanding the nature of things, and to point out how that way of understanding is illustrated by a survey of the mutations of human experience. Each book can be read separately; but they supplement each other's omissions or compressions.

The books that have chiefly influenced my *general way* of looking at this historical topic are Gibbon's *Decline and Fall,* Cardinal Newman's *Essay on the Development of Christian Doctrine,* Paul Sarpi's *History of the Council of Trent,* Henry Osborn Taylor's *The Mediæval Mind,* Leslie Stephen's *English Thought in the Eighteenth Century,* and various well-known collections of letters. While on the subject of literature, I venture to commend to the notice of those interested in an earlier development of English Thought, and also in good literature, the sermons of the Elizabethan and Jacobean divines. Also H. O. Taylor's *Thought and Expression in the Sixteenth Century* presents the currents and cross-currents of thought in those times. The twentieth century, so far as it has yet advanced, bears some analogy to that predecessor in European history, both in clash of thought and in clash of political interest.

In Part II, dealing with Cosmology, I have made constant use of two books published by the Oxford University Press in 1928, namely, *A Commentary on Plato's Timæus,* by Professor A. E. Taylor of the University of Edinburgh, and *The Greek Atomists and Epicurus,* by Dr. Cyril Bailey, Tutor of Balliol College, Oxford.

Use has already been made of some parts of the book in response to invitations which I had the honour to receive. The main substance of Chapters I, II, III, VII, VIII was delivered as the four Mary Flexner Lectures at Bryn Mawr College, during the session 1929-30: they have not been hitherto published. Also Chapter IX, *Science and Philosophy*—not previously published—was delivered as the Davies Lecture in Philosophy, at the Institute of Arts and Sciences, Columbia University, March, 1932. Chapter VI, *Foresight,* was delivered as a lecture at the Harvard Business School, and by the request of Dean W. B. Donham was published as a preface to his book, *Business Adrift,* McGraw-Hill Book Company, Inc., New York, 1931. Also Chapter XVI, *Objects and Subjects,* was delivered as the presidential address to the eastern division of the American Philosophical Association, at New Haven, December, 1931; and has since been published in *The Philosophical Review,* Vol. XLI, 1932, Longmans, Green, and Company, New York.

PREFACE

Some unpublished lectures, delivered at Dartmouth College, New Hampshire, in 1926, embodied a preliminary sketch of the topic of this book. They were concerned with the two levels of ideas which are required for successful civilization, namely, particularized ideas of low generality, and philosophic ideas of high generality. The former set are required to reap the fruit of the type of civilization immediately attained; the latter set are required to guide the adventure toward novelty, and to secure the immediate realization of the worth of such ideal aim.

I am indebted to my wife for many ideas fundamental to the discussion; and also for the great labour of revision of the successive drafts of the various chapters.

ALFRED NORTH WHITEHEAD.

Harvard University
September, 1932

CONTENTS

xi

CONTENTS

PART IV
CIVILIZATION

PART I
SOCIOLOGICAL

CHAPTER I

INTRODUCTION

SECTION I. In its widest possible extension the title of this book—Adventures of Ideas—might be taken as a synonym for The History of The Human Race, in respect to its wide variety of mental experiences. In this sense of the title, the Human Race must experience its own history. It cannot be written in its total variety.

Throughout this book I propose to consider critically the *sort* of history which ideas can have in the life of humanity, and to illustrate my thesis by an appeal to some well-known examples. The particular topics chosen for illustration will be dictated by the arbitrary limitations of my own knowledge, and by the consideration of their general interest and importance in our modern life. Also for our purpose in the book the notion of History includes the present and the future together with the past, affording a mutual elucidation and wrapped in common interest. For the facts in detail we shall be dependent upon that great band of critical scholars whose labours today, and for the past three centuries, lay upon mankind the obligation to deepest reverence.

Theories are built upon facts; and conversely the reports upon facts are shot through and through with theoretical interpretation. Direct visual observation is concerned with the vision of coloured shapes in motion—'questionable shapes'. Direct aural observation is concerned with auditions of sounds. But some contemporary observer of such shapes and noises, for example, some envoy resident at a foreign Court, interpreting the so-called 'bare' facts, states that 'he interviewed the minister of state, who manifested considerable emotion and explained with great clearness the measures with which he would meet the impending crisis'. In such ways contemporary evidence is contemporary interpretation, including the assumption of data other than these bare sensa.

In some subsequent age the critical scholar in accordance with his own theoretical judgments selects from bygone contemporary observations: he criticizes the contemporary observers, and gives his own interpretations of the contemporary evidence. We thus arrive at 'pure history', according to the faith of the school of history prevalent in the latter part of the nineteenth century. This notion of historians, of history devoid of æsthetic prejudice, of history devoid of any reliance on metaphysical principles and cosmological generalizations, is a figment of the imagination. The belief in it can only occur to minds steeped in provinciality,—the provinciality of an epoch, of a race, of a school of learning, of a trend of interest—, minds unable to divine their own unspoken limitations.

The historian in his description of the past depends on his own judgment as to what constitutes the importance of human life. Even when he has rigorously confined himself to one selected aspect, political or cultural, he still depends on some decision as to what constitutes the culmination of that phase of human experience and as to what constitutes its degradation. For example, considering the political history of mankind, Hegel saw in the Prussian State of his date its culmination: a generation later Macaulay saw that culmination in the English constitutional system of his date. The whole judgment on thoughts and actions depend upon such implicit presuppositions. You cannot consider wisdom or folly, progress or decadence, except in relation to some standard of judgment, some end in view. Such standards, such ends, when widely diffused, constitute the driving force of ideas in the history of mankind. They also guide the composition of historical narrative.

In considering the history of ideas, I maintain that the notion of 'mere knowledge' is a high abstraction which we should dismiss from our minds. Knowledge is always accompanied with accessories of emotion and purpose. Also we must remember that there are grades in the generality of ideas. Thus a general idea occurs in history in special forms determined by peculiar circumstances of race and of stage of civilization. The higher generalities rarely receive any accurate verbal expression. They are hinted at through their special forms appropriate to the age in question. Also the emotional accompaniments are partly due to the vague feeling of importance derived from the superior generality, and partly due to the special interest of special forms in which generalities make their appearance. Some people are stirred by a flag, a national anthem; others by the vague feeling of the form of civilization which their country stands for. In most people the two origins of emotion are fused together.

Gibbon's history demonstrates a twofold tale. It tells of the Decline and Fall of the Roman Empire through a thousand years. We see the greatness of that Empire at its height, its military organization, its provincial administration, its welter of races, the rise and clash of two religions, the passage of Greek philosophy into Christian theology. Gibbon displays before us the greatness and the littleness of soldiers and of statesmen, of philosophers and of priests, the pathos, the heroism, the grossness of the general multitude of humanity. He shows us the happiness of mankind and the horrors which it has endured.

But throughout this history, it is Gibbon who speaks. He was the incarnation of the dominant spirit of his own times. In this way his volumes also tell another tale. They are a record of the mentality of the eighteenth century. They are at once a detailed history of the Roman Empire, and a demonstration of the general ideas of the silver age of the modern European Renaissance. This silver age, like its Roman counterpart seventeen hundred years earlier, was oblivious of its own imminent destruction by the impact of the Age of Steam and of Democracy, the counterparts of the Barbarians and of the Christians. Thus Gibbon narrates the Decline and Fall of the Roman Empire and exemplifies the prelude to the Decline and Fall of his own type of culture.

SECTION II. The history of ideas is dominated by a dichotomy which is illustrated by this comparison of Steam and Democracy in recent times to Barbarians and Christians in the classical civilization. Steam and Barbarians, each in their own age, were the senseless agencies driving their respective civilizations away from inherited modes of order. These senseless agencies are what Greek writers sometimes [e.g. in the Timæus of Plato, and passim throughout general literature] call 'compulsion' [ἀνάγκη], and sometimes 'violence' [βία]. They are apt to speak of 'compulsion' when these agencies appear with a general coördination among themselves, and of 'violence' when they appear as a welter of sporadic outbursts. It is one task of history to display the types of compulsion and of violence characteristic of each age. On the other hand, Democracy in modern times, and Christianity in the Roman Empire, exemplify articulated beliefs issuing from aspirations, and issuing into aspirations. Their force was that of consciously formulated ideals at

odds with the ancestral pieties which had preserved
modulated existing social institutions. For example, we
the Christian theologian, Clement of Alexandria, exhorting
his contemporaries to shun custom [συνήθεια]. These
Christian ideals were among the persuasive agencies re-
fashioning their respective ages.

The well-marked transition from one age into another
can always be traced to some analogues to Steam and
Democracy, or—if you prefer it—to some analogues to
Barbarians and Christians. Senseless agencies and formulated aspirations coöperate in the work of driving mankind
from its old anchorage. Sometimes the period of change is
an age of hope, sometimes it is an age of despair. When
mankind has slipped its cables, sometimes it is bent on the
discovery of a New World, and sometimes it is haunted by
the dim sound of the breakers dashing on the rocks ahead.
The Fall of the Roman Empire occurred in a prolonged age
of despair: Steam and Democracy belong to an age of hope.

It is easy to exaggerate the contrast between these two
kinds of ages of transition. It all depends upon the surviving records. Whose feelings do they express? After all,
even during the worst period of the decline of Rome the
barbarians were enjoying themselves. To Attila and his
hordes their incursion into Europe was an enjoyable episode
diversifying the monotonous round of a pastoral life. But
we have preserved for us hymns and ejaculations of senti-
nels in North Italian towns as they paced the walls amid
the gathering gloom of a winter's night:—'From the fury
of the Huns, Good Lord deliver us.' In this instance it seems
easy to discriminate; barbarism and civilization were at
odds with each other, and we stand for civilization. I waive
the point that we now know something about the social
state of central Asia at that epoch, and that the imagination

of a sentinel on the walls of Padua or Aquileia was not quite adequate in its presentation of the Huns.

In every age of well-marked transition there is the pattern of habitual dumb practice and emotion which is passing, and there is oncoming of a new complex of habit. Between the two lies a zone of anarchy, either a passing danger or a prolonged welter involving misery of decay and zest of young life. In our estimate of these agencies everything depends upon our standpoint of criticism. In other words, our history of ideas is derivative from our ideas of history, that is to say, upon our own intellectual standpoint.

Mankind is not wholly dumb, and in this respect it differs from other races of animals. Yet in the history of the world of animals even among the ancestors of men, there have been transitions of patterns of habit which exemplify a history of forms of behaviour devoid of any contemporary intellectual expression, either in the form of antecedently expressed purpose or in the form of subsequently expressed reflection. For example, at a remote period urged by the growth of forests some mammals ascended trees and became apes; and then later, after the lapse of some vast period, urged by the decay of forests, the same race descended from trees and became men.

We have here history on its senseless side, with its transitions pushed forward either by rainfall and trees, or by brute barbarians, or by coal, steam, electricity and oil. Yet even the senseless side of history refuses to accept its own proper category of sheer senselessness. The rainfall and the trees are items in a majestic order of nature: Attila's Huns had their own intellectual point of view in some respects surprisingly preferable to that of the degenerate Romans: the age of coal and steam was pierced through and through by the intellectual abilities of particular men who urged forward the transition. But finally, with all this qualification, rainfall and Huns and steam-engines represent brute necessity, as conceived in Greek thought, urging forward mankind apart from any human conception of an end intellectually expressed. Fragmentary intellectual agencies coöperated blindly to turn apes into men, to turn the classic civilization into mediaeval Europe, to overwhelm the Renaissance by the Industrial Revolution. Men knew not what they did.

SECTION III. The fragment of human history, upon which this book is concentrated, is concerned with the transmission of civilization from the Near East to Western Europe. The topic is limited to the story of the energizing of two or three main ideas, whose effective entertainment constitutes civilization. These ideas are traced in outline from their status in the ancient world of the Near East up to the present time. The boundaries of a civilization are indefinite, whether we are speaking of geography or of time, or of essential character. This vagueness more especially characterizes the eastern boundaries of Western Europe, and the boundaries of the Near East. Also these boundaries fluctuate as the centuries pass. In its latest phase of brilliance the Near East touched the Atlantic Ocean. But during its earlier period of greatness, before the age of the Greeks, it stretched from the Nile Valley to Mesopotamia, and from the Indian Ocean to the Euxine and the Caspian Seas. It also penetrated into the Ægean Basin, and later into the Western Mediterranean. But the Near East is only important for this discussion in its function of the origin and the background of modern Europe.

The whole point of the present enquiry is to demonstrate those factors in Western civilization which jointly constitute a new element in the history of culture. Of course no novelty is wholly novel. Factors which were present sporadically and as the dreams of individuals, or as a faint tinge upon other modes of mentality, received a new importance in the later civilization of Europe. The question is to understand how the shift of emphasis happened, and to recognize the effects of this shift upon the sociology of the Western World. In this way we obtain some presuppositions of thought which the detailed criticism of modern sociological development requires. We can then discern the status of the impulses which are driving forward the World of mankind.

In the story of this transmission of civilization from East to West, the Hebrew, the Hellenic, and the Hellenistic epochs can, with equal reason, be considered together, *either* as outposts of the Near East in the process of differentiating itself into the first phase of European mentality, *or* as the earliest groups of Europeans to receive the torch and successfully to assert their spiritual independence. Between them, the Hebrews and the Greeks introduced into Europe, and into the latest phase of the Near East, notions concerning the status of mankind in general, and of individual men in particular, and a discipline and direction in the general exercise of mentality, which in their combination have started the modern phase of progress within the European races. The first part of this book is occupied with the most general aspect of the sociological functions arising from, and issuing into, ideas concerning the human race; and the second part is concerned with modern cosmological principles which also are the outcome of ancient Greek and Hebrew thought. A simple-minded interest in ideas with one or other of these two types of generality is the main source from which mankind acquires novelty of outlook.

CHAPTER II

THE HUMAN SOUL

SECTION I. In any human society, one fundamental idea tingeing every detail of activity is the general conception of the status of the individual members of that group, considered apart from any special preëminence. In such societies as they emerge into civilization, the members recognize each other as individuals exercising the enjoyment of emotions, passions, comforts and discomforts, perceptions, hopes, fears, and purposes. Also there are powers of intellectual understanding involving discrimination of details of characters, judgments of 'true or false', and of 'beautiful or ugly', and of 'good or bad'. We pass our lives vaguely and flittingly entertaining groups of such experiences, and we attribute like ways of existence to others.

But in the early stages of civilization such experiences and beliefs are mere matters of course. They provoke no abrupt reflective reaction isolating them for thoughtful inspection. Accordingly there is no modification of habit arising from the valuation of human beings as such. Thus the various members of a society find themselves cherishing each other, destroying, obeying or commanding, as the case may be. There is a communal organization, and there are beliefs about it slowly forming themselves into explanations.

We are to discuss the later phases when civilization has reached its modern height, a period of three thousand years at the most. Thinkers have now arisen. The notion of duty has dawned and received some definition. Above all the notion of a psyche,—that is, of a mind—has dawned. In its first phase of gradual emergence, this great notion was instinctively used as a master-key to make intelligible the baffling occurrences of nature. The two most obvious characteristics of Nature, writes Lytton Strachey,[1] are loveliness and power. The beauty dawned later upon human intelligences than did its power. Also in early phases of thought the powers of nature became the minds of Nature—minds bestial, ruthless, and yet placable. In all stages of civilization the popular gods represent the more primitive brutalities of the tribal life. The progress of religion is defined by the denunciation of gods. The keynote of idolatry is contentment with the prevalent gods.

The factor in human life provocative of a noble discontent is the gradual emergence into prominence of a sense of criticism, founded upon appreciations of beauty, and of intellectual distinction, and of duty. The moral element is derivative from the other factors in experience. For otherwise there is no content for duty to operate upon. There can be no mere morality in a vacuum. Thus the primary factors in experience are first the animal passions such as love, sympathy, ferocity, together with analogous appetitions and satisfactions; and secondly, the more distinctly human experiences of beauty, and of intellectual fineness, consciously enjoyed. Here the notion of intellectual distinction, or of fineness, is somewhat broader than that of 'truth', which is ordinarily cited in this connection. There is a grandeur of achievement in the delicate adjustment of thought to thought, which is independent of the mere blunt question of truth. We may term it 'beauty'. But intellectual beauty, however capable of being hymned in terms relevant

[1] Cf. *Books and Characters,* Chapter on 'The Poetry of Blake'.

to sensible beauty, is yet beautiful by stretch of metaphor. The same consideration applies to moral beauty. All three types of character partake in the highest ideal of satisfaction possible for actual realization, and in this sense can be termed that beauty which provides the final contentment for the Eros of the Universe.

For European thought, the effective expression of this critical discontent, which is the gadfly of civilization, has been provided by Hebrew and Greek thought. Its most adequate expression, so far as concerns literary delicacy and definition of the issues involved, is to be found in Plato's dialogues. We there find him criticizing the customary gods of the poets—indeed he would banish all poets—, and analyzing the capacities latent in the human soul. The religion of Plato is founded on his conception of what a God can be, with gaze fixed upon forms of eternal beauty; and his sociology is derived from his conception of what man can be, in virtue of a nature, which for its full description requires terms applicable to the nature of gods. Between them, the Hebrews and the Greeks provided a program for discontent. But the value of their discontent lies in the hope which never deserted their glimpses of perfection.

SECTION II. The intellectual agencies involved in the modification of epochs are the proper subject of this book. When we examine them we find a rough division into two types, one of general ideas, the other of highly specialized notions. Among the former, there are the ideas of high generality expressing conceptions of the nature of things, of the possibilities of human society, of the final aim which should guide the conduct of individual men. In each age of the world distinguished by high activity there will be found at its culmination, and among the agencies leading to that culmination, some profound cosmological outlook, implicitly accepted, impressing its own type upon the current springs of action. This ultimate cosmology is only partly expressed, and the details of such expression issue into derivative specialized questions of violent controversy. The intellectual strife of an age is mainly concerned with these latter questions of secondary generality which conceal a general agreement upon first principles almost too obvious to need expression, and almost too general to be capable of expression. In each period there is a general form of the forms of thought; and, like the air we breathe, such a form is so translucent, and so pervading, and so seemingly necessary, that only by extreme effort can we become aware of it.

In order to find an example capable of ready expression, we must descend below the utmost generality. In the region of political theory, consider the divergence of outlook in the classical Mediterranean civilization. Think of the differences between Pericles and Cleon, Plato and Alexander the Great, Marius and Sulla, Cicero and Cæsar. Yet they all agreed in one fundamental notion which lies at the base of all political theory. Throughout the Hellenic and Hellenistic Roman civilizations—those civilizations which we term 'classical'—it was universally assumed that a large slave population was required to perform services which were unworthy to engage the activities of a fully civilized man. In other words in that epoch a civilized community could not be self-sustaining. A comparatively barbarous substratum had to be interwoven in the social structure, so as to sustain the civilized apex. This assumption that a complex urban civilization requires a base of slavery was so universal, both in practice and in implicit presuppositions, that we may assume it to be derived from some well-founded reason in the conditions permitting the formation of the earlier phases of civilized life. The Egyptians wanted bricks, so they captured the Hebrews.

The confusion of tongues associated with the tower of Babel may be historically doubtful in the form of the surviving legend: it is at least well-found as a reference to the confusion of races amid the slave populations supplying the mechanized man-power for the building of cities.

Now in respect to the political factions of the ancient world nothing has yet been settled. Every problem which Plato discusses is still alive today. Yet there is a vast difference between ancient and modern political theories. For we differ from the ancients on the one premise on which they were all agreed. Slavery was the presupposition of political theorists then; Freedom is the presupposition of political theorists now. In those days the penetrating minds found a difficulty in reconciling their doctrine of slavery to certain plain facts of moral feeling and of sociological practice; and in these days our sociological speculations find a difficulty in reconciling our doctrine of freedom to another group of plain facts, perplexing, irreconcilable, only to be conceived as a hateful brute necessity. Yet, when all such qualifications have been made, Freedom and Equality constitute an inevitable presupposition for modern political thought, with an admixture of subsequent lame qualification; while Slavery was a corresponding presupposition for the ancients, with their admixture of lame qualification. For both sets of thinkers God has been a great resource: a lot of things, which won't work on Earth, can be conceived as true in his sight. Ancients and Moderns in respect to this question face in directly opposite directions.

SECTION III. This growth of the idea of the essential rights of human beings, arising from their sheer humanity, affords a striking example in the history of ideas. Its formation and its effective diffusion can be reckoned as a triumph —a chequered triumph—of the later phase of civilization.

We shall find out how general ideas arise and are diffused, if we examine the sort of history which belongs to this particular instance.

The great classical civilization is remarkable for two facts. First, it constituted a culmination of slavery, especially at the height of the Roman Empire. At that moment slavery reached its height, in necessity, in quantity, in horror, and in danger. In earlier, simpler communities slavery may have been conceived as an accidental mercy, a favour granted to a few fortunate communities or to a few fortunate individuals within any community. But for a thousand years of the classical civilization, to be civilized was to be a slave-owner. Some slave-owners were kind, some were brutal: probably, they were mostly mediocre. In Plato's Symposium Agathon, the host, is represented with a uniform well-bred kindliness both towards his slaves and his guests. Cicero and the younger Pliny exhibit themselves in their Letters as kindly masters. But on the whole the Roman capitalists with their vast estates exemplify the necessity for ancient civilization that it be built upon iniquity. Efficiency spelt Brutality. When such evils culminate, either they are corrected by the introduction of some new principle, or they destroy society. In the case of the classical civilizations, these alternatives were not exclusive: they both happened.

We now come to the second fact for which the classical period was remarkable. It was the first period which introduced moral principles forming an effective criticism of the whole system. The Athenians were slave-owners: but they seem to have humanized the institution. Plato was an aristocrat by birth and by conviction, also he must have owned slaves. But it is difficult to read some of his Dialogues without an uneasy feeling about the compulsory degradation of mankind. Also the Stoic lawyers of the Roman Empire in-

troduced a legal reformation largely motived by the principle that human nature has essential rights. But neither the
humane slave-owners, nor the inspired Plato, nor the clear-
headed lawyers, initiated any campaign against slavery.
They accepted it as a matter of course. It was presupposed
in the very structure of society; and such necessity limits
the scope of all generalities. Distinctions were introduced,
the sort of distinctions which are conclusive so long as you
know that in practice you have got to accept them.

We see here the first stage of the introduction of great
ideas. They start as speculative suggestions in the minds of
a small, gifted group. They acquire a limited application to
human life at the hands of various sets of leaders with
special functions in the social structure. A whole literature
arises which explains how inspiring is the general idea, and
how slight need be its effect in disturbing a comfortable
society. Some transition has been produced by the agency
of the new idea. But on the whole the social system has
been inoculated against the full infection of the new principle. It takes its place among the interesting notions which
have a restricted application.

But a general idea is always a danger to the existing
order. The whole bundle of its conceivable special embodiments in various usages of society constitutes a program of
reform. At any moment the smouldering unhappiness of
mankind may seize on some such program and initiate a
period of rapid change guided by the light of its doctrines.
In this way, the conception of the dignity of human nature
was quietly energizing in the minds of Roman officials,
producing somewhat better government and nerving men
like Marcus Aurelius to rise to the height of their appointed
task. It was a worthy moral force, but society had been
inoculated against its revolutionary application. For six hun-

dred years, the ideal of the intellectual and moral grandeur of the human soul had haunted the ancient Mediterranean world. It had in a way transformed the moral ideas of mankind: it had readjusted religions: and yet it had failed to close with the basic weakness of the civilization in which it flourished. It was the faint light of the dawn of a new order of life.

SECTION IV. In the midst of this period of progress and decadence, Christianity arose. In its early form it was a religion of fierce enthusiasm and of impracticable moral ideals. Luckily these ideals have been preserved for us in a literature which is almost contemporary with the origin of the religion. They have constituted an unrivalled program for reform, which has been one element in the evolution of Western civilization. The progress of humanity can be defined as the process of transforming society so as to make the original Christian ideals increasingly practicable for its individual members. As society is now constituted a literal adherence to the moral precepts scattered throughout the Gospels would mean sudden death.

Christianity rapidly assimilated the Platonic doctrine of the human soul. The philosophy and the religion were very congenial to each other in their respective teachings; although, as was natural, the religious version was much more specialized than the philosophic version. We have here an example of the principle that dominates the history of ideas. There will be a general idea in the background flittingly, waveringly, realized by the few in its full generality—or perhaps never expressed in any adequate universal form with persuasive force. Such persuasive expression depends on the accidents of genius; for example, it depends on the chance that a man like Plato appears. But this general idea, whether expressed or implicitly just below the surface of conscious-

ness, embodies itself in special expression after special expression. It condescends so as to lose the magnificence of its generality, but it gains in the force of its peculiar adaptation to the concrete circumstances of a particular age. It is a hidden driving force, haunting humanity, and ever appearing in specialized guise as compulsory on action by reason of its appeal to the uneasy conscience of the age. The force of the appeal lies in the fact that the specialized principle of immediate conduct exemplifies the grandeur of the wider truth arising from the very nature of the order of things, a truth which mankind has grown to the stature of being able to feel though perhaps as yet unable to frame in fortunate expression.

The greatness of Christianity—the greatness of any valuable religion—consists in its 'interim ethics'. The founders of Christianity and their earlier followers firmly believed that the end of the world was at hand. The result was that with passionate earnestness they gave free reign to their absolute ethical intuitions respecting ideal possibilities without a thought of the preservation of society. The crash of society was certain and imminent. 'Impracticability' was a word which had lost its meaning; or rather, practical good sense dictated concentration on ultimate ideas. The last things had arrived: intermediate stages were of no account.

This consideration was of more influence in framing the mentality of the earlier followers than in the initial foundation of the religion. It enabled these followers to transmit in their full purity the primitive notions. But the religion arose in a more tranquil atmosphere although highly sensitive in regard to religious emotion, and with some admixture of apocalyptic belief. The Galilean peasantry, having regard to their climate and simplicity of life, were neither rich nor poor: they were unusually intellectual for a peasantry, by reason of their habits of study of historical and religious records: they were protected from disturbance, from within or from without, by the guardian structure of the Roman Empire. They had no responsibility for the maintenance of this complex system. Their own society was of the simplest; and they were ignorant of the conditions by which the Empire arose, of the conditions requisite for its efficiency, and of the conditions necessary for its preservation. They were ignorant even of the services which the Empire was rendering them. The alternation of procurators was like that of the seasons, some were better and some were worse; but all alike, seasons and procurators of Judaea, issued from an inscrutable order of things.

The tone of life of this peasantry provided an ideal environment in which concepts of ideal relations between rational beings could be formulated—concepts devoid of ferocity, concepts gracious, kindly, and shrewd, concepts in which mercy prevailed over judicial classification. In this ideal world forgiveness could be stretched to seventy times seven, whereas in the real world of the Herods and the Roman Empire a sevenfold forgiveness touched upon the impracticable. But the Galilean people were unconcerned with the discipline of the Roman legions, with the imperial inspection of the doings of proconsuls, and with the complexities of a legal system which was to impose an order upon multitudinous transactions, stretching from the hills of Scotland to the marshes of Mesopotamia. A gracious, simple mode of life, combined with a fortunate ignorance, endowed mankind with its most precious instrument of progress—the impracticable ethics of Christianity.

A standard had now been created, expressed in concrete illustrations foolproof against perversions. This standard is a gauge by which to test the defects of human society. So

long as the Galilean images are but the dreams of an unrealized world, so long they must spread the infection of an
uneasy spirit.

SECTION V. In ethical ideals we find the supreme example
of consciously formulated ideas acting as a driving force
effecting transitions from social state to social state. Such
ideas are at once gadflies irritating, and beacons luring, the
victims among whom they dwell. The conscious agency of
such ideas should be contrasted with senseless forces, floods,
barbarians, and mechanical devices. The great transitions
are due to a coincidence of forces derived from both sides
of the world, its physical and its spiritual natures. Mere
physical nature lets loose a flood, but it requires intelligence
to provide a system of irrigation.

The ethical ideas, embodied in the great religions, Christianity for instance, though representing a high approach to
final generality, are yet specializations of the Platonic generality. Partly these ethical intuitions are a direct application of metaphysical doctrine for the determination of practice. The ethical principle is then a parable illuminating the
superior generality on which it depends. Thus the codes of
all religions also embody the particular temperaments and
stages of civilization of their adherents. No religion can be
considered in abstraction from its followers, or even from
its various types of followers. Religious ideas represent
highly specialized forms of general notions. Sometimes
these specializations are concrete embodiments with peculiar beauty and aptness: sometimes they are the result of a
throw back to barbaric brutality. Neither religions nor individual men demonstrate their sanctity by their ejaculations. We find however this whole bundle of more special
notions, legal, political, ethical, religious, driving forward
human life, and deriving a force of grandeur from their

various exemplifications of the mystery of the human soul in its journey toward the source of all harmony. It is a story of crime, misunderstanding, profanation. Great ideas enter into reality with evil associates and with disgusting alliances. But the greatness remains, nerving the race in its slow ascent.

In the Middle Ages institutional Christianity was honourably distinguished as a driving force toward the grander intuitions. Unfortunately, in accordance with the habits of all institutions, it adapted itself to its environment. It became an instrument of conservation instead of an instrument of progress. After a short period of progressive energy, the Reformation Churches again accepted the same idolatrous rôle. On the whole, well-established religious institutions are to be reckoned among the conservative forces of society. They soon become the grand support of what Clement had termed 'communal custom'. But the ultimate ideals, of which they profess themselves the guardians, are a standing criticism of current practices.

Accordingly the next resurgence of the notion of the essential greatness of the human soul is associated with the sceptical humanitarianism of the eighteenth century. We have arrived at the Age of Reason and the Rights of Man. This great French age of thought has remade the presuppositions of the civilized world, in speculation, in science, and in sociological premises. It was derived from the English thought of the seventeenth century, Francis Bacon, Isaac Newton, and John Locke. Also it gained inspiration from the English revolutions of the same epoch. But the English modes always retained the note of insularity. The French broadened, clarified, and universalized. They thus made world-wide, ideas which such a man as Edmund

Burke could only grasp in their application to one race, and even at times to one island.

But the thought of John Locke survived also in England. Its influence was reinforced by the general pride in the doctrines of freedom embodied in the English Common Law. There was thus a Whiggish tinge even to Tory Parliaments in those days. In this way the British Government was the first government to make effective two decisive steps in the abolition of slavery. Two parliaments determined the new policies. They were composed of aristocratic landowners and evangelical bankers and merchants, one parliament Tory and the other Whig. The first step was the abolition of the British slave-trade in 1808, and the second step was the purchase and freeing of all slaves in the British Dominions in the year 1833. This latter operation cost twenty million pounds at a time of grave financial difficulty.

But the problem was comparatively simple for the English people. None the less this action constituted a foretaste of the final triumph of that same wavering alliance of philosophy, law, and religion which had its first success in the reforms of the Roman Imperial system. We notice that a great idea in the background of dim consciousness is like a phantom ocean beating upon the shores of human life in successive waves of specialization. A whole succession of such waves are as dreams slowly doing their work of sapping the base of some cliff of habit: but the seventh wave is a revolution—'And the nations echo round'. In the last quarter of the eighteenth century, Democracy was born, with its earliest incarnations in America and in France; and finally it was Democracy that freed the slaves. In the modern world, Democracy has a deeper import than among the ancients. At last, in the nineteenth century, the fundamental question of slavery has been explicitly faced. In Europe, it was already a decaying institution, slowly withdrawing from slavery to serfdom, from serfdom to feudalism, from feudalism to aristocracy, from aristocracy to legal equality, from legal equality to careers effectively open to talent. But the question was assuming a new and menacing form by reason of the impact of the European and Arabian races upon the African tribes.

So modern Democrats, in the nineteenth century, nerved themselves to face the question of Slavery, explicitly and with thoroughness. The slow working of ideas is thereby illustrated. Two thousand years had elapsed since the foundation of Plato's Academy, since the reforms of the Stoic lawyers, since the composition of the Gospels. The great program of reform bequeathed by the classical civilization was achieving another triumph.

SECTION VI. The slow issue of general ideas into practical consequences is not wholly due to inefficiency of human character. There is a problem to be solved, and its complexity is habitually ignored by impetuous seekers. The difficulty is just this:—It may be impossible to conceive a reorganization of society adequate for the removal of some admitted evil without destroying the social organization and the civilization which depends on it. An allied plea is that there is no known way of removing the evil without the introduction of worse evils of some other type.

Such arguments are usually implicit. Even the wisest are unable to conceive the possibility of untried forms of social relations. Human nature is so complex that paper plans for society are to the statesman not worth even the price of the defaced paper. Successful progress creeps from point to point, testing each step. It is not difficult to frame the sort of defence that Cicero would have advanced, if challenged on the question of slavery. The Roman Government, he would have said, is the one hope for the human race. Destroy Rome; and Where will you find the firmness of the Roman Senate, the discipline of its legions, the wisdom of its lawyers, the restraints upon misgovernment, the appreciative protection of Greek learning? But he would not have said this. His genius would have risen to prophecy, and he would have foreseen and quoted the lines of Virgil on the mission of the Eternal City.

In fact, we do know exactly the stand taken upon this very question by the lawyers, Pagan and Christian, and by the bishops and popes, of the five centuries succeeding Cicero. Among them were statesmen with more than Cicero's practical sagacity, and his equals in moral sensibility. They introduced careful legal restraints upon the powers of the masters; they protected some of the essential rights of slaves. But they preserved the institution. Civilization, Hellenic and Roman, was preserved intact for more than seven centuries after the death of Plato. The slaves were the martyrs whose toil made progress possible. There is a famous statue of a Scythian slave sharpening a knife. His body is bent, but his glance is upward. That figure has survived the ages, a message to us of what we owe to the suffering millions in the dim past.

We may ask, Would Rome have been destroyed by a crusade for the abolition of slavery in the time of Cicero or in the time of Augustus? Throughout the whole period of classical civilization the foundations of social order could scarcely sustain the weight upon them—the wars between states, the surrounding barbarians, the political convulsions, the evils of the slave system. In the age from the birth of Cicero to the accession of Augustus to undisputed power, the whole structure almost collapsed, before it had finished its appointed task. Even earlier, it had nearly met its fate, and later by a few centuries came the final collapse. It is impossible to doubt the effect of any vigorous effort for the immediate abolition of the only social system that men knew. It may be better that the heavens should fall, but it is folly to ignore the fact that they will fall.

Suppose that, in the middle of the nineteenth century, the shock that overwhelmed the Confederate States in the American Civil War had equally overwhelmed the whole of North America and the whole of Europe. The sole hope of progressive civilization would have been lost. We may speculate about a recovery, but of that we know nothing. In the ancient world, the dangers were immeasurably greater.

SECTION VII. The argument of the previous section can be generalized. It amounts to this:—that the final introduction of a reform does not necessarily prove the moral superiority of the reforming generation. It certainly does require that that generation exhibits reforming energy. But conditions may have changed, so that what is possible now may not have been possible then. A great idea is not to be conceived as merely waiting for enough good men to carry it into practical effect. That is a childish view of the history of ideas. The ideal in the background is promoting the gradual growth of the requisite communal customs, adequate to sustain the load of its exemplification.

Many factors contributed to the final inversion of sociological theory, from the presupposition of slavery to the presupposition of freedom. The chief factor has already been mentioned, namely, the sceptical, humanitarian movement of the eighteenth century, of which Voltaire and Rousseau were among the chief exponents, and the French Revolution the culmination.

Thus in a sense, and more especially when we consider the whole world-wide movement, religion was in the background. But in one section of this stirring of mankind the religious motive was among the chief agencies. Throughout the Anglo-Saxon world, English and American, the Wesleyan protestant revival was in full activity. It had been reserved for a great French historian, Elie Halévy, to point out the full sociological significance of this episode. The Methodist preachers aimed at saving men's souls in the next world, but incidentally they gave a new direction to emotions energizing in this world. The movement was singularly devoid of new ideas, and singularly rich in vivid feelings. It is the first decisive landmark indicating the widening chasm between the theological tradition and the modern intellectual world. From the earliest Greek theologians to Jerome and Augustine: from Augustine to Aquinas: from Aquinas to Luther, Calvin, and Suarez: from Suarez to Leibniz and John Locke: every great religious movement was accompanied by a noble rationalistic justification. You may disagree with the theologians—indeed it is impossible to agree with all of them—but you cannot complain that they have been unwilling to indulge in rational argument. The Middle Ages argued, Luther defended ninety-seven theses, Calvin produced his Institute, the Council of Trent argued on and off for eighteen years, the judicious Hooker argued, at the Synod of Dort Arminians and Calvinists argued.

The great Methodist movement more than deserves the eulogies bestowed on it. But it can appeal to no great intellectual construction explanatory of its modes of understanding. It may have chosen the better way. Its instinct may be sound. However that may be, it was a notable event in the history of ideas when the clergy of the western races began to waver in their appeal to constructive reason. More recently scientists and critical philosophers have followed the Methodist example.

In an age of aristocracy in England, the Methodists appealed to the direct intuitions of working men and of retail traders concerned with working men. In America they appealed to the toiling, isolated groups of pioneers. They brought hope, fear, emotional release, spiritual insight. They stemmed the inroads of revolutionary ideas. Also, allowing for many qualifications, they must be credited with one supreme achievement. They made the conception of the brotherhood of man and of the importance of men, a vivid reality. They had produced the final effective force which hereafter made slavery impossible among progressive races.

In the history of ideas the great danger is oversimplification. It is true that the Methodists produced the final wave of popular feeling which drove the anti-slavery movement to success. But the Methodist movement succeeded because it came at the right time. In this section we are discussing the religious influences. During the sixteenth, seventeenth, and eighteenth centuries the Church of Rome—to use a Quaker phrase—had a 'concern' for the races, groaning under European exploitation, which far surpassed that of the combined Protestant churches. The priests did not consider the problem in terms of human freedom. But, not to speak of the rest of the world, in America alone the heroism of the Catholic missionaries extended their self-sacrifice from the northern to the southern icefields. It is impossible to doubt but that their example kept alive a sensitiveness of the European conscience respecting the obligations of men to men.

Neither the Catholics, nor the Methodists, gave the first

modern formulation of an explicit purpose to procure the abolition of slavery. This supreme honour belongs to the Quakers, and in particular to that Apostle of Human Freedom, John Woolman. Also the American Civil War was the tremendous episode constituting the climax of this sombre journey of civilization toward the light.

Thus in the evolution of the strands of thought which constituted the final stage in the destruction of the iniquitous slave-foundation of civilization, there are interwoven the insights and the heroisms of sceptical humanitarians, of Catholics, of Methodists, of Quakers. But the intellectual origin of the movement is to be traced back for more than two thousand years to the speculations of the philosophical Greeks upon functions of the human soul, and its status in the world of flux.

Section VIII. In this chapter the story of the translation of the Greek metaphysical speculations into the sociological concept of human freedom has been only half told. In the next chapter I shall consider in more detail some nineteenth century criticisms of this whole movement towards Democracy and Freedom. But, so far as it has gone, the story illustrates the extreme difficulty of expressing in language the final generalities. The importance of man as the supreme example of a living organism is beyond question. Yet when we try to express the general notions thus involved, and their bearing upon conduct, at every step controversy arises. The immense history of Plato's metaphysical concept of the soul, with its influence on religion, and on social theory, carries this moral decisively.

Human life is driven forward by its dim apprehension of notions too general for its existing language. Such ideas cannot be grasped singly, one by one in isolation. They require that mankind advances in its apprehension of the general nature of things, so as to conceive systems of ideas elucidating each other. But the growth of generality of apprehension is the slowest of all evolutionary changes. It is the task of philosophy to promote this growth in mentality. In so far as there is success, the specialized applications of great ideas are purified from their gross associations with savage fancies. The Carthaginians were a great civilized trading nation. They belonged racially to one of the great progressive sections of mankind. They traded from the shores of Syria, throughout the Mediterranean Sea, up the Atlantic Coast of Europe, to the tin mines of Cornwall in England. They circumnavigated Africa. They ruled Spain and Sicily and North Africa. Yet, when Plato was speculating, this great people could so conceive the supreme powers of the Universe that they sacrificed their children to Moloch as an act of religious propitiation. The growth in generality of understanding makes such savagery impossible in corresponding civilizations today.

Human Sacrifice, Human Slavery are instances of great intuitions of religion and of civilized purposes expressing themselves by means of inherited brutalities of instinctive behaviour. Direct religious intuitions, even those of the purest origin, are in danger of allying themselves with lower practices and emotions which in fact pervade existing society. Religion lends a driving force to philosophy. But in its turn, Speculative philosophy guards our higher intuitions from base alliances by its suggestions of ultimate meanings, disengaged from the facts of current modes of behaviour.

The history of ideas is a history of mistakes. But through all mistakes it is also the history of the gradual purification of conduct. When there is progress in the development of favourable order, we find conduct protected from relapse into brutalization by the increasing agency of ideas consciously entertained. In this way Plato is justified in his saying, The creation of the world—that is to say, the world of civilized order—is the victory of persuasion over force.

CHAPTER III

THE HUMANITARIAN IDEAL

Section I. In the previous chapter we considered the combined influence of philosophy, law, and religion, upon the evolution from the notion of society based upon servitude to that of society based upon individual freedom. To this transformation philosophy contributed its generality, law contributed the constructive ability, religion the moral energy. By themselves and apart from correction by the Platonic philosophy, the religions derived from Western Asia were tinged with the mentality of the older civilizations of that region. They conceived the universe in terms of despots and slaves. None of these religions have been able wholly to shake off the horrible implications latent in such a conception. But the fortunate coalescence of the initial Christian institutions with the philosophic Platonic doctrines provided the Western Races with a beautiful sociological ideal, intellectually expressed, and closely allied with intermittent bursts of emotional energy. Unfortunately, interwoven with this ideal in Christian theology and in the patterns of Christian emotion, there has survived throughout history the older concept of a Divine Despot and a slavish Universe, each with the morals of its kind.

The theme of the former chapter has been the agency of these sociological ideals in the transformation of society. They constitute the intellectual side of the transformation, combined with an explanation how such intellectual concepts acquired driving force. In the present chapter we first glance at accessory causes, and then proceed to the criticism of the humanitarian ideal, a criticism which has been gathering strength since its origin in the nineteenth century. Finally, the barest sketch of a reply to this criticism is suggested.

The growth of technology is the greatest among the accessory causes which weakened the necessity for slavery. But this agency hardly came into play before the seventeenth century. Till that time the technology of the ancients, in their prime, probably surpassed that of the moderns. From that century onward, technological advance has more than satisfied the complex demands for effective labour, without recourse to slavery. Of course, the fixed order of society in a well-managed feudal system must not be confused with slavery, even in its application to the agricultural labourers at the base of the whole structure. Each order had its rights and duties, and in the happier examples of later feudalism the villagers were quite competent to go to law with their feudal chief. The system was very liable to degenerate into practical slavery, and often did so. Indeed, there is evidence[1] that, during the early Norman period in England, there was a relatively small class of slaves whose lives were at the arbitrary will of their owners. But the slave-trade shocked the conscience of those times. William the Conqueror legislated against it, and Bishops denounced it. In those times, it must be remembered, to be attached to the land was a protection as well as a restriction. It was the basis of a recognized status in an organized society—so far as the social system was organized, and was not a welter of violence.

[1] Cf. *Mediæval England,* pp. 100, 101, by Mary Bateson, T. Fisher Unwin, London 1903, and G. P. Putnam's Sons, New York.

The modern evolution of big business involves a closer analogy to feudalism, than does feudalism to slavery. In fact, the modern social system with its variety of indispensable, interlocked avocations necessitates such organization. The only questions at issue are the freedom of individuals to circulate among the grades, and satisfactory legal conceptions of the variety of relations of the grades with each other. Individualists and socialists are merely debating over the details of the neo-feudalism which modern industry requires. The self-sufficing independent man, with his peculiar property which concerns no one else, is a concept without any validity for modern civilization. Unfortunately this notion has been embodied in ancient moral codes applicable to Syrian deserts, and has reappeared tingeing western political theory in the commercial epoch immediately succeeding the decay of mediaeval feudalism. But it is not the practicable alternative to a slave society. The problem of social life is the problem of the coördination of activities, including the limits of such coördination.

The sense of the unity of civilization fostered by the Catholic Church, the general similarities of mankind throughout Europe, and the simplicities of life in the middle ages, are probably the main reasons why mediaeval wars were dissociated from slave-raiding expeditions. We hear of Saxon slaves in the slave-market in Rome. But that was in the lifetime of Gregory the Great, and the Saxons were not Christians. Indeed, whenever the European races came into contact with non-Christian foreign races, they seem to have had no compunction about slavery. We read of Saracen slaves, of the enslavement of the indigenous American tribes, and, above all, of negro slavery. But thanks to the growth of technology concurrently with the advance of civilization, the European races have avoided slavery in temperate climates. Finally, the humanitarian movement of the eighteenth century, combined with a religious sense of the kinship of men, has issued in the settled policy of the great civilized governments to extirpate slavery from the world.

SECTION II. This success came only just in time. For before and during the nineteenth century, several strands of thought emerged whose combined effect was in direct opposition to the humanitarian ideal. At the moment when the 'brotherhood of man' triumphed, the intellectual world was meditating on political economy conceived in terms of unrestrained competition, on Malthus' iron law that the mass of the population must always press on the limits of bare subsistence, and on the zoölogical law of natural selection by which an iron environment crushed out the less favoured species, and on Hume's criticism of the notion of the soul. This new trend of thought was in its immediate origin British and is to be compared and contrasted with the antecedent Wesleyan movement. In neither case did the leaders intend the sociological effects which followed from their efforts. It is often the case that the originators belong to the antecedent epoch, and stand outside the epoch of their followers. The Methodist preachers did not intend to transform society, their object was to save souls. In like manner, Adam Smith was a typical figure of the eighteenth century enlightenment.

He and Hume are two of the last great Scotchmen who mark the traditional affiliation of Scotland with France, which had survived from the earlier centuries of joint antagonism to England. At their date the intellectual life of Edinburgh and Glasgow is not to be assimilated with that of England. Throughout the greater part of the eighteenth century, during its central portion, the intellectual life of England, so far as concerns any originative energy, is negligible. Indeed, one of the reasons for the separation of America from England was that the particular circumstances of English life were not applicable to America, and that England was not fermenting with any universal ideas capable of specialization for American conditions. English influence survived, it is true, in the Common Law; but, apart from that exception, the mentality of men like Jefferson and Franklin was French. There was the homeland of their thoughts. It has required the whole of the activity of the nineteenth century, from 1790 onward, to reconstruct the intellectual influence of England on the outside world. In the eighteenth century, France looked to England; but it was to the England of the seventeenth century, Bacon, Newton, Locke and the Regicides. In order to understand the intellectual history of Europe, it is essential to remember the collapse of Germany during and after The Thirty Years' War, to remember the collapse of Italy owing to the supersession of the Mediterranean trade route to the East, owing to the Catholic Reaction with its activity of censorship, and owing to the domination of Spaniards and Habsburgs, and to remember the collapse of England owing to absorption in the commercial expansion of the eighteenth century—in the words of the old song, 'When George and pudding-time came round'. In the eighteenth century France carried the 'White Man's Burden' of intellectual advance.

Perhaps it was owing to the loss of the habit of speculative thoroughness, that in the revival of intellectual activity in England the issue of the emerging lines of thought was not discerned. Hume's flux of impressions and of reactions to impressions, each impression a distinct, self-sufficient existence, was very different to the Platonic soul. The status of man in the universe required re-considering. 'What is man that thou art mindful of him?' The brotherhood of man at the top of creation ceased to be the well-defined foundation for moral principles. There seems no very obvious reason why one flux of impressions should not be related to another flux of impressions in the relative status of master to slave. To put the matter at its very lowest, the point requires arguing. It is no answer to point out that Hume and Huxley were united in their dislike of slavery—certainly Huxley, probably Hume. The question is what reason could they give, apart from their own psychological inheritance from the Platonic religious tradition. For example, in Book III, of his *Treatise,* Part II, Section I, Hume writes, "In general, it may be affirm'd that there is no such passion in human minds, as the love of mankind, merely as such, independent of personal qualities, or services, or of relation to ourself." This sentence seems very remote from the Catholic missionaries in America, from the Quaker John Woolman, or from the free-thinking Thomas Paine. In some mysterious way, they all cared for 'mankind, merely as such'.

Section III. In the Middle Ages of Europe the keynote of sociological theory is 'coördination'. The Church coördinated religious speculations; the Feudal System coördinated the intimate structure of society; the Empire—or, Was it the Church? Here dispute crept in—coördinated the Governments of the provincial regions, Counts, Dukes, Kings, and City-Republics. In the provinces of theology and of clerical organization, the success was considerable. To a less degree the Feudal system effected its purpose. No other system can be suggested which at that time and in those circumstances could have replaced it successfully: although the towns with their commercial and artisan populations

stood outside it, more particularly in Italy. The Empire
was a failure mitigated by a few successes. The Church,
as an agent of large-scale political organization, was more
successful than the Empire. Its agents were better educated,
and—allowing for many exceptions—had a higher morale.
Also its influence extended to regions which the Empire
never reached. But, on the whole, the attempts at large-scale
organization of Europe were a failure. There is a pathetic
interest in Dante's *De Monarchia* with its initial premise
of the desire of mankind for peace and quietness. We have
only to remember the state of Europe at that time, the state
of Italy, and Dante's own life. Indeed, men do long for
peace and quietness but their desire is chequered by other
impulses. The Middle Ages were always haunted by the
ghost of the old Roman Empire, with its message of vast
success in the imposition of order upon men.

The Renaissance men read the classical authors, and decisively ignored the ideals of the Roman statesmen. Plato,
perhaps, would have been gratified by the attention his
works then received. But he would have been horrified at
the outburst of individualism. In the men of the Italian
Renaissance Plato would have recognized reproductions of
the character of the younger Dionysius of Syracuse. At the
time the incongruity was not perceived. But the inevitable
issues followed. Finally in the nineteenth century, amid
the triumph of humanitarian principles, the basic positions
of the social theories derived from Platonism and Christianity were questioned. Previously, they had never been
fully acted on. They were impracticable. But they had not
been questioned as a social ideal.

SECTION IV. The collapse of the Middle Ages was, in
one of its aspects, a revolt against coördination. The new
keynote is expressed in the word 'competition'—

'Thou shalt not murder, but tradition
Approves all forms of competition.'

Private life now dominated the social life of Europe in all
its special forms—The Right of Private Judgment, Private
Property, The Competition of Private Traders, Private
Amusement. The notion that every action is at once a
private experience and a public utility had to be born again.
It sickened and died with the disappearance of the 'mediaeval
mind'. Wherever men looked, they saw 'competition' written across the face of things. Nations arose, and men
thought of nations in terms of international competition.
They examined the theory of trade, and they construed its
interactions in terms of competition, mitigated by 'higgling.'
They considered the bounty of nature in the provision of
food, and they saw the masses of mankind competing for
insufficient supplies. They saw the fecundity of nature in
the provision of a myriad species of living things, and they
construed the explanation in terms of the competition of
species. What the notions of 'form' and 'harmony' were
to Plato, that the notions of 'individuality' and 'competition' were to the nineteenth century. God had placed his
bow in the skies as a symbol; and the strip of colours,
rightly read, spelt 'competition.' The prize to be competed
for was 'life'. Unsuccessful competitors died; and thus, by a
beautiful provision of nature, ceased from constituting a
social problem.

Now it is quite obvious that a much needed corrective
to an unqualified, sentimental humanitarianism is here
being supplied. Strife is at least as real a fact in the world as
Harmony. If you side with Francis Bacon and concentrate
on the efficient causes, you can interpret large features of
the growth of structure in terms of 'strife'. If, with Plato,
you fix attention on the end, rationally worthy, you can in-

terpret large features in terms of 'harmony'. But until some outline of understanding has been reached which elucidates the interfusion of strife and harmony, the intellectual driving force of successive generations will sway uneasily between the two.

There have been many interpretations of special aspects of European society in terms of strife: Machiavelli's 'Prince', the political policies of the great Renaissance Monarchs, Charles the Fifth, Philip the Second, Francis the First, Henry the Eighth, Henri Quatre, William the Silent, Queen Elizabeth. The people, thus indicated, found strife. They could not evade it. Fleets, armies, hatreds, assassin's daggers, burnings at the stake, insurrections were there as real present facts. To survive, as persons or as nations, meant force and policy suppressing competitors. Harmony crept in under the guise of the joy of the adventure, of faculties stretched to the full. But such harmony was a secondary effect, merely Romance gilding Strife.

In the hands of theologians both in the Middle Ages and in the first period of its supersession, the Platonic-Christian tradition leant heavily towards its mystical religious side. It abandoned this world to the Evil Prince thereof, and concentrated thought upon another world and a better life. Plato himself explicitly considers this solution at the end of his dialogue, the *Republic*. But he there gives it another twist to that adopted by later theologians. He conceives the perfect Republic in Heaven as an immediate present possession in the consciousness of the wise in the temporal world. Thus for Plato, at least in his mood when he concluded this dialogue, the joy of heaven is realizable on earth: the wise are happy. Theoretically, this doctrine also tinged mediaeval Christianity. But in practice there has always been the temptation to abandon the immediate ex-

perience of this world as a lost cause. The shadows pass—
says mystical Religion. But they also recur, and recur—
whispers the Experience of Mankind. Be tranquil, they
will end—rejoins Religion. The mystical religion which
most whole-heartedly adopts this attitude is Buddhism. In
it despair of this world is conjoined with a program for the
world's abolition by a mystic tranquillity. Christianity has
wavered between Buddhistic renunciation, and its own impracticable ideals culminating in a crude Millennium within
the temporal flux. The difference between the two consists
in the difference between a program for reform and a program for abolition. I hazard the prophecy that that religion will conquer which can render clear to popular understanding some eternal greatness incarnate in the passage of
temporal fact.

SECTION V. The political, liberal faith of the nineteenth
century was a compromise between the individualistic,
competitive doctrine of strife and the optimistic doctrine of
harmony. It was believed that the laws of the Universe were
such that the strife of individuals issued in the progressive
realization of a harmonious society. In this way, it was
possible to cherish the emotional belief in the Brotherhood
of Man, while engaging in relentless competition with all
individual men. Theoretically, it seemed possible to con-
ciliate the belief with the practice without the intrusion of
contradiction. Unfortunately, while this liberalism was winning triumph after triumph as a political force in Europe
and America, the foundations of its doctrine were receiving
shock after shock.

The new industrial system which should have been a
triumph for the liberal doctrines, did not work well. It
had first developed in England under treatment exclusively
dictated by the doctrines of economic liberalism. On this

point, in their treatment of the manufacturing and mining industries, the English Tories at first were as orthodox as the English Whigs. Unfortunately after two generations of such industrial development, the widespread misery at the base of the whole organization, in the mines, in the factories, in the slums, aroused the public conscience. This foundation of social relations upon individualism and competition, with no mitigating practices, was not working well under the new industrial conditions, such as mining for raw materials and mechanized manufacturing for finished products. At least this judgment holds for the old, comparatively crowded, nations of Europe. England was the pioneer and tried the system whole-heartedly. It failed. The evidence is scattered through the records of the two decades from 1830 to 1850. For example it can be found summarized in any life of the Lord Shaftesbury of the period—a great philanthropist—, in some of Disraeli's early novels, in the joint writings of J. L. Hammond and Barbara Hammond, dealing with the state of the labourers, town and country. The mere doctrines of freedom, individualism, and competition, had produced a resurgence of something very like industrial slavery at the base of society.

The industrial politics of the nineteenth century in Europe can only be understood by remembering this fact. The pure doctrine of nineteenth-century liberalism failed. During the decade of the eighteen forties and since, in England and in every European country a series of remedial industrial measures were introduced. The great liberal leaders, Cobden, Bright, and even Gladstone, were either opposed, or were notably cold, to these measures. They infringed the purity of the liberal doctrine. The important internal division of the political liberals in England was not the prominent one between Radicals and Whigs. It was the division between the pure liberals and the modified liberals. These modified liberals were in some ways nearer to the old Tories. They repudiated the liberal doctrine of an atomistic society. Unfortunately for the liberal political party in England, its later leaders, Gladstone, Lord Hartington, Asquith belonged to the pure liberal faction. If Campbell-Bannerman had been somewhat abler and, what is still more important, if he had lived, political history in England would have been different. As it was, in the last phase, English political liberalism under Asquith's leadership was engaged in direct opposition, or apathy, in respect to every reform which it was the task of a reforming political party to undertake—the Women's movement, Education, Industrial Reorganization. During the seventy years of its greatest triumphs, from 1830 onward, English liberalism was slowly decaying by its failure to acquire a coherent system of practicable ideals. On the whole, the pure liberals retained command of the political machine in England, from Mr. Gladstone in the last third of the nineteenth century to Mr. Asquith in the opening phase of the twentieth century.

Notwithstanding this reluctance of the great representative liberals, before the middle of the century a whole new movement of social coördination arose, in the form of Governmental measures, regulative of mining, of factories, of slum areas. The Industrial System then spread to Germany, where the necessity for coördination and the failure of free competition were at once taken for granted. The early form of the industrial doctrine of liberalism was never even tried in that country. But the modification of the liberal doctrines came grudgingly; and its failure generated a new formulation of an old idea. Karl Marx proclaimed the doctrine of 'The Class War'. The learned economists are unanimous in telling us that *Das Kapital* does not express a sound scientific doctrine, which will stand comparison with the facts. The success of the book—for it is still with us as a power— can then only be accounted for by the magnitude of the evils ushered in by the first phase of the industrial revolution.

The early liberal faith that by the decree of benevolent Providence, individualistic competition and industrial activity, would necessarily work together for human happiness had broken down as soon as it was tried. Perhaps a more enlightened training of the directing classes was required. Then coördination should mainly be directed towards education and sociological training: Perhaps, governmental agency regulating the conditions of all employments was the proper corrective: Perhaps the State, controlled by the workers, should be the sole employer. All these suggestions are still matters of fierce debate. In some country or other almost every solution has been tried. But no one now holds that, apart from some further directive agency, mere individualistic competition, of itself and by its own self-righting character, will produce a satisfactory society.

Unfortunately, the Malthusian doctrine, in its popular rendering, affirmed that as a law of nature the masses of mankind could never emerge into a high state of well-being. Still worse, biological science drew the conclusion that the destruction of individuals was the very means by which advance was made to higher types of species. This was the famous doctrine of Natural Selection, promulgated in 1859, by Charles Darwin. This exclusive reliance upon Natural Selection was not characteristic of Darwin's own theory. For him, it was one agency among many others. But, in the form in which the doctrine reigned in thought from that day to this, Natural Selection was the sole factor to be seriously considered. As applied to human society this theory is a challenge to the whole humanitarian movement.

The contrast between the dominant theories of Lamarck
and Darwin made all the difference. Instead of dwelling
on the brotherhood of man, we are now directed to procure
the extermination of the unfit. Again the modern doctrines
of heredity, gained partly from the experience of breeders
of stock, partly from practical horticulturists, partly from
the statistical researches of Francis Galton, Karl Pearson,
and their school, partly from the laws of heredity discovered
by Mendel, the Austrian Abbot, who published his unnoticed researches comtemporaneously with the publication
of Darwin's *Origin of Species,*—these doctrines have all
weakened the Stoic-Christian ideal of democratic brotherhood.

Religion by itself has always wavered between that conception and the despot-slaves conception of God and his
creatures. But the democratic liberalism of the late eighteenth and early nineteenth centuries was the triumph of the
Stoic-Christian strain of thought. In Hume's criticism of
the doctrine of the soul, in the breakdown of pure unmiti-
gated competitive individualism as a practical working system, in the Malthusian doctrine of the pressure of population on the means of subsistence, in the scientific doctrine of
the elimination of the unfit as the engine of progress, in the
Galtonian and Mendelian doctrines of heredity, in the rejection of the Lamarckian doctrine that usage can raise the
standard of fitness,—in the concurrence of all these strands
of thought the liberalism of the early nineteenth century
lost its security of intellectual justification.

SECTION VI. There are two intellectual movements to be
set on the other side of the account. One is Jeremy Bentham's legal reformation based on the Utilitarian Principle
of 'The Greatest Happiness of The Greatest Number': the
other is Auguste Comte's 'Religion of Humanity', that is to

say, Positivism. Most of what has been practically effective, in morals, in religion, or in political theory, from their day to this has derived strength from one or other of these men. Their doctrines have been largely repudiated as theoretical foundations, but as practical working principles they dominate the world. On the whole, their influence has been democratic. They have swept away mysterious claims of privileged orders of men, based on mystical intuitions originated by religion or philosophy. They carried back to the Roman Stoic lawyers, though they repudiated the ultimate metaphysical doctrines of Stoicism. They were in effect a resurrection of this Stoic legal movement, but devoid of its intellectual grandeur. From another point of view, they recurred to the scientific revolt against metaphysics, led by Newton, in the seventeenth century. They extended this revolt to moral and political theory.

For two thousand years, Platonic philosophic theories and Christian intuitions had furnished the intellectual justification for the slow growth in Western Europe of emotions of respect and friendliness between man and man—the notion of brotherhood. These emotions are at the basis of all social groups. As relatively blind emotions they must pervade animal society, namely, the urge to coöperate, to help, to feed, to cherish, to play together, to express affection. Among mankind these fundamental feelings reign with great strength within limited societies. But the range of human intelligence,—its very foresight as to dangers and opportunities, the power of the imaginative entertaining of differences between group and group, of their divergencies of habit and sentiment—this range of intelligence has produced a ferocity of inversion of this very sentiment of interracial benevolence. Mankind is distinguished by its strength of tribal feeling, and conversely it is also distinguished by far-reaching malign exploitation and inter-tribal warfare. Also the tribal feeling is apt to be chequered by limitations of benevolence to special sections within the boundary of the same community.

For two thousand years philosophy and religion had held up before Western Europe the ideal figure of man, as man, and had claimed for it a supreme worth. Under this urge, Jesuits had gone to Patagonia, John Woolman had denounced slavery, Tom Paine had revolted against social oppression and against the doctrine of original sin. These Jesuits, these Quakers, and these Freethinkers differed among themselves. But they owed their emotions towards men, as men, to the generalization of feeling produced by the joint influence of philosophy and religion.

Jeremy Bentham and Auguste Comte accepted these generalized emotions as ultimate moral intuitions, clear matter of fact, requiring no justification and requiring no ultimate understanding of their relations to the rest of things. They discarded metaphysics. In so doing, they effected an immense service to democratic liberalism. For they produced a practicable program of reform, and practicable modes of expression which served to unite men whose ultimate notions differed vastly.

Unfortunately, owing to the advance of scientific theory, the relations of the emotions to the rest of things refused to be ignored. In the evolution of life Nature is implacable: Nature discriminates. Whence comes this universal benevolence 'The Religion of Humanity' should be replaced by a cult of a select assortment of Humanity: 'The Greatest Happiness of the Greatest Number' should be replaced by 'The Humane Extinction of Inferior Specimens'. Hume denies that there is any 'such passion . . . as the love of mankind merely as such'. Modern science gives a plausible explanation why no such passion is required. It can only stand in the way of the scavenging process of evolution. If any people are subject to this passion, of course they will act on it. But no reason can be given why we should inculcate the passion in others, or why we should pervert legislation to subserve the ends of such an unreasonable emotion. I am certainly in greater sympathy with Bentham and Comte than with this deduction from Hume and modern Zoölogy. But, if it proves nothing else, the deduction does show that Bentham and Comte were mistaken in thinking that they had found a clear foundation for morals, religion, and legislation, to the exclusion of all ultimate cosmological principles. On the surface, their pet doctrines are just as liable to sceptical attack as metaphysical dogmas ever were. They have gained nothing in the way of certainty by dropping Plato and Religion.

More ultimate reasons are required either to justify discriminations in the mixture, or to provide a reconstructed justification for the doctrine of regard to man, as man. Further mere 'survival value' is not sufficient: for there are conditions which stamp out just those types which we find ourselves most willing to preserve amid happiness.

SECTION VII. Auguste Comte founded his Positivism on the assured results of science, the physical and moral science of his own day. He died in 1857, and two years later Darwin published his *Origin of Species*. We have already discussed some of the difficulties for the Religion of Humanity introduced by the subsequent phases of the Evolution Theory. Such a foundation may be adequate to shape the methodology of a group of men with limited interests at some definite date. But certainly this adequacy does not arise from any adequate clarity of the point of view. Many a worshipper obtains his purpose of spiritual consolation by bowing towards the sunrise and muttering an incantation; but he may be totally unable to render any coherent account of the grounds, metaphysical or pragmatic, which render his procedure effective.

Apart from this difficulty of conciliating the physical with the mental sciences, physical science, taken by itself, has some difficulty with its own fundamental notions. This perplexity is relevant to Platonic religious tradition whose fortunes and specializations we have been tracing. We can classify the topics of physical science under four headings:— (1) The true and real things which endure, (2) The true and real things which occur, (3) The abstract things which recur, (4) The Laws of Nature. An example of the first heading is a piece of rock, or—to pass beyond mere physical science—the individuality of a human being, his soul, as Plato would have it. An example of the second kind is any happenings, in a street, in a room, in an animal body, or—again to pass beyond mere physical science—our individual complex experience within a tenth of a second. An example of the third type is the shape of a rock. It seems doubtful whether a shade of colour, or the qualitative element in the performance of a musical symphony, are to be reckoned as concerned with nature or mentality. But certainly they recur. On the other hand a *sort* of feeling of affection is a recurrence which belongs decidedly to the mental side of things. An example of the fourth heading is the Law of Gravitation, or the geometrical Relations of Things.

I am not going to plunge into a metaphysical discussion at the close of a chapter, already sufficiently complex. But it is relevant to point out, how superficial are our controversies on sociological theory apart from some more fundamental determination of what we are talking about. The four topics above at once suggest a host of perplexing questions, which have puzzled thinkers from the time of Plato to the present time. In these two chapters we have been tracing the history of three very different types of thought, (a) the Platonic-Religious ideas, (b) Individualistic, Competitive ideas of Commercial Society, (c) the idea of physical science. Also each of these types involves internal complexities. Now we may hold, indeed I think we must hold, that each of these strains of theory is the outcome of valid intuitions and embodies truths about the nature of things which cannot be set aside. It seems an easy solution to hold that each type of idea is within its own sphere autonomous. In that case, the controversies arise from the illegitimate poaching of one type over the proper territory of some other type. For example, it is fashionable to state that religion and science can never clash because they deal with different topics. I believe that this solution is entirely mistaken. In this world at least, you cannot tear apart minds and bodies. But as soon as you try to adjust ideas you find the supreme importance of making perfectly clear, what you are talking about. It is fatal to oscillate uncritically from the things which endure to the things which occur, and from the things which occur to the things which recur. Discussions based on no metaphysical clarity in the discrimination of endurance, occurrence, recurrence, can be made sophistically to prove anything.

For example, in the statement of the Utilitarian Principle, we find the phrase 'The Greatest Happiness of The Greatest Number'. Evidently this phrase has a meaning, at least sufficient for us to take it as a rough guide to action. But when we use the formula as a criticism of the other points of view we are entitled to ask what it means. The 'Happiness' is evidently a recurrent, and it is differentiated into grades of intensity, so that one occurrence may be more intense than another in point of Happiness. But what is meant by the addition of the Happinesses of different occurrences. There is no occurrence with the Happiness of this addition sum. At least, if there be such an occurrence, it ought to be indicated in the principle, and this indication will lead us in the direction of the discarded Platonism. Again, we must know the relation of the endurances to the occurrences in order to understand the principle. As usually employed, the phrase refers to the greatest number of men. It therefore refers to endurances and not to occurrences. But can we really correlate the happinesses of three shortlived men with that of one longlived man? Then again there are the qualitative differences between different types of happiness. Finally we conclude that before we can profitably proceed with this discussion, it is necessary to attain some clarity in our metaphysical notions respecting endurances, occurrences, and things that recur.

SECTION VIII. We now pass to Science and ask whether it provides us with any clear notions, independently of a metaphysical discussion. Science is founded on the notion of Law,—The Laws of Nature. The notion is that there are many things in the world, whose behaviour towards each other always exemplifies fixed rules. These rules are evidently indicating recurrences which never fail to recur. Yet here a perplexity arises as to the connection of the Laws with the behaving things. Behaviours differ widely in a city—New York, for instance—, in a forest, in a subtropical desert, in an Arctic icefield. Also, to travel further, they differ widely on the Moon, on the atmosphere of the Sun, in the interior of a dense star, in inter-stellar space.

This is very superficial. We all know that if we analyse the things into molecules the laws of chemistry are the same in the city, the forest, the desert and the icefield. These laws of chemistry express the mutual behaviour of molecules, packed with sufficient closeness. But molecules are analysable. Things behave very differently amid a close pack of molecules from their behaviour amid the vibrations of so-called empty space. The chemical laws are merely relevant to the inter-relations of molecules. In empty space we are driven back to the fundamental electromagnetic laws controlling the flux of energy. At this point we have to stop our regression, merely because our penetration has come to an end.

But there is no reason to doubt, that the laws are the outcome of the environment of electromagnetic occasions. This whole process of regression suggests an inversion of ideas. The laws are the outcome of the character of the behaving things: they are the 'communal customs' of which Clement spoke. This conception should replace the older idea of given things with mutual behaviour conditioned by imposed laws. What we know of external nature is wholly in terms of how the various occasions in nature contribute to each other's natures. The whole environment participates in the nature of each of its occasions. Thus each occasion takes its initial form from the character of its environment. Also the laws which condition each environment merely express the general character of the occasions composing that environment. This is the doctrine of the definition of things in terms of their modes of functioning.

But we are now drawing close to the impracticable ethics of Christianity. The ideals cherished in the souls of men enter into the character of their actions. These inter-actions within society modify the social laws by modifying the occasions to which those laws apply. Impracticable ideals are a program for reform. Such a program is not to be criticized by immediate possibilities. Progress consists in modifying the laws of nature so that the Republic on Earth may conform to that Society to be discerned ideally by the divination of Wisdom.

In these two chapters, we have been considering the adventures in the history of Europe of a great idea. Plato conceived the notion of the ideal relations between men based upon a conception of the intrinsic possibilities of human character. We see this idea enter into human consciousness in every variety of specialization. It forms alliances with allied notions generated by religion. It differentiates its specializations according to the differentiations of the diverse religions and diverse scepticisms associated with it. At times it dies down. But it ever recurs. It is criticized, and it is also a critic. Force is always against it. Its victory is the victory of persuasion over force. The force is the sheer fact of what the antecedent volume of the world in fact contains. The idea is a prophecy which procures its own fulfillment.

The power of an ideal consists in this. When we examine the general world of occurrent fact, we find that its general character, practically inescapable, is neutral in respect to the realization of intrinsic value. The electromagnetic occasions and the electromagnetic laws, the molecular occasions and the molecular laws, are all alike neutral. They condition the sort of values which are possible, but they do not determine the specialties of value. When we examine the specializations of societies which determine values with some particularity, such specializations as societies of men, forests, deserts, prairies, icefields, we find, within limits, plasticity. The story of Plato's idea is the story of its energizing within a local plastic environment. It has a creative power, making possible its own approach to realization.

CHAPTER IV

ASPECTS OF FREEDOM

SECTION I. The cultural history of Western Civilization for the period illuminated by written records can be considered from many aspects. It can be conceived under the guise of a steady economic progression, diversified by catastrophic collapses to lower levels. Such a point of view emphasizes technology and economic organization. Alternatively, history can be conceived as a series of oscillations between worldliness and other-worldliness, or as a theatre of contest between greed and virtue, or between truth and error. Such points of view emphasize religion, morality, and contemplative habits eliciting generalizations of thought. Each mode of consideration is a sort of searchlight elucidating some of the facts, and retreating the remainder into an omitted background. Of course in any history, even with a restricted topic, limited to politics, or to art, or to science, many points of view are in fact interwoven, each with varying grades of generality.

One of the most general philosophic notions to be used in the analysis of civilized activities is to consider the effect on social life due to the variations of emphasis between Individual Absoluteness and Individual Relativity. Here 'absoluteness' means the notion of release from essential dependence on other members of the community in respect to modes of activity, while relativity means the converse fact of essential relatedness. In one of their particularizations these ideas appear in the antagonism between notions of freedom and of social organization. In another they appear in the relative importance to be ascribed to the welfare of the state and to the welfare of its individual members. The character of each epoch as to its social institutions, its jurisprudence, its notions of ideal ends within the range of practicability, depends largely upon those various patches of activity within which one or other of these notions, individual absoluteness or individual relativity, is dominant for that epoch. No period is wholly controlled by either one of these extremes, reigning through its whole range of activities. Repression in one direction is balanced by freedom in others. Military discipline is severe. In the last resort individual soldiers are sacrificed to the army. But in many fields of human activity soldiers are left completely unfettered both by regulation and by custom. For members of university faculties the repressions and the freedoms are very different from those which obtain for soldiers.

Distribution of emphasis between absoluteness and relativity is seemingly arbitrary. Of course there is always a historical reason for the pattern. Frequently the shifting of emphasis is to be ascribed to the general tendency to revolt from the immediate past—to interchange black and white wherever we find them. Also the transformation may be a judgment upon dogmas held responsible for inherited failures. It should be one function of history to disengage such a judgment from the irritation due to transient circumstances.

More often changes in the social pattern of intellectual emphasis arise from a shift of power from one class or group of classes, to another class, or group of classes. For example, an oligarchic aristocratic government and a democratic government may each tend to emphasize social organization, that is to say, the relativity of individuals to the state. But governments mainly satisfying the trading and professional classes, whether nominally they be aristocratic, democratic, or absolute, emphasize personal freedom, that is to say, individual absoluteness. Governments of the latter kind have been that of Imperial Rome with its middle class imperial agents, and its middle class stoic lawyers, and in its happiest period its middle class emperors; and that of England in the eighteenth and nineteenth centuries.

With the shift of dominant classes, points of view which in one epoch are submerged, only to be detected by an occasional ripple, later emerge into the foreground of action and literary expression. Thus the various activities of each age—governmental, literary, scientific, religious, purely social—express the mentalities of various classes in the community whose influence for those topics happens to be dominant. In one of his speeches on the American Revolution, Burke exclaims, "For heaven's sake, satisfy *somebody*."

Governments are best classified by considering who are the 'somebodies' they are in fact endeavouring to satisfy. Thus the English government of the first sixty years of the eighteenth century was, as to its form and its persons, aristocratic. But in policy it was endeavouring to satisfy the great merchants of the City of London and of the City of Bristol. Their dissatisfaction was the immediate source of danger. Sir Robert Walpole and William Pitt, the Great Commoner, personify the changing moods of this class, in the earlier period sick of wars, and later imperialistic.

In a period when inherited modes of life are operating with their traditional standard of efficiency, or inefficiency, the class to be actively satisfied may be relatively restricted, for example, the merchants of eighteenth century England. The majority will then be relatively quiescent, and conservative statesmen, such as Walpole, will be anxious to do nothing to stir the depths—'*Quieta non movere.*' Walpole was an active reformer in respect to trade interests, otherwise a conservative.

The corresponding statesmen in France were actively concerned with the interests of the Court whose power was based on a bureaucracy (legal, administrative, and ecclesiastical) and an army. As in contemporary England, the personnel of the whole French organization, civil and military, was aristocratic and middle class. French politics ran more smoothly, but unfortunately for France its active political element was more divorced from the main interests of the country than the active element in England, though in each country government exhibited its periods of insight and folly. The French emphasis was towards coördination, the English towards individual freedom. In the latter portion of this century, in England the more active class politically were the rural landowners. Note for instance the way in which, at the end of his political life, Burke hugs the improbable belief that he understood agriculture. Also the municipality of the City of London was in the earlier period an element of support for the government, and— until the excesses of the French Revolution—in the later period an element of opposition.

In the later period the oncoming industrial revolution absorbed the energies of that English industrial class, whom at the earlier period the slogan, 'The Protestant Succession' had stirred to political activity because for them it spelled 'Industrial Freedom'. The mass of the people were now, towards the end of the century, stirring uneasily, as yet ignorant of the ways in which their interests were being determined, and with its better members engaged in saving their souls according to the directions of John Wesley.

Finally out of this welter, after a delay caused by the wars of the French Revolution, the Victorian epoch emerged. The solution was merely temporary, and so is the planet itself.

SECTION II. ιn our endeavour to understand sociological change we must not concentrate too exclusively on the effect of abstract doctrine, verbally formulated and consciously assented to. Such elaborate intellectual efforts play their part in preserving, or transforming, or destroying. For example, the history of Europe is not to be understood without some reference to the Augustinian doctrines of original sin, of divine grace, and of the consequent mission of the Catholic church. The history of the United States requires in addition some knowledge of the English political doctrines of the seventeenth century, and of French thought in the eighteenth century. Men are driven by their thoughts as well as by the molecules in their bodies, by intelligence and by senseless forces. Social history, however, concentrates on modes of human experience prevalent at different periods. The physical conditions are merely the background which partially controls the flux of modes and of moods. Even here we must not over-intellectualize the various types of human experience. Mankind is the animal at the head of the Primates, and cannot escape habits of mind which cling closely to habits of body.

Our consciousness does not initiate our modes of functioning. We awake to find ourselves engaged in process, immersed in satisfactions and dissatisfactions, and actively modifying, either by intensification, or by attenuation, or by the introduction of novel purposes. This primary procedure which is presupposed in consciousness, I will term Instinct. It is the mode of experience directly arising out of the urge of inheritance, individual and environmental. Also, after instinct and intellectual ferment have done their work, there is a decision which determines the mode of coalescence of instinct with intelligence. I will term this factor Wisdom. It is the function of wisdom to act as a modifying agency on the intellectual ferment so as to produce a self-determined issue from the given conditions. Thus for the purpose of understanding social institutions, this crude three-fold division of human nature is required: Instinct, Intelligence, Wisdom.

But this division must not be made too sharply. After all, intellectual activity is itself an inherited factor. We do not initiate thought by an effort of self-consciousness. We find ourselves thinking, just as we find ourselves breathing and enjoying the sunset. There is a habit of daydreaming, and a habit of thoughtful elucidation. Thus the autonomy of thought is strictly limited, often negligible, generally beyond the threshold of consciousness. The ways of thought of a nation are as much instinctive—that is to say, are subject to routine—as are its ways of emotional reaction. But most of us believe that there is a spontaneity of thought which lies beyond routine. Otherwise, the moral claim for freedom of thought is without meaning. This spontaneity of thought is, in its turn, subject to control as to its maintenance and efficiency. Such control is the judgment of the whole, attenuating or strengthening the partial flashes of self-determination. The whole determines what it wills to be, and thereby adjusts the relative importance of its own inherent flashes of spontaneity. This final determination is its Wisdom or, in other words, its subjective aim as to its own nature, with its limits set by inherited factors.

Wisdom is proportional to the width of the evidence made effective in the final self-determination. The intellectual operations consist in the coördination of notions derived from the primary facts of instinctive experience into a logically coherent system. Those facts, whose qualitative aspects are thus coördinated, gain importance in the final self-determination. This intellectual coördination is more readily achieved when the primary facts are selected so as to dismiss the baffling aspects of things into intellectual subordination. For this reason intellectual activity is apt to flourish at the expense of Wisdom. To some extent, to understand is always to exclude a background of intellectual incoherence. But Wisdom is persistent pursuit of the deeper understanding, ever confronting intellectual system with the importance of its omissions. These three elements, Instinct, Intelligence, Wisdom, cannot be torn apart. They integrate, react, and merge into hybrid factors. It is the case of the whole emerging from its parts, and the parts emerging within the whole. In judging social institutions, their rise, their culmination, and their decay, we have to estimate the types of instinct, of intelligence, and of wisdom which have coöperated with natural forces to develop the story. The folly of intelligent people, clear-headed and narrow-visioned, has precipitated many catastrophes.

However far we go back in recorded history, we are within the period of the high grade functioning of mankind, far removed from mere animal savagery. Also, within that period it would be difficult to demonstrate that mankind has improved upon its inborn mental capacity. Yet there can be no doubt that there has been an immense expansion of the outfit which the environment provides for the service of thought. This outfit can be summarized under the headings, modes of communication, physical and mental, writing, preservation of documents, variety of modes of literature, critical thought, systematic thought, constructive thought, history, comparison of diverse languages, mathematical symbolism, improved technology providing physical ease. This list is obviously composed of many partially redundant and overlapping items. But it serves to remind us of the various ways in which we have at our service facilities for thought and suggestions for thought, far beyond those at hand for our predecessors who lived anywhere from two to five thousand years ago. Indeed the last two hundred years has added to this outfit in a way which may create a new epoch unless mankind degenerates. Of course, a large share of this outfit had already accumulated between two and three thousand years ago. It is the brilliant use which the leading men of that millennium made of their opportunities which makes us doubt of any improvement in the native intelligence of mankind.

But the total result is that we now discern a certain simple-mindedness in the way our predecessors adjusted themselves to inherited institutions. To a far greater extent the adjustment was a matter of course, in short, it was instinctive. In the great period they discovered what we have inherited. But there was a naïvety about the discovery, a surprise. Instinctive adaptation was so pervasive that it was unnoticed. Probably the Egyptians did not know that they were governed despotically, or that the priests limited the royal power, because they had no alternative as a contrast either in fact or in imagination. They were nearer in their thoughts to the political philosophy prevalent in an anthill.

Another aspect of this fact is that in such societies, relativity is stressed rather than individual freedom. Indeed, in the earlier stages freedom is almost a meaningless notion. Action and mood both spring from an instinct based upon ancestral coördination. In such societies, whatever is not the outcome of inherited relativity, imposing coördination of action, is sheer destructive chaos. Alien groups are then evil groups. An energetic prophet hewed Agag in pieces. Unfortunately the spiritual descendants of Samuel still survive, archaic nuisances.

SECTION III. We can watch some of the episodes in the discovery of freedom. About fourteen hundred years before Christ the Egyptian king Akhnaton evidently belonged to an advanced group who thought for themselves and made a step beyond the inherited religious notions. Such groups, with flashes of free thought, must have arisen sporadically many times before, during countless thousands of years, some successful and most of them failures. Otherwise the transition to civilization, as distinct from the mere diversity of adaptations of thoughtless customs, could never have arisen. Bees and ants have diverse social organizations; but, so far as we know, neither species is in any sense civilized. They may enjoy thoughtless adaptations of social customs. Anyhow their flashes of freedom are below the level that we can discern. But Akhnaton, having exercised his freedom, evidently had no conception of freedom as such. We have all the evidence archæology can provide, that he rigidly endeavoured to impose his notions upon the thoughts and customs of the whole Egyptian nation. Apparently he failed; for there was a reaction. But reactions never restore with minute accuracy. Thus in all probability there remained a difference which the evidence before us is unable to discriminate.

A more successful group were the Hebrew prophets about eight or nine hundred years later. Spurred by the evils of their times they exercised a freedom in the expression of moral intuition, and fitted out the character of Jehovah with the results of their thoughts. Our civilization owes to them more than we can express. They constitute one of the few groups of men who decisively altered history in any intimate sense. Most spectacular upheavals merely replace one set of individuals by another analogous set; so that history is mostly a barren change of names. But the Hebrew prophets really produced a decisive qualitative alteration, and what is still more rare, a change for the better; yet the conception of freedom never entered into the point of view of the Jehovah of the prophets. Intolerance is the besetting sin of moral fervour. The first important pronouncement in which tolerance is associated with moral fervour, is in the Parable of the Tares and the Wheat, some centuries later.

Subsequent examples of intolerance supervening upon the exercise of freedom are afforded by the Christian Church after its establishment by Constantine, and by the Protestants under the guidance of Luther and Calvin. At the period of the Reformation mankind had begun to know better and so charity of judgment upon the Reformers begins to wear thin. But then charity is a virtue allied to tolerance, so we must be careful. All advanced thinkers, sceptical or otherwise, are apt to be intolerant, in the past and also now. On the whole, tolerance is more often found in connection with a genial orthodoxy. The apostles of modern tolerance—in so far as it exists—are Erasmus, the Quakers, and John Locke. They should be commemorated in every laboratory, in every church, and in every court of law. We must however remember that many of the greatest seventeenth century statesmen and thinkers, including John Locke, owed their lives to the wide tolerance of the Dutch Republic.

Certainly these men were not the originators of their admirable ideas. To find the origins we must go behind them for two thousand years. So slow is translation of idea into custom. We must however first note that the examples cited have all been concerned with religion. There are other forms of behaviour, active and contemplative. The Athenians have given us the first surviving instance of the explicit recognition of the importance of tolerance in respect to varieties of social behaviour. No doubt antecedent civilizations must have provided many practical examples of it. For example, it is difficult to believe that in big metropolitan cities such as Babylon and Nineveh, there was much detailed supervision of social behaviour. On the other hand, the ways of life in Egypt seem to have been tightly organized. But the first explicit defence of social tolerance, as a requisite for high civilization, is found in the speech of Pericles as reported by Thucydides. It puts forth the conception of the organized society successfully preserving freedom of behaviour for its individual members. Fifty years later, in the same social group, Plato introduced deeper notions from which all claims for freedom must spring. His general concept of the psychic factors in the Universe stressed them as the source of all spontaneity, and ultimately as the ground of all life and motion. The human psychic activity thus contains the origins of precious harmonies within the transient world. The end of human society is to elicit such psychic energies. But spontaneity is of the essence of soul. Such in outline is the argument from Platonic modes of thought to the importance of social freedom.

Plato's own writings constitute one prolonged apology for freedom of contemplation, and for freedom for the communication of contemplative experiences. In the persistent exercise of this right Socrates and Plato lived, and it was on its behalf that Socrates died. There are exceptional passages, but throughout the bulk of the Dialogues Socrates and Plato are engaged in expressing manners of thought. Hardly ever is there a passage which can be directly translated into a particular action. The conclusions of the Republic will work only in heaven. The great exception is The Laws, which is a minutely practical scheme for the establishment of small city-states of the type then prevalent in the Ægean area. The Thucydidean Pericles stresses the other side. He is thinking of the activities of the individual citizens. The peculiar civilization of the speech arises from its stress upon the æsthetic end of all action. A Barbarian speaks in terms of power. He dreams of the superman with the mailed fist. He may plaster his lust with sentimental morality of Carlyle's type. But ultimately his final good is conceived as one will imposing itself upon other wills. This is intellectual barbarism. The Periclean ideal is action weaving itself into a texture of persuasive beauty analogous to the delicate splendor of nature.

The establishment of freedom requires more than its mere intellectual defence. Plato above all men introduced into the world this further essential element of civilization. For he exhibited the tone of mind which alone can maintain a free society, and he expressed the reasons justifying that tone. His Dialogues are permeated with a sense of the variousness of the Universe, not to be fathomed by our intellects, and in his Seventh Epistle he expressly disclaims the possibility of an adequate philosophic system. The moral of his writings is that all points of view, reasonably coherent and in some sense with an application, have something to contribute to our understanding of the universe, and also involve omissions whereby they fail to include the totality of evident fact. The duty of tolerance is our finite homage to the abundance of inexhaustible novelty which is awaiting the future, and to the complexity of accomplished fact which exceeds our stretch of insight.

Thus two types of character must be excluded from those effectually promoting freedom. One type belongs to those who despair of attaining any measure of truth, the Sceptics. Such temperaments can obviously have no message for those who hold that thought does count. Again the pursuit of freedom with an intolerant mentality is self-defeating. For all his equipment of imagination, learning, and literary magnificence in defence of freedom, the example of Milton's life probably does as much to retard the cause as to advance it. He promotes a frame of mind of which the issue is intolerance.

The ancient world of paganism was tolerant as to creeds. Provided that your actions conformed, your speculations were unnoticed. Indeed, one mark of progress beyond purely instinctive social relations is an uneasy feeling as to the destructive effect of speculative thought. Creeds are at once the outcome of speculation and efforts to curb speculation. But they are always relevant to it. Antecedently to speculation there can be no creeds. Wherever there is a creed, there is a heretic round the corner or in his grave. Amid the great empires, Egyptian, Mesopotamian, and Hittite, and with the discovery of navigation, the intercourse between races promoted shrewd comparisons gradually broadening into speculative thought. In its beginnings this shift in human mentality must have developed slowly. Where there is no anticipation, change has to wait upon chance, and peters out amid neglect. Fortunately the Bible preserves for us fragments of the process as it affected one gifted race at a nodal point. The record has been written up by editors with the mentality of later times. Thus the task of modern scholars is analogous to an endeavour to recover the histories of Denmark and Scotland from a study of Hamlet and Macbeth. We can see initial antagonisms broadening into speculative attempts to rationalize the welter. We can watch Samuel and Agag succeeded by Solomon

and the Queen of Sheba. There are the meditations of Job
and his friends, the prophetical books, and the 'wisdom'
books of the Bible. And with a leap of six hundred years
one version of the story ends with the creed of the Council
at Nicæa.

SECTION IV. The episode of Greek civilization during its
short phase of independence created a new situation. Speculation was explicitly recognized. It was ardently pursued.
Its various modes and methods were discovered. The relation of the Greeks to their predecessors is analogous, as to
stretch of time and intensity of effect, to that of the second
phase of the modern industrial revolution during the last
fifty years to the first phase which in truth sprawls over the
long centuries from the fifteenth century to the close of the
nineteenth.

By reason of its inheritance from the episode of Hellenic
culture the Roman Empire was more self-conscious than its
predecessors in its treatment of the problem of liberty and
of the allied problem of social institutions. So far as concerns Western Europe, the origin of the Mediaeval civilization must be dated from the Emperor Augustus and the
Journeys of St. Paul. For the Byzantine, Semitic, Egyptian
area, the date must be pushed back to the death of Alexander the Great, and the renaissance of Græco-Egyptian
learning. For the first two centuries after Augustus the
former area, centered in Italy, was incomparably the more
important. Latin literature is the translation of Hellenic
culture into the mediaeval modes of thought, extending that
period to end with the French Revolution. Throughout
that whole period culture was backward looking. Lucretius,
Cicero, Virgil were mediaevals in their relation to Hellenic
literature and speculation; though they lacked the Semitic
factor. After that first Latin period, the notable contribu-

tions to thought, Pagan, Christian, and Mahometan, all derive from the eastern region, with the important exception of Augustine. Finally, the centre of culture again swings westward, as the Eastern civilization collapses under the prolonged impacts of Tartars and Turks. The notes of these three allied cultures, the Eastern, the Latin, and the later European, are scholarly learning, recurrence to Hellenic speculation re-stated in creedal forms, imitative literatures stressing humane aspirations, the canalization of curiosity into professional grooves, and—in the West—a new grade of intelligence exhibited in the development of a variety of social institutions. It is this last factor which has saved the progress of mankind.

The new epoch in the formation of social institutions unfolded itself very gradually. It is not yet understood in its full importance. Social philosophy has not grasped the relevant principles, so that even now each case is treated as a peculiar fact. But the problem of liberty has been transformed by it. The novelty consists in the deliberate formation of institutions, embodying purposes of special groups, and unconcerned with the general purposes of any political state, or of any embodiment of tribal unity playing the part of a state. Of course any big empire involves a coalescence of diverse tribes, customs, and modes of thought. But in the earlier examples, each subject race had its own status in the complex empire, and its ways of procedure were part of the imperial system. Also there must have been complex modes of behaviour, peculiar to the various races, inherited and tolerated as a matter of course. In the case of the smaller units such as the Greek city states, we find a condition of affairs in which all corporate action is an element in state-policy. The freedom was purely individual, never corporate. All incorporation, religious or secular, was communal, or patriarchal. The saying, "Render unto Cæsar the things that are Cæsar's and unto God the things that are God's" was uttered by Christ in the reign of Tiberius, and not by Plato four hundred years earlier. However limited may be the original intention of the saying, very quickly God was conceived as a principle of organization in complete disjunction from Cæsar.

It is interesting to speculate on the analogies and differences between the deaths of Socrates and of Paul. Both were martyrs. Socrates died because his speculative opinions were held to be subversive of the communal life. It is difficult to believe that the agents of Claudius, or Nero, or Galba, were much concerned with Paul's speculative opinions as to the ways of God to man. Later on, Lucian's opinions were as unorthodox as Paul's. But he died in his bed. Unfortunately for Paul, as he journeyed he left behind him organized groups, indulging in activities uncoördinated with any purposes of state. Thus imperial agents were alarmed, and sympathized with popular prejudice. Indeed, we know exactly what one of the best of the Roman Emperors about half a century later thought of the matter. Trajan in his letter to the younger Pliny dismisses Christian Theology as negligible. He is even unconcerned with their organization into groups, so long as no overt action emerges affronting the traditional association of the state with religion. Yet he recognizes that the Christians will fit into no current political philosophy, and that they represent corporate actions on the verge of the intolerable. Thus if circumstances unearth them, they are to be questioned, dismissed if possible, but punished when their actions become glaring. It is interesting to compare the Christians in the Roman Empire, from Nero to Trajan, with the Communists in modern America.

Trajan shews himself as a fine statesman dealing with the faint dawn of a new epoch, not understood, and indeed not yet understood. The old organization of mankind was being affected by the influence of the new width of intellectuality due to Hellenism. Organizations mainly derived from blind inheritance, and affected by the intellect only in detail and in interpretation, are to receive the shock of other types founded primarily on the intellectual appreciation of private ends, that is to say, of ends unconcerned with the State. What Henry Osborn Taylor has termed 'rational consideration' is becoming a major force in human organization. Of course, Plato and Aristotle exhibited rational consideration on a magnificent scale. But a group of thinkers do not necessarily constitute a political force. Centuries, sometimes thousands of years, have to elapse before thought can capture action. It is typical of this gap, that Aristotle's manuscripts are said to have been stowed in a cellar for two hundred years, and that even to this day Plato is mainly valued as a religious mystic and a supreme literary artist. In these latter functions, Plato represents the world he inherited and not the world he created. Perhaps these constitute his best part. But he played two rôles.

The situation in the Roman Empire was in effect novel. Pericles had conceived a freedom for private actions, of a certain civilized type within narrowly restricted bounds. Plato voices the claim for contemplative freedom. But the Empire was faced with the claim for freedom of corporate action. Modern political history, from that day to this, is the confused story of the strenuous resistance of the State, and of its partial concessions. The Empire reasserted the old doctrine of the divine Emperor; but also yielded by admitting as legal principle the Stoic doctrine of the Voice of Nature. The Middle Ages compromised with the doc-

trine of the two swords. In recent times, the State is fighting
behind its last ditch, which is the legal doctrine of sovereignty. The thought of the seventeenth and eighteenth centuries rationalized its political philosophy under the fiction
of the 'Original Contract'. This concept proved itself
formidable. It helped to dismiss the Stuarts into romance,
to found the American Republic, and to bring about the
French Revolution. Indeed, it was one of the most timely
notions known to history. Its weakness is that it antedates
the era of the importance of rational consideration, and
overestimates the political importance which at any time
reason has possessed. The antagonistic doctrine was that of
the 'Divine Right of Kings', which is the ghost of the
'divine Emperor'.

SECTION V. Political philosophy can claim no exemption
from the doctrine of the golden mean. Unrestricted liberty
means complete absence of any compulsory coördination.
Human society in the absence of any compulsion is trusting
to the happy coördination of individual emotions, purposes,
affections, and actions. Civilization can only exist amid a
population which in the mass does exhibit this fortunate
mutual adaptation. Unfortunately a minority of adverse individual instances, when unchecked, are sufficient to upset
the social structure. A few men in the whole caste of their
character, and most men in some of their actions, are anti-
social in respect to the peculiar type of any society possible
in their time. There can be no evasion of the plain fact
that compulsion is necessary and that compulsion is the
restriction of liberty.

It follows that a doctrine as to the social mingling of
liberty and compulsion is required. A mere unqualified demand for liberty is the issue of shallow philosophy, equally
noxious with the antithetical cry for mere conformation to

standard pattern. Probably, there can be no one solution of this problem adapted to all the circumstances of human societies which have been and will be. We must confine ourselves to the way in which at the present day the issue is being adjusted in the western civilization, European and American.

Roughly speaking, the main effectiveness of this solution presupposes a wide distribution of institutions founded upon professional qualifications and exacting such qualifications. Obviously the canalization of a variety of occupations into professions is a pre-requisite. Here the term Profession means an avocation whose activities are subjected to theoretical analysis, and are modified by theoretical conclusions derived from that analysis. This analysis has regard to the purposes of the avocation and to the adaptation of the activities for the attainment of those purposes. Such criticism must be founded upon some understanding of the natures of the things involved in those activities, so that the results of action can be foreseen. Thus foresight based upon theory, and theory based upon understanding of the nature of things, are essential to a profession. Again the purposes of a profession are not a simple bundle of definite ends. There is a general purpose, such as the curing of sickness, which defines medicine. But in a multitude of ways every human body might be in a better state of biological fitness, and might easily be worse. There has in every case to be a selection of ends dependent partly on intrinsic importance if attained, and partly upon practicability of attainment. It is for this reason that the practice of a profession cannot be disjoined from its theoretical understanding, and *vice versa*. We do however find it necessary to specialize even further, not only within some department of that profession, such as surgery, but also either to a major consideration of its theory or to a major devotion to its current practice.

The antithesis to a profession is an avocation based upon customary activities and modified by the trial and error of individual practice. Such an avocation is a Craft, or at a lower level of individual skill it is merely a customary direction of muscular labour. The ancient civilizations were dominated by crafts. Modern life ever to a greater extent is grouping itself into professions. Thus ancient society was a coördination of crafts for the instinctive purposes of communal life, whereas modern society is a coördination of professions. Without question the distinction between crafts and professions is not clear-cut. In all stages of civilization, crafts are shot through and through with flashes of constructive understanding, and professions are based upon inherited procedures. Nor is it true that the type of men involved are to be ranked higher in proportion to the dominance of abstract mentality in their lives. On the contrary, a due proportion of craftsmanship seems to breed the finer types. The brilliant ability, in proportion to population, of Europe in the fifteenth, sixteenth, and seventeenth centuries suggests that at about that period the best harmony had been reached. Pure mentality easily becomes trivial in its grasp of fact.

The organization of professions by means of self-governing institutions places the problem of liberty at a new angle. For now it is the institution which claims liberty and also exercises control. In ancient Egypt the Pharaoh decided, acting through his agents. In the modern world a variety of institutions have the power of action without immediate reference to the state. This new form of liberty which is the autonomous institution limited to special purposes, was especially exemplified in the guilds of the middle ages; and that period was characterized by a remarkable growth of civilized genius. The meaning that—in England at least—was then assigned to the word 'liberty' illustrates the projection of the new social structure upon the older form of customary determination. For a 'liberty' did not then mean a general freedom, but a special license to a particular group to organize itself within a special field of action. For this reason 'liberties' were sometimes a general nuisance.

Of course the Catholic Church was the great 'liberty' which first confronted the Roman Empire, and then dominated mediaeval life. In its early stages it is seen in its proper theoretical relation to other autonomous societies. For example in the pagan Empire, its legal status seems to have been analogous to that of the pagan burial societies; although the status of the Church property before the age of Constantine has not yet been finally elucidated by scholars. But in the middle ages, the Church so towered above other institutions that it out-rivalled the state itself. Accordingly its analogy to secular guilds and to other professional institutions such as universities was obscured by its greatness. The Catholic Church had another characteristic of priceless value. It was, so far as concerned Europe, universal, that is to say, Catholic. Until the approach of the Renaissance there were no European nations in the modern sense. But the Church transcended all governmental boundaries, all racial divisions and all geographic divisions. It was a standing challenge to any form of communal despotism, a universal 'liberty'.

SECTION VI. From the beginning of the sixteenth century this first form of institutional civilization, with its feudalism, its guilds, it universities, its Catholic Church, was in full decay. The new middle classes, whether scholars or traders, would have none of it. They were individualists. For them the universities were secondary, the monasteries were a nuisance, the Church was a nuisance, feudalism was a nuisance, the guilds were a nuisance. They wanted good order, and to be let alone with their individual activities. The great thinkers of the sixteenth and seventeenth centuries were singularly detached from universities. Erasmus wanted printers, and Bacon, Hervey, Descartes, Galileo, Leibniz, wanted governmental patronage, or protection, more than university colleagues, mostly reactionary. When Luther, Descartes, Galileo, or Leibniz shifted his residence, it was not to find a better university, but a more suitable government—a Duke who would protect, a Prince who would pay, or a Dutch Republic which would not ask questions. Nevertheless, the universities survived the change better than other institutions. In some ways it was a great time for them, though they shrank to be national. What finally emerged was the modern national organization of Europe with the sovereign state dictating every form of institutional organization, as subordinate elements for its own purposes. This was a recurrence to that earlier form of human organization which showed its faint signs of decay during the period of the Roman Empire. Naturally there were great differences. For nothing is ever restored. In fact the reaction was a failure, because mankind has outgrown the simplicities of the earlier form of civilization.

The political philosophy of the modern era was a retrogression, based upon a recurrence to the philosophers and lawyers of the old classical civilizations. The Middle Ages, in the simplified form of the relations of Church with State, were considering the problem of a civilization in which men owed a divided allegiance to many intersecting institutions pursuing diverse ends. This is the real problem in a world dominated by fraternity derived from the catholic diffusion of ideas, and from the international distribution of property. The solution provided by the doctrine of the sole sovereignty of the state, however grateful to protestants and to sovereigns, is both shocking and unworkable, a mere stick with which to beat Papists in the sixteenth and seventeenth centuries, a mere way to provide policemen for the counting-houses of merchants. But, amid this reactionary triumph of Periclean individualism in the political philosophies of the eighteenth and nineteenth centuries, there was an outcrop of institutions based upon the vigour of modern intellectual interests. These institutions, even when national, were concerned with interests impartial among the nations. These were the centuries in which science triumphed, and science is universal. Thus scientific institutions, though in form national, informally established a Catholic league. Again the advance of scholarship, and of natural science, transformed the professions. It intellectualized them far beyond their stage of advance in earlier times. Professions first appear as customary activities largely modified by detached strains of theory. Theories are often wrong; and some of the earlier professional doctrines erred grievously and were maintained tenaciously. Doctrines emerged as plausible deductions, and survived as the wisdom of ancestors. Thus the older professional practice was rooted upon custom, though it was turning towards the intellectual sunlight. Here and there individuals stood out far in advance of their colleagues. For example, in the fourteen hundred years separating Galen from Vesalius, the standard of European medical practice was not to be compared with the attainments of either of these men. Also more than a century after Vesalius, Charles the Second, of England, on his deathbed was tortured by physicians employing futile remedies customary at that time. Again, as a designing engineer Leonardo da Vinci was unequalled until the advent of Vauban and James Watt. In the earlier centuries the professional influence, as a general sociological fact, was mainly a welter of bygone flashes of intelligence relapsing into customary procedures. It represented the continual lapse of intellect into instinct. But the culmination of science completely inverted the rôles of custom and intelligence in the older professions. By this inversion professional institutions have acquired an international life. Each such institution practices within its own nation, but its sources of life are world-wide. Thus loyalties stretch beyond sovereign states.

Perhaps the most important function of these institutions is the supervision of standards of individual professional competence and of professional practice. For this purpose there is a complex interweaving of universities and more specialized institutions. The problem of freedom comes in here. For it is not opinions which are censured, but learning and ability. Thus in the more important fields of thought, opinion is free and so are large divergencies of practice. The community is provided with objective information as to the sort of weight to be attached to individuals and as to the sort of freedom of action which may safely be granted. Whatever is done can be subjected to the test of general professional opinion, acting through this network of institutions. Further, even large freedom can now be allowed to non-professional individuals. For the great professional organizations, so long as they are efficient, should be able to demonstrate the dangers of extravagant notions. In this way, where sudden action is not in question, reason has obtained an entrenchment which should be impregnable. Indeed individual freedom, standing apart from organization, has now its indispensable rôle. For all organizations are liable to decay, and license for outside criticism is the best safeguard for the professions.

Also the sovereign state of modern legal theory has its sphere of action and its limitation. The state represents the general wisdom of the community derived from an experience broader than the topics of the various sciences. The rôle of the state is a general judgment on the activity of the various organizations. It can judge whether they welcome ability, whether they stand high among the kindred institutions throughout the world. But where the state ceases to exercise any legitimate authority is when it presumes to decide upon questions within the purview of sciences or professions.

For example, in the teaching profession it is obvious that young students cannot be subjected to the vagaries of individual teachers. In this sense, the claim for the freedom of teaching is nonsense. But the general community is very incompetent to determine either the subject matter to be taught or the permissible divergences to be allowed, or the individual competence. There can be only one appeal, and this is to general professional opinion as exhibited in the practice of accredited institutions. The appeal is catholic. The State of Tennessee did not err in upholding the principle that there are limits to the freedom of teaching in schools and colleges. But it exhibited a gross ignorance of its proper functions when it defied a professional opinion which throughout the world is practically unanimous. Even here that State is hardly to be blamed. For the current political philosophy of sovereignty is very weak as to the limitations of moral authority. Of course whoever at any moment has physical power has that power of physical compulsion, whether he be a bandit, or a judge, or political

ruler. But moral authority is limited by competence to attain
those ends whose immediate dominance is evident to enlightened wisdom. Political loyalty ceases at the frontiers
of radical incapacity.

The functions of professional institutions have been considered in some detail because they constitute a clear-cut
novelty within modern societies. There were faint anticipations in the ancient world, for example the schools at
Athens, in particular those founded by Plato, Aristotle, and
the Stoics, and elsewhere the great foundation at Alexandria.
Also later the theologians of the Christian Church formed
another professional group which even stretched its claim
to authority beyond all bounds of good sense. It is by reason
of these anticipations, and of the legal developments of the
Roman and Byzantine schools of law, that the beginnings
of the modern world, in respect to the problem of freedom
and of moral authority, have been placed as early as Alexander and Augustus.

SECTION VII. In the immediate present, economic organization constitutes the most massive problem of human relationships. It is passing into a new phase, and presents confused outlines. Evidently something new is developing.
The individualistic liberalism of the nineteenth century has
collapsed, quite unexpectedly. So long as the trading middle
classes were dominant as the group to be satisfied, its doctrines were self-evident. As soon as industrialism and education produced in large numbers the modern type of
artisan, its whole basis was widely challenged. Again the
necessity for large capital, with the aid of legal ingenuity
produced the commercial corporation with limited liability.
These fictitious persons are exempt from physiological death
and can only disappear by a voluntary dissolution or by
bankruptcy. The introduction into the arena of this new

type of 'person' has considerably modified the effective
meaning of the characteristic liberal doctrine of contractual
freedom. It is one thing to claim such freedom as a natural
right for human persons, and quite another to claim it for
corporate persons. And again the notion of private property had a simple obviousness at the foot of Mount Sinai
and even in the eighteenth century. When there were
primitive roads, negligible drains, private wells, no elaborate
system of credit, when payment meant the direct production of gold-pieces, when each industry was reasonably self-
contained—in fact when the world was not as it is now—
then it was fairly obvious what was meant by private property, apart from any current legal fictions. Today private
property is mainly a legal fiction, and apart from such legal
determination its outlines are completely indefinite. Such
legal determination is probably, indeed almost certainly, the
best way of arranging society. But the 'voice of nature' is
a faint echo when we are dealing with it. There is a striking
analogy between the hazy notions of justice in Plato's Republic, and the hazy notions of private property today.
The modern artisan, like Thrasymachus of old, is apt to
define it as 'the will of the stronger'.

Of course these extremes as to the nature of property—
simple-minded assertion and simple-minded denial—are
exaggeration. The whole concept of absolute individuals
with absolute rights, and with a contractual power of forming fully defined external relations, has broken down. The
human being is inseparable from its environment in each
occasion of its existence. The environment which the occasion inherits is immanent in it, and conversely it is immanent in the environment which it helps to transmit. The
favorite doctrine of the shift from a customary basis for
society to a contractual basis, is founded on shallow soci-

ology. There is no escape from customary status. This status is merely another name for the inheritance immanent in each occasion. Inevitably customary status is there, an inescapable condition. On the other hand, the inherited status is never a full determination. There is always the freedom for the determination of individual emphasis. In terms of high-grade human society, there is always the customary fact as an essential element in the meaning of every contractual obligation. There can be no contract which does not presuppose custom, and no custom leaving no loophole for spontaneous contract. It is this truth that gives vitality to the Anglo-American Common Law. It is an instrument, in the hands of skilled experts, for the interpretation of explicit contract in terms of implicit status. No code of verbal statement can ever exhaust the shifting background of presupposed fact. What does alter for dominant interests within each social system is the relative importance of the contractual and customary factors in general conscious experience. This balance, fortunate or unfortunate, largely depends on the type of social inheritance provided by that society. But contract is a mode of expression for spontaneity. Otherwise it is meaningless, a futile gesture of consciousness.

In the end nothing is effective except massively coördinated inheritance. Sporadic spontaneity is composed of flashes mutually thwarting each other. Ideas have to be sustained, disentangled, diffused, and coördinated with the background. Finally they pass into exemplification in action. The distinguishing mark of modern civilization is the number of institutions whose origin can be traced to the initial entertainment of some idea. In the ancient civilizations thought was mainly explanatory. It was only creative in respect to individual actions. But the corporate actions preceded thought. The ancient Gods, either as notions or as persons, did not create the thunderstorm, they explained it. Jehovah did not create the Hebrew tribal emotions, he explained them. He never made a covenant which initiated Hebrew history; the notion of the covenant was an explanatory idea. It was influential; but the idea arose as an explanation of the tribal history. Nevertheless it intensified a preëxisting fact. The Old Testament is on the verge of the dividing line between ancient and modern. This watershed is Hellenism. The difference is only one of proportion, of more or less. But a sufficient change of proportion makes all the difference. In the last phase of ancient life there is a haunting feeling that corporate actions ought to have originated from ideas. Thus their historical imagination unconsciously imported types of explanation of their past which were faintly relevant to their own present: explanations fantastic, incredible, fit only for exposure by scholars. It was the shadow of the future thrown back onto the past.

Returning to the economic side of life, in the ancient world there were economic transactions between tribes and between states, and there were also the economic activities of craftsmen, merchants, and bankers. There was communal activity and individual activity. Cicero's financial worries are preserved for us in his letters to Atticus. They are very analogous to Gibbon's letters to Holroyd, which are characteristic of educated Europe in the eighteenth century. Certainly Cicero's affairs were sufficiently complex. It is not in that respect that the ancient world fell short. It would be worth sacrificing a good deal of Latin literature to know what Atticus thought of Cicero's financial position. Even after two thousand years it is difficult not to entertain a friendly anxiety on the subject. Perhaps as Cicero put his head out of the litter he had been dreaming of bankruptcy, when the sword of the soldier gave him death.

That ancient world is modern both in the physical facts which await us, and in the ripples of anxiety arising from its social intricacies. At that time the human mind was singularly powerful for the generation of ideas. To the epoch between Plato and Justinian, we can trace our philosophical ideas, our religious ideas, our legal ideas, and the model of modern governmental organization. We can recognize Pliny as he discusses whether the parents should serve on the board of governors of the Grammar School he had founded. Sidonius Apollinaris is an anticipation of many New England gentlemen, ecclesiastic and lay. But within that period the ferment of ideas had not persisted for a sufficient time to transform society by a profusion of corporations originated by explicit thought. In particular the great commercial corporations awaited modern times, The Bank of St. George at Genoa, The Bank of England, The great trading companies to India and the East. Atticus was a banker; but he was not the president of a banking corporation. Private wealth was deposited in pagan temples; but temples were corporations devoted to the customary rites of religion. The state taxes were farmed by private corporations of Roman capitalists. Here we approach modern notions. Yet after all the *publicani* were engaged in performing one of the direct services of the state. Their actions were communal and traditional with a tinge of modern modes of incorporation. No doubt many anticipations of modern commercial institutions can be found. Those times lie within the modern world. But it was modern commerce in its infancy. Indeed, the examples quoted of modern commercial activity belong to an intermediate period, and only recently has the influence of ideas produced its full economic effect. But wherever ideas are effective, there is freedom.

SECTION VIII. Unfortunately the notion of freedom has

been eviscerated by the literary treatment devoted to it. Men of letters, artists in symphonies of pictorial imagination, have staged the shock of novel thought against tradition. The concept of freedom has been narrowed to the picture of contemplative people shocking their generation. When we think of freedom, we are apt to confine ourselves to freedom of thought, freedom of the press, freedom for religious opinions. Then the limitations to freedom are conceived as wholly arising from the antagonisms of our fellow men. This is a thorough mistake. The massive habits of physical nature, its iron laws, determine the scene for the sufferings of men. Birth and death, heat, cold, hunger, separation, disease, the general impracticability of purpose, all bring their quota to imprison the souls of women and of men. Our experiences do not keep step with our hopes. The Platonic Eros, which is the soul stirring itself to life and motion, is maimed. The essence of freedom is the practicability of purpose. Mankind has chiefly suffered from the frustration of its prevalent purposes, even such as belong to the very definition of its species. The literary exposition of freedom deals mainly with the frills. The Greek myth was more to the point. Prometheus did not bring to mankind freedom of the press. He procured fire, which obediently to human purpose cooks and gives warmth. In fact, freedom of action is a primary human need. In modern thought, the expression of this truth has taken the form of 'the economic interpretation of history'.

The fact that the 'economic interpretation' is itself a novel thought arising within the last sixty or seventy years illustrates an important sociological fact. The literary world through all ages belonged mainly to the fortunate section of mankind whose basic human wants have been amply satisfied. A few literary men have been in want throughout their lives, many have occasionally suffered. The fact shocks us. It is remembered because it is rare. The fortunate classes are oblivious to the fact that throughout the ages the masses of mankind have lived in conscious dread of such disaster— a drought, a wet summer, a bad harvest, a cattle disease, a raid of pirates. Also the basic needs when they are habitually satisfied cease to dominate thought. Delicacies of taste displace the interest in fullness of stomach. Thus the motives which stir the fortunate directing classes to conscious activity have a long range forecaste and an æsthetic tinge:— Power, glory, safety in the distant future, forms of government, luxury, religion, excitement, dislike of strange ways, contemplative curiosity, play. Mankind survived by evolving a peculiar excitability whereby it quickly adapts itself to novel circumstance. This instability is quickly diverted to some simple form of the more abstract interests of the minority. The great convulsions happen when the economic urge on the masses has dove-tailed with some simplified ideal end. Intellect and instinct then combine, and some ancient social order passes away. But the masses of the population are always there, requiring at least a minimum of satisfaction, with their standard of life here higher and there lower, also rising or falling. Thus, even when the minority is dominant, the plain economic facts of life must be the governing force in social development. Yet in general the masses are intellectually quiescent, though the more ideal ends of the minority, good and bad, permeate the masses, directing policies according to the phantasies of the generations. And the primary demand for freedom is to be found in the general urge for the accomplishment of these general ends, which are a fusion of ideal and economic policies, making the stuff of history. In so far as a population is dominated by some general appetition, freedom presents no peculiar problem to the statesman. The tribal actions are shaped inevitably, and that group of mankind is pushed towards accomplishment or frustration.

In modern states there is a complex problem. There are many types of character. Freedom means that within each type the requisite coördination should be possible without the destruction of the general ends of the whole community. Indeed, one general end is that these variously coördinated groups should contribute to the complex pattern of community life, each in virtue of its own peculiarity. In this way individuality gains the effectiveness which issues from coördination, and freedom obtains power necessary for its perfection.

This is the hope of the statesman, the solution which the long course of history is patiently disclosing. But it is not the intuition which has nerved men to surpass the limitations of mankind. After all, societies of primates, of animals, of life on the earth's surface, are transient details. There is a freedom lying beyond circumstance, derived from the direct intuition that life can be grounded upon its absorption in what is changeless amid change. This is the freedom at which Plato was groping, the freedom which Stoics and Christians obtained as the gift of Hellenism. It is the freedom of that virtue directly derived from the source of all harmony. For it is conditioned only by its adequacy of understanding. And understanding has this quality that, however it be led up to, it issues in the soul freely conforming its nature to the supremacy of insight. It is the reconciliation of freedom with the compulsion of the truth. In this sense the captive can be free, taking as his own the supreme insight, the indwelling persuasion towards the harmony which is the height of existence.

CHAPTER V

FROM FORCE TO PERSUASION

SECTION I. The gradual development of Persuasive Agencies in the communal life of mankind was not wholly due to the energizing of ideas. Indeed the very habit of intellectual activity was promoted by the slow natural development of persuasive intercourse within the social life of each community, and between different communities. Evidently the existence of each family group involves a mixture of love, dependence, sympathy, persuasion, and compulsion. There can never have been any period when the gentler modes of human relations were wholly absent. Indeed the ferocity may have been the later development, due to the increase of intelligent self-interest. It may easily have arisen as a strain of character necessary for preservation, and have developed into an overgrowth checking upward evolution beyond a low level of life. We find civilized communities struggling with two kinds of compulsion. There are the natural necessities, such as food, warmth, and shelter. There are also the necessities for a coördination of social activities. This coördination is produced partly by instinctive habit, sustained by flashes of good sense, partly by the compulsion exercised by other members of the community, and partly by reasonable persuasion. In so far as the area of reasonable persuasion widens, an environment has been provided within which the higher mental activities and the subtler feelings can find their use and their enjoyment. But with the growth of intellect the range of necessity diminishes. Some command over nature has been attained. Thus a widespread reliance on persuasion produces its reward in the shape of an upward evolution. At least, it produces conditions favourable to such an upward trend.

In this chapter, we consider the effect of some of the natural necessities, such as food and clothing, and also the effect of activities, such as commerce, which naturally promote the persuasive reactions within society, and between societies. Also we consider the transition of these agencies into various types of restlessness.

Such activities, energizing for centuries, indeed for thousands of years, lie behind the intellectual ferment which we find driving onward the Hebrew prophets and the Greek philosophers. Indeed, apart from the continuing vigour of such agencies, the intellectual life of mankind would wither, without roots, and without any material content for thought or purpose.

SECTION II. The term Commerce, as used in this chapter, will have an enlarged sense. It will include the interchange of material commodities, and their manufacture for the purpose of such interchange. It will also include the management of currency, which is a conventionalized commodity, possibly but not necessarily possessing some intrinsic value of its own apart from its use as currency. Finally we shall extend the meaning of the term even beyond these limits, passing beyond the bounds of material things. In its most general sense, the commerce of mankind involves every species of interchange which proceeds by way of mutual persuasion.

All commercial values are psychological, that is to say, they are measured by the desire widely spread among sec-

tions of mankind to acquire the numerous articles in question. Such desire may be closely connected with some physical necessity arising out of possession or deprivation, for
example, the satisfaction of hunger or starvation. When
there is a complete absence of any such physical necessity or
æsthetic fact, so that the sole advantages of possession depend on the possibility of renewed exchange, we are essentially concerned with currency founded on credit. In this
field of human behaviour the psychological peculiarities of
mankind produce their fullest effect. Very often, even in
connection with currencies, there is no explicit contract,
but the advantage of possession consists in the belief as to
the stability of certain habits of mankind, habits which are
not founded on physical necessities for the preservation of
life. For example, gold currencies depend for their prestige
upon the habit of highly prizing the possession of gold. This
habit has a long and complex history. One comparatively
late element in this history is the well-established use of
coined gold pieces as a medium of exchange. Another element is the unfounded belief that the value of gold is still
mainly independent of its use as currency, by reason of its
æsthetic and metallurgic uses. Another element is the well-
founded belief that so long as gold is generally used as currency, no Government can arbitrarily increase its stock of
gold pieces. All of these characteristics of gold are alterable. A chemical discovery in the remote future may render
the production of gold as easy as that of paper currency-
notes. The superstitious reverence for gold may pass away.
The governments of the world may prefer paper currencies,
perhaps for the very reason that they can increase the number of paper notes at their arbitrary will, thus freeing society
from one type of physical compulsion. But the fundamental

fact is that so long as the generality of mankind deem gold to be wealth, then it is wealth; and as soon as this opinion passes, gold then becomes a metal of subsidiary importance.

Currencies represent only one particular case of this dependence on habits of mankind. All producers and retail traders are in this position. One extreme example is afforded by the commerce in religious emblems, such as the production of idols for worship in Central Africa, or the production of black gowns for the vesture of Calvinistic or Unitarian preachers in some countries. However, most commodities belong to a mixed type. In temperate climates dress is a physical necessity, but fashions of dress depend upon taste and are in fact very alterable. Even food, though a more pressing necessity than dress, in modern times includes an abundance of alternatives. The upshot of all these considerations is that the doctrines of Commerce have to be founded upon assumptions concerning necessities, habits, technology, and prevalent knowledge. But habits, technology, and knowledge are variable from epoch to epoch, and even in any one epoch differ in different sections of humanity. Thus any theory of Commerce depends upon presuppositions as to the populations concerned, and cannot be extended beyond these limits apart from a direct investigation of the wider populations. For example, any considerable change in technology alters in effect the populations, and thus requires a corresponding shift in commercial theory. This conclusion has been well-known to the great masters of economic doctrine. But certainly it has not been adequately attended to by the majority of people engaged in the theory or the practice of commerce or in its political regulation. The classical political economy which dominated the nineteenth century was largely based upon sociological observation of the middle classes of northern Europe

and northern America in the eighteenth century, also with
some reference to Mediterranean commerce of earlier epochs.
Everything else, discernible in other sections of the European populations or in other continents, was dismissed as
irrelevant interruption to the pure practice of perfect
commerce.

The development of economics was, in truth, affected by
the moralizing tendency of the class mainly concerned.
Their ideal of commercial activity as the main occupation of
perfected civilization led to the consideration of economic
laws which *should* hold, and to the neglect of economic procedures which in fact *did* hold. For example, in England in
the mid-nineteenth century radical manufactures opposed
the enactment of adulteration laws, basing their action on
the axiom *Caveat emptor*. In this instance their individualistic doctrine of society, combined with their presupposition
that respectable men and women are mainly engaged in
safeguarding all details of their commercial interests, led
them to neglect questions of prevalent fact. In the study of
ideas, it is necessary to remember, that insistence on hard-
headed clarity issues from sentimental feeling, as it were a
mist, cloaking the perplexities of fact. Insistence on clarity
at all costs is based on sheer superstition as to the mode in
which human intelligence functions. Our reasonings grasp
at straws for premises and float on gossamers for deductions.

SECTION III. Another instance of ill-judged simplification
is the use made of the Malthusian Law of Population. This
law, in any reasonably accurate statement, is undeniable.
The increase of population apart from checks on impulse, or
on childbearing, or on survival, proceeds by a law with
some analogy to geometric progression. Also, apart from
these checks, the numerical factor of the geometric increase

is greater than unity by a difference which is not negligible. Again the means of subsistence—food, clothing, shelter—, so far as they are provided by appliances of given types, can only be increased by the production of additional appliances of these types. Such additional production, even if variable, must conform to the general type of arithmetical progression. But a geometric progression will always overtake an arithmetic progression. It was then concluded, as a conse-quence of this Malthusian Law, that population will always overtake the means of subsistence. The further inference was then drawn that, apart from short exceptional periods, the normal structure of society was that of a comparatively affluent minority subsisting on the labours of a teeming population checked by starvation and other discomforts.

These sociological conclusions, if true, are of enormous importance to commerce, in the enlarged sense in which we have used that term. For, in the first place, the normal structure of society is now defined. It consists of the fortunate few, and of the semi-destitute many. Thus producers must, in the long run, design their production to suit these types of customers. Again the hope of improving the social system by a humane adjustment of social conditions in factories must be abandoned. It is of course possible, here and there, as the result of isolated charity. But in the long run, there must be a pool of labour, starving and destitute, ready to work on the wages of bare subsistence. Factories taking ad-vantage of such cheap labour will drive out of trade those managed on fanciful humanitarian lines. Hence the final improvement of the social system is mirage. In so far as medicine saves life, there will be only more to starve.

These sociological conclusions from the Malthusian Law assume first that all the restraints upon increase of mankind are secondary in their effect until they are raised to dominance by excessive population. Secondly they assume that within the span of time required for the operation of the Malthusian Law, sudden increases of productive power, due to improved technology will not be introduced. Perhaps such improved technology may even require additional population. Thirdly they assume that the geographic situation of the population concerned will not be seriously affected by migration. In truth there is a complex situation depending on the balance of many factors. By arbitrarily seizing upon one or two factors, and by relegating the remainder to the status of secondary disturbances, almost any law of population can be deduced. Thus the Malthusian Law, with its sociological consequences, is not an iron necessity. It is a possibility inherent in the facts, which may afford an interpretation of the circumstances of some human societies, perhaps of all.

A recourse to observation at once discloses the importance of the doctrine of Malthus. China and India both afford examples of societies which illustrate his law. They contain large populations whose standard of life is perilously near to the margin of subsistence. We must conclude, therefore, that for nearly half the human race, Malthus has provided an interpretation for some of the dominant facts of history occurring within the last few centuries, and perhaps stretching into a longer period. Now India and China are instances of civilized societies which for a long period in their later history maintained themselves with arrested technology and with fixed geographical location. They provided the exact conditions required for the importance of the Malthusian Law.

When we turn to the European races the evidence is more perplexing. The superficial fact is that during the eleven centuries from the age of Charlemagne to the present day a persistently increasing population has been accompanied by an equally persistent rise in the general standard of life. Thus any simple-minded Malthusian correlation of density of population with deficiency in the necessaries of life does not apply. Of course, the stock answer to this conclusion is that the checks, which the leading Malthusians have always explicitly recognized, have intervened to delay the inevitable issue. But Europe, even Western Europe, is a large region, and a thousand years is a long time, about one-sixth of the whole past of civilization within the historical period. The plain truth is that during this period and over that area, the so-called checks were such that the Malthusian law represented a possibility, unrealized and of no importance. Also these checks were not even in proportion to the density of the population. For examples the plagues depended mainly on insanitary habits, and the densities of rats, insects, and microbes. At the time of the Black Death, a Malthusian discussing the excessive birth rate would have been talking irrelevant nonsense. Soap, water, and drains were the key to the situation. The Thirty Years' War halved the population of Germany. It was due to many causes, a few creditable, but most of them discreditable. An excessive population in Germany has never been mentioned among them. Of course there was plenty of misery in the Middle Ages, and during the Renaissance. For example, we read of Peasants' risings. But this misery certainly did not prevail in any proportion to density of population. Thus, in the early years of the sixteenth century, Flanders which was thickly populated was notably more prosperous than the country-districts in Germany where, at that time, there was a rising of the peasants. Of course the reasons for this contrast are too obvious to be worth mentioning. But among these reasons, the fact emerges that the Malthusian Law is largely irrelevant for the discussion of sociological conditions in Europe.

SECTION IV. Nevertheless there have been such occasions of relevance. It is a mistake to discuss the development of Western Europe in isolation. The history of Europe has been decisively influenced by its reactions with the Near East. Here the term Near East is used to denote that large region, including three metropolitan districts, on its coastal boundaries,—Constantinople, Mesopotamia, and the Delta of the Nile, and also including the Arabian Desert with its fertile fringes, and the plateaus and mountains of Asia Minor. The history of civilization in the Old World is the history of the internal development of the four continental regions fringing Asia, namely, China, India, The Near East, and Europe. These four histories cannot be understood apart from a study of the reactions of these vast regions on each other. For example, the Hellenic and Hellenistic epochs comprise the story of how the ancient civilization of the Near East brought to birth the new civilization of Europe, and how European civilization asserted its independence of the social system to which it owed its nurture. The subsequent collapse of the older civilization is the tragedy of history, foreshadowed by the decline of the Roman Empire whose imperial system had reverted to Eastern ideals.

The reactions between mediaeval Europe and the Near East can be classified under four headings, Malthus, Religion, Technology, Commerce. It must be remembered, however, that all the major crises in the story were precipitated by a concurrence of many causes. It is a great mistake in sociological theory to link impulse towards activity with abject destitution. In fact, when a population has sunk its standard of life to the marginal level for subsistence, the poverty of life weakens the impulse towards adventure. The

Malthusian impulse towards conquest arises when a well-nurtured, hardy population is only beginning to feel the pressure of its numbers on its resources. There was no evidence of starvation at the Courts of Central Asia or among the Arabian tribes. Probably there was a growing hard dullness of life provoking unrest. But the active stimulants for the eruptions of the Tartar and Arabian tribes were adventure, the dream of fabulous luxury, religion. The dream of luxury is the first, and more dangerous, phase of the Malthusian pressure on a population. It arises before the inroad of enfeeblement. But the initial phase of emotional unrest can take a more intellectual form, and clothe itself in religious concepts. A new mass-religion can then arise, with the mission to subdue the Earth and destroy the infidels. In fact, it is a commonplace of history, that the pressure of population upon its resources is one main ingredient in the catastrophic reactions between large regions, and between diverse classes within the same social system. On the whole, catastrophes are disastrous to civilization. They are a plunge into the unknown; and civilization is not the average result of raw nature. It depends upon the long-time operation of selective agency.

Three reasons stand out to explain why the internal conditions in Europe, for more than a thousand years, reduced to insignificance the operation of the Malthusian Law. They are, Expansion of Commerce, Development of Technology, and Discovery of Empty Continents. All these causes are interconnected. Also the activities involved in each can be represented as due to a population seeking means of subsistence. But the point is that mankind has developed an unstable sensitivity in respect to its emotional and intellectual functions. Thus in fortunate societies faint signs of economic pressure develop disproportionate forms of adventure, physical and intellectual. Avocations are initiated as means of subsistence: they end as passions. The result in Europe has been the introduction of novelties, of Commerce, of Scientific Technology, and of Geographic Knowledge, which have entirely masked sociological consequences of the Malthusian type.

The central activity from which the other two developed was Commerce. We are speaking of Europe from the Age of Charlemagne onwards. If we had included the six hundred years preceding that Age, the migration of Peoples within Europe was one main factor. But in the period under review these great migrations were over. The diffusion of the Scandinavian Northmen was still in progress. But this migration was hardly a mass movement. It is best conceived as the diffusion of the ablest governing class that Europe has ever seen,—Canute and his Danes, Norman Barons in France, and in England, and in Southern Italy. Also their direct activities were not such as to mask the Malthusian Laws. They introduced order, and good order is a condition for the increase of population. Order, as such, gives no reason for escape from the consequences of an increasing population. Also an enumeration of some main interests of the epoch is not to the point. For example, the various activities of the Catholic Church, the scholastic controversies, the Holy Roman Empire, architecture, the artistic and literary interests of the Renaissance, the Reformation, had no direct bearing on the evasion of Malthusian consequences arising from the increase of population. Granting the increase of population, History has only disclosed three ways of escape,—expanding Commerce, improving Technology, and utilization of Empty Regions. The most fundamental of all sociological classifications is that between civilized societies for which one or more of these conditions do obtain, and those for which they do not obtain. In the wide sense of the term, Commerce covers all three conditions. Thus Commerce is one central factor, essential for a prosperous civilization. As soon as there is an arrest, when expansion, improvement, and novel utilization cease, then slowly and imperceptibly a blight settles upon the populations concerned. China and India survived, with populations blighted by hopeless poverty, the Roman Empire fell by reason of the blight, the Near East is the store-house of buried cities recording ancient magnificence. The central factor is Commerce; and more than that, it is Commerce developed adventurously.

In the first three hundred years of the slow development of the Feudal System after Charlemagne, we see a population barely gaining a livelihood by hard toil. This state of things exemplifies the application of Malthus' Doctrine in the primitive stages of civilization. The only way of coping with an increase of population was to cut down another forest, and arithmetically to add field to field, till fertile land was fully occupied. Also fertility itself became exhausted, so that until the close of the eighteenth century fallow fields bore witness to the iron limits that nature set to agriculture. The essence of technology is to enable mankind to transcend such limitations of unguided nature. For example, the rotation of the crops, the scientific understanding of fertilizers and of genetics, have already altered the bounds set to food production.

In those early times the Malthusian Laws set their limits to life. The 'checks' were operating, and population hardly increased. The slow growth of Commerce, the foundation of centres of trade with the peculiar privileges of the burgesses and the guilds, the strange knowledge of the Jews, pilgrims, the glimpses of the Near East provided by Medi-

terranean trade, and later by the Crusades, the intelligence
housed in the great monasteries—all these factors gradually
removed the repression of raw nature upon the possibilities
of human existence. European life began to approach the
standards of the Near East and of China so far as concerned
technology and general commercial activities. But these
older civilizations were about to face new limitations, equally
inexorable, granting their stage of technology and of social
organization.

SECTION V. Nature is plastic, although to every prevalent
state of mind there corresponds iron nature setting its
bounds to life. Modern history begins when Europeans
passed into a new phase of understanding which enabled
them to introduce new selective agencies, unguessed by the
older civilizations. It is a false dichotomy to think of Nature
and Man. Mankind is that factor *in* Nature which exhibits
in its most intense form the plasticity of nature. Plasticity
is the introduction of novel law. The doctrine of the Uniformity of Nature is to be ranked with the contrasted doctrine of magic and miracle, as an expression of partial truth,
unguarded and uncoördinated with the immensities of the
Universe. Our interpretations of experience determine the
limits of what we can do with the world.

For the purpose of understanding how it happened that
European life escaped the restrictions which finally bound
China, India, and The Near East, it is important to recap-
ture the attitude towards Commerce prevalent in various
epochs. I do not mean records of trade, but records of the
kinds of mentality governing commercial relations. We can
only understand a society by knowing what sort of people
undertook what sort of functions in that society. It must be
remembered that China and Bagdad, at the height of their
prosperity, exhibited forms of human life in many ways

more gracious than our own. They were great civilizations. But they became arrested, and the arrest is the point of our enquiry. We have to understand the reasons for the greatness and the final barriers to advancement. Of course, such an ambitious design is absurd. It would mean the solution of the main problem of sociology. What can be done, is to note some indications of relevant tones of mind apparently widely spread in various districts at different epochs.

There is ample evidence of active Commerce in China and the Near East in ancient times, contemporary with the pre-Hellenic and Hellenic periods of the Ægean Basin. There are Codes of Law which determine commercial problems. Also among the early inscriptions recovered from Babylon and Nineveh there are a mass of records of private transactions between merchants. Three thousand years ago the importance of credit would have been no news either in Mesopotamia or in China. Also there was foreign trade beyond the boundaries of the Near East. There are evidences of ocean-borne trade between India and Egypt, perhaps even between China and Egypt, with Ceylon as an intermediary. Also Central Asia was nearing its last phase of prosperity before it faded out into desert. It seems to have provided the route for a flourishing overland trade between China and the Near East. Thus these great civilizations were supported by internal trade and by external trade with each other. Also there was the whole coast-line of semi-barbarous Europe,—the shores of the Black Sea, the shores of the Western Mediterranean, the Atlantic coasts of Europe.

Having regard to relative backwardness of the art of navigation then, compared with the same art in the fifteenth and sixteenth centuries after Christ, the boldness of the Phœnician sailors and the enterprise of their traders at least equals that in any of the later feats. It is impossible to be more

than absolutely fearless: and considering the dim geographic knowledge possessed by the ancients, the Phœnicians
must be allowed the fame of having displayed that extremity
of courage. The Greeks were bold sailors, but the Phœnicians led the way. There is no reason to believe that in later
times a Greek or a Roman vessel ever saw a coast-line not
previously visited by Phœnician traders. Also, remembering
Hanno's voyage in the sixth century before Christ, the whole
oceanic coast-line of Africa was explored by the men of the
Near East, where western Europeans did not venture till
the lapse of nigh two thousand years. In the last few hundred years, European races have been apt to forget the greatness of the Near East, whose populations, with no predecessors to guide them, carried mankind from the stage of
semi-barbarism only half-erect from the soil, to peaks of
civilized life, in art, in religion, and in adventure, which
remain unsurpassed. Their civilization in its prime was
founded on Expanding Commerce, Development of Technology, and Discovery of Empty Continents. But in this list
one item has been omitted, The Souls of Men.

The vigour of the Near East survived the first effort to
establish a widespread European civilization. This European attempt was embodied in the Western portion of the
Roman Empire. It was sustained during four hundred and
fifty, or five hundred years. The limits of this period may
be approximately assigned from Cæsar and Augustus at the
commencement down to the taking of Rome by Alaric in
the year 410 A.D. The failure did not consist in the decline
and fall of its political institutions. Such state-systems are
transient expedients upon the surface of civilization. The
real failure consists in the fact that in the year 600 A.D.,
Western Europe was less civilized than in the year 100 A.D.,
and was far behind the Eastern Mediterranean during the

third and fourth centuries before Christ. Pope Gregory, the
Great, would have been poor company for Sophocles, Aristotle, Eratosthenes, or Archimedes. Gregory was the man
for his time. But the delicacies of civilization—in art, or in
thought, or in human behaviour—were then at a discount.

In every sense of the term, the Western Empire had
lacked expansive force. Across the Rhine and the Danube
the northern forests were impenetrable. On the west, the
Atlantic Ocean was trackless. With the minor exception of
the conquest of Britain, all attempt at physical expansion
ceased after Varus lost the legions of Augustus. The Western
Empire in all its ramifications was a purely defensive institution, in its sociological functionings and in its external behaviour. Its learning lacked speculative adventure. In no
sense, however we stretch the metaphor, did it discover a
New World. Unfortunately life is an offensive, directed
against the repetitious mechanism of the Universe. It is
the thesis of this discussion that a policy of sociological defence is doomed to failure. We are analysing those types
of social functioning which provide that expansion and
novelty which life demands. Life can only be understood as
an aim at that perfection which the conditions of its environment allow. But the aim is always beyond the attained fact.
The goal is some type of perfected things, however lowly
and basically sensual. Inorganic nature is characterized by
its acceptance of matter of fact. In nature, the soil rests,
while the root of the plant pursues the sources of its refreshment. In the Western Empire there was no pursuit. Its
remnants of irritability were devoid of transcendent aim.

Of course Christianity was a tremendous exception. But
on the whole, in its immediate effect it was a destructive
agency. Its disregard of temporal fact, based on apocalyptic
prophecy, was too extreme. It was not till its first few cen-

turie< were passed that it began to acquire a fortunate worldliness. Indeed the translation of Eastern modes of thought—
Semitic, Greek, and Egyptian—to Western Europe had
the unfortunate effect of making the ideal side of civilization appear more abstract than it was in the lands and the
epochs of its origin. It had this effect in the Near East
itself when by the lapse of time circumstances altered. For
the early Hebrews, their God was a personage whose aims
were expressible in terms of the immediate political and
social circumstances. Their religious notions had singularly
slight reference to another World. The absorption of the
Greek philosophers in the city life of their times is evident.
But in other times and, still more, in other lands, such
thoughts and ideals took on an abstract tinge. They had
lost their practical application. The notion arose that the
man of culture and the man of ideal aim was a stranger
in the busy world. It is true that such a notion haunted
Plato. But it dominated Augustine. Yet in Augustine's
age, towards the close of the century after Constantine, the
mission of the Church for the reformation of this World
was in its first phase. The obstinate survival of the present
World was upsetting the unworldly tactics of the early
Christians.

But the civilization of the Near East, including its Byzantine fringe, contained other sources of vigour, preserving
it from the decadence of its Western off-shoot. The true
successors of Alexander, the men who realized his fabled
dream of extending the Near Eastern civilization from
the Tigris to the western shores of the Mediterranean, belonged to the age of Justinian and to the age of Mahometan expansion. Justinian's success was incomplete. It was
a false dawn. But the Mahometans represent the complete
triumph of the Near East, after it had absorbed the novel

ingredients introduced by Hellenism and Hebrewism, its two great off-shoots destined to re-create civilization. Thus there are two peaks to the Near Eastern Culture. The earlier is embodied in the first known examples of high civilization in Babylon and Egypt. The metaphor of a peak here fails; for this earlier type of life maintained itself for long ages. The advent of the Persians represents a transitional period. They almost antedated the Mahometans. But the times were not ready.

The distinction separating the Byzantines and the Mahometans from the Romans is that the Romans were themselves deriving the civilization which they spread. In their hands it assumed a frozen form. Thought halted, and literature copied. The Byzantines and the Mahometans were themselves the civilization. Thus their culture retained its intrinsic energies, sustained by physical and spiritual adventure. They traded with the far East: they expanded westward: they codified law: they developed new forms of art: they elaborated theologies: they transformed mathematics: they developed medicine. In this final period of Near Eastern greatness the Jews played the same part as did the Greeks during the Persian epoch. Finally, the Near East as a centre of civilization was destroyed by the Tartars and the Turks.

Luckily for Europe, the more northern thrust of the Tartars across Russia seems to have been checked by the forests of Poland and the more southern hills and mountains. These conquerors of the Near East were never civilized in any effective sense of the term. During the later centuries, the Turkish pressure on Europe constituted merely the threat of Europe produced by a lower civilization, an ingenious compound of primitive brutality and decadent refinement. In the eighteenth and nineteenth centuries much history was written under the impression that the Turks were the authentic representatives of the previous Near Eastern civilization. Thus the early Greeks were staged as its opponents and not as its derivatives. In fact the long pupillage of Europe to the Near East was entirely misrepresented.

SECTION VI. At the close of the Dark Ages Europe started upon its second effort after civilization with three main advantages: its Christian ethics: its instinct for legal organization transcending local boundaries, derived from the Church and the reminiscence of the Empire: and thirdly its wider inheritance of antecedent thought, gradually disclosing itself as Hebrew, Greek, and Roman literatures. The total effect was the increased sense of the dignity of man, as man. There has been a growth, slow and wavering, of respect for the preciousness of human life. This is the humanitarian spirit, gradually emerging in the slow sunrise of a thousand years.

The creation of the world—said Plato—is the victory of persuasion over force. The worth of men consists in their liability to persuasion. They can persuade and can be persuaded by the disclosure of alternatives, the better and the worse. Civilization is the maintenance of social order, by its own inherent persuasiveness as embodying the nobler alternative. The recourse to force, however, unavoidable, is a disclosure of the failure of civilization, either in the general society or in a remnant of individuals. Thus in a live civilization there is always an element of unrest. For sensitiveness to ideas means curiosity, adventure, change. Civilized order survives on its merits, and is transformed by its power of recognizing its imperfections.

Now the intercourse between individuals and between social groups takes one of two forms, force or persuasion.

Commerce is the great example of intercourse in the way of persuasion. War, slavery, and governmental compulsion exemplify the reign of force. The weakness of the Near Eastern civilizations consisted in their large reliance upon force. The growth of persuasive intercourse within the texture of society became halted. These civilizations never eradicated a large reliance upon the sway of conquerors over conquered populations, and upon the rule of individual masters over slaves. This habit of dominance spread its infection beyond these limits. A rule of men over women remained an established feature of highly civilized societies. It survived as a hang-over from barbarism. But its demoralizing effects increased with civilization. This inequality of men and women seems to have been based upon physical superiorities, and the absorption of women in the birth and care of children. Anyhow it issued in the degradation of women below the level of the males. Thus these eastern races entered upon the fatal experiment of maintaining themselves at two levels of culture, and of dominating subject populations at yet a third level. The enjoyment of power is fatal to the subtleties of life. Ruling classes degenerate by reason of their lazy indulgence in obvious gratifications.

Commerce followed upon the gradual acquirement of means for easy locomotion in small groups. Whole communities had wandered, gradually shifting to other environments. But travel and return, undertaken by small groups or even by individual men, is an enterprise of entirely different character. It requires either open country, free from forest barriers, or the navigation of rivers and seas. The strangers arrive in small groups. They are thus under no temptation to dominate, and excite no fear. Commerce may stabilize itself into a steady traditional routine. This halt in progress has happened over large areas for long periods of time. But on the whole, Commerce is unstable. It brings together groups of men with different modes of life, different technologies, and different ways of thought. Apart from Commerce, the mariners' compass, with the vast theory which it has suggested, would never have reached the shores of the Atlantic, and printing would not have spread from Pekin to Cairo.

The expanding Commerce of mediaeval and modern Europe was promoted in the first place by the great roads which were the legacy from the Roman Empire, by the improving art of navigation which enabled the indented coastline to be utilized, and by the sense of unity promoted by the Catholic Church and Christian ethics. There were pirates, and feudal wars, and rough sporadic disorder. But men from different regions, of different races, and of different occupation were meeting together on the basis of free persuasion. Even the feudal castle, though it often harboured men with the mentality of gangsters, was more apt for defence than for offence. Also feudal levies, with their short periods of service, were mostly effective as defensive forces. In later times the evils of this system outweighed its merits. But in its origin it can be compared to the modern police, quite as aptly as to the modern army. Of course it differed from both. The point is that the feudal castle was mostly a sensible mode of self-protection for a peaceful district. The merit of Commerce lies in its close relation to technology. The novelty of experience promoted by Commerce suggests alternatives in ways of production. Again European technology was fertilized from another source. The art of clear thinking, of criticism of premises, of speculative assumption, of deductive reasoning—this great art was discovered, at least in embryo, by the Greeks, and was inherited by Europe. Like other inventions it has often been disastrously misused

But its effect on intellectual capacity can only be compared
with that of fire and iron and steel for the production of the
blades of Damascus and Toledo. Mankind was now armed
intellectually, as well as physically.

Curiosity was now progressive. The static wisdom of the
proverbs of Solomon, and of the Wisdom Books of the Bible,
has been supplanted by Euclid's Elements, by Newton's
Physics, by the modern epoch in industry. 'All the rivers
run into the sea; there is nothing new under the sun', was
the final judgment of the Near East. When we have allowed
for all its brilliance, and for its many modes of activity, this
great civilization finally sank under the barren criticism of
disillusioned sensualists. It is the nemesis of the reign of
force, of the worship of power, that the ideals of the semi-
divine rulers centre upon some variant of Solomon's magnificent harem of three hundred wives and seven hundred
concubines. The variation may be towards decency, but it
is equally decadent. Christianity has only escaped from the
Near East with scars upon it.

SECTION VII. In this rapid survey of the rise and fall of
civilizations, we have noted four factors which decisively
govern the fate of social groups. First, there stands the
inexorable law that apart from some transcendent aim the
civilized life either wallows in pleasure or relapses slowly
into a barren repetition with waning intensities of feeling.
Secondly, there stands the iron compulsion of nature that
the bodily necessities of food, clothing, and shelter be provided. The rigid limits which are thereby set to modes of
social existence can only be mitigated by the growth of an
understanding by which the interplay between man and the
rest of nature can be adjusted. Thirdly, the compulsory
dominion of men over men has a double significance. It
has a benign effect so far as it secures the coördination of

behaviour necessary for social welfare. But it is fatal to extend this dominion beyond the barest limits necessary for this coördination. The progressive societies are those which most decisively have trusted themselves to the fourth factor which is the way of persuasion. Amidst all the activities of mankind there are three which chiefly have promoted this last factor in human life. They are family affections aroused in sex relations and in the nurture of children, intellectual curiosity leading to enjoyment in the interchange of ideas, and—as soon as large-scale societies arose—the practice of Commerce. But beyond these special activities a greater bond of sympathy has arisen. This bond is the growth of reverence for that power in virtue of which nature harbours ideal ends, and produces individual beings capable of conscious discrimination of such ends. This reverence is the foundation of the respect for man as man. It thereby secures that liberty of thought and action, required for the upward adventure of life on this Earth.

CHAPTER VI

FORESIGHT

SECTION I. By the phrase Historical Foresight, I mean something quite different from the accurate exercise of Scientific Induction. Science is concerned with generalities. The generalities apply, but they do not determine the course of history apart from some anchorage in fact. There might have been many alternative courses of history conditioned by the same laws. Perhaps, if we knew enough of the laws, then we should understand that the development of the future from the past is completely determined by the details of the past and by these scientific laws which condition all generation. Unfortunately our knowledge of scientific laws is woefully defective, and our knowledge of the relevant facts of the present and the past is scanty in the extreme. Thus as the result of all our science, we are ignorant of that remote epoch when there will be a second collision between the sun and a passing star, we are ignorant of the future of life on the earth, we are ignorant of the future of mankind, we are ignorant of the course of history a year hence, we are ignorant of most of the domestic details of our lives tomorrow, we are even ignorant of the term that has been set to our own existence.

This catalogue of ignorances at once reminds us that our state is not that of blank absence of knowledge. Our ignorance is suffused with Foresight. Also the basis of our defect in foresight is our scant knowledge of the relevant detailed facts in past and present which are required for the application of the scientific laws. Where the circumstances are comparatively simple, as in Astronomy, we know that the facts and the astronomical laws provide an apparatus of great accuracy in forecast. The main difficulty in Historical Foresight is the power of collecting and selecting the facts relevant to the particular type of forecast which we wish to make. Discussions on the method of science wander off onto the topic of experiment. But experiment is nothing else than a mode of cooking the facts for the sake of exemplifying the law. Unfortunately the facts of history, even those of private individual history, are on too large a scale. They surge forward beyond control.

It is thus evident that this topic of Historical Foresight is not to be exhausted by a neat description of some definite methods. It is faced with two sources of difficulty, where science has only one. Science seeks the laws only, but Foresight requires in addition due emphasis on the relevant facts from which the future is to emerge. Of the two tasks required for Foresight, this selection amid the welter is the more difficult. Probably a neat doctrine of Foresight is impossible. But what can be done is to confine attention to one field of human activity, and to describe the type of mentality which seems requisite for the attainment of Foresight within that field. The present state of the world, and the course of the discussions in this book, suggest the field of Commercial relations. This field will therefore be chosen to illustrate the function of ideas in the provision of anticipation and purpose.

To avoid misunderstanding I must disclaim the foolish notion that it is possible for anyone, devoid of personal experience of commerce, to provide useful suggestions for its detailed conduct. There is no substitute for first-hand practice. Also the word 'commerce' is here used in the largest sense of that term, in which it includes a variety of activities. Any useful theory, capable of immediate application to specific instances, must depend on a direct knowledge of the relevant reactions of men and women composing that society, or perhaps group of nations, within which the specific business in question is to flourish. In this discussion there is no pretence of such detailed knowledge.

There remains, however, the question of the general type of mentality which in the present condition of the world will promote the general success of a commercial community. Such a type is, of course, very complex. But we are considering one unquestioned element in it, namely Foresight, and will discuss the conditions for its development and its successful exercise.

Some people are born with astounding knacks of the mind. For example, there are calculating boys who can perform intricate operations of mental arithmetic in a flash, there are also other sorts of peculiar faculties of divination; in particular there are men with a knack of shrewdness in judging circumstances within the narrow range of their immediate observation. But after all, bankers prefer that their clerks should learn arithmetic, and trained geologists are preferred to men with divining rods. In the same way, there are general conditions of training which promote the development of a wider type of foresight.

It is a great mistake to divide people into sharp classes, namely, people with such-and-such a knack and people without it. These trenchant divisions are simply foolish. Most humans are born with certain aptitudes. But these aptitudes can easily remain latent unless they are elicited into activity by fortunate circumstances. If anyone has no aptitude of a certain type, no training can elicit it. But, granted the aptitude, we can discuss the ways of training it. Foresight depends upon understanding. In practical affairs it is a habit. But the habit of foreseeing is elicited by the habit of understanding. To a large extent, understanding can be acquired by a conscious effort and it can be taught. Thus the training of Foresight is by the medium of Understanding. Foresight is the product of Insight.

Section II. The general topic to be understood is the entire internal functioning of human society, including its technologies, the biological and physical laws on which these technologies depend, and including the sociological reactions of humans depending on fundamental psychological principles. In fact, the general topic is sociology in the broadest sense of the term, including its auxiliary sciences. Such a width of understanding is, of course, beyond the grasp of any single human. But no part of it is entirely foreign to the provision of foresight in business. Such a complete understanding is a coöperative enterprise; and a business community maintains its success for long periods so far as its average foresight is dominated by some approach to such general understanding.

We shall comprehend better the varieties of individual understanding which go to complete this general equipment of an ideal business community, if we commence by considering the contrast between understanding and routine.

Routine is the god of every social system; it is the seventh heaven of business, the essential component in the success of every factory, the ideal of every statesman. The social machine should run like clockwork. Every crime should be followed by an arrest, every arrest by a judicial trial, every trial by a conviction, every conviction by a punishment, every punishment by a reformed character. Or, you can conceive an analogous routine concerning the making of a motor car, starting with the iron in the ore, and the coal in the mine, and ending with the car driving out of the factory and with the President of the Corporation signing the dividend warrants, and renewing his contracts with the mining Corporations. In such a routine everyone from the humblest miner to the august president is exactly trained for his special job. Every action of miner or president is the product of conditioned reflexes, according to current physiological phraseology. When the routine is perfect, understanding can be eliminated, except such minor flashes of intelligence as are required to deal with familiar accidents, such as a flooded mine, a prolonged drought, or an epidemic of influenza. A system will be the product of intelligence. But when the adequate routine is established, intelligence vanishes, and the system is maintained by a coördination of conditioned reflexes. What is then required from the humans is receptivity of special training. No one, from President to miner, need understand the system as a whole. There will be no foresight, but there will be complete success in the maintenance of the routine.

Now it is the beginning of wisdom to understand that social life is founded upon routine. Unless society is permeated, through and through, with routine, civilization vanishes. So many sociological doctrines, the products of acute intellects, are wrecked by obliviousness to this fundamental sociological truth. Society requires stability, foresight itself presupposes stability, and stability is the product of routine. But there are limits to routine, and it is for the discernment of these limits, and for the provision of the consequent action, that foresight is required.

The two extremes of complete understanding and of complete routine are never realized in human society. But of the two, routine is more fundamental than understanding, that is to say, routine modified by minor flashes of short range intelligence. Indeed the notion of complete understanding controlling action is an ideal in the clouds, grotesquely at variance with practical life. But we have under our eyes countless examples of societies entirely dominated by routine. The elaborate social organizations of insects appear to be thoroughgoing examples of routine. Such organizations achieve far-reaching, complex purposes: they involve a differentiation of classes, from cows to serfs, from serfs to workers, from workers to warriors, from warriors to janitors, and from janitors to queens. Such organizations have regard to needs in a distant future, especially if the comparatively short space of life of the individual insects is taken into account as the unit of measurement.

These insect societies have been astoundingly successful, so far as concerns survival power. They seem to have a past extending over tens of thousands of years, perhaps of millions of years. It is the greatest of mistakes to believe that it has required the high-grade intelligence of mankind to construct an elaborate social organization. A particular instance of this error is the prevalent assumption that any social routine whose purposes are not obvious to our analysis is thereby to be condemned as foolish. We can observe insects performing elaborate routine actions whose purposes they cannot possibly understand, which yet are essential either for their own individual survival or for race-survival.

But these insect societies have one great characteristic in common. They are not progressive. It is exactly this characteristic that discriminates communities of mankind from communities of insects. Further, this great fact of progressiveness, be it from worse to better, or from better to worse, has become of greater and greater importance in Western civilization as we come to modern times. The rate of change has increased even in my life-time. It is possible that in future ages mankind may relapse into the stage of stable societies. But such a relapse is extremely unlikely within any span of time which we need take into account.

SECTION III. The recent shortening of the time-span between notable changes in social customs is very obvious, if we examine history. Originally it depended upon some slow development of physical causes. For example, a gradual change of physical configuration such as the elevation of mountains: the time-span for such a change is of the order of a million years. Again, a gradual change of climate: the time-span for such a change is of the order of five-thousand years. Again a gradual over-population of the region occupied by some community with its consequent swarming into new territories: having regard to the huge death-rate of pre-scientific ages, the time-span for such a change was of the order of five-hundred years. Again, the sporadic inventions of new technologies, such as the chipping of flints, the invention of fire, the taming of animals, the invention of metallurgy: in the pre-scientific ages, the average time-span for such changes was, at least, of the order of five-hundred years. If we compare the technologies of civilizations west of Mesopotamia at the epochs 100 A.D., the culmination of the Roman Empire, and 1400 A.D., the close of the Middle Ages, we find practically no advance in technology. There was some gain in metallurgy, some elaboration of clockwork, the recent invention of gun powder with its influence all in the future, some advance in the art of navigation, also with its influence in the future. If we compare 1400 A.D. with 1700 A.D., there is a great advance; gunpowder, and printing, and navigation, and the technique of commerce, had produced their effect. But even then, the analogy between life in the eighteenth century and life in the great period of

ancient Rome was singularly close, so that the peculiar
relevance of Latin literature was felt vividly. In the fifty
years between 1780 and 1830, a number of inventions came
with a rush into effective operation. The age of steam power
and of machinery was introduced. But for two generations,
from 1830 to 1890, there was a singular uniformity in the
principles of technology which were regulating the structure
of society and the usages of business.

The conclusion to be drawn from this survey is a momentous one. Our sociological theories, our political philosophy,
our practical maxims of business, our political economy,
and our doctrines of education, are derived from an unbroken tradition of great thinkers and of practical examples,
from the age of Plato in the fifth century before Christ to
the end of the last century. The whole of this tradition is
warped by the vicious assumption that each generation will
substantially live amid the conditions governing the lives of
its fathers and will transmit those conditions to mould with
equal force the lives of its children. We are living in the
first period of human history for which this assumption is
false.

Of course in the past, there were great catastrophes: for
example, plagues, floods, barbarian invasions. But, if such
catastrophes were warded off, there was a stable, well-known
condition of civilized life. This assumption subtly pervades
the premises of political economy, and has permitted it to
confine attention to a simplified edition of human nature.
It is at the basis of our conception of the reliable business
man, who has mastered a technique and never looks beyond his contracted horizon. It colours our political philosophy and our educational theory, with their overwhelming
emphasis on past experience. The note of recurrence dominates the wisdom of the past, and still persists in many

forms even where explicitly the fallacy of its modern application is admitted. The point is that in the past the time-span of important change was considerably longer than that of a single human life. Thus mankind was trained to adapt itself to fixed conditions.

Today this time-span is considerably shorter than that of human life, and accordingly our training must prepare individuals to face a novelty of conditions. But there can be no preparation for the unknown. It is at this point that we recur to the immediate topic, Foresight. We require such an understanding of the present conditions, as may give us some grasp of the novelty which is about to produce a measurable influence on the immediate future. Yet the doctrine, that routine is dominant in any society that is not collapsing, must never be lost sight of. Thus the grounds, in human nature and in the successful satisfaction of purpose, these grounds for the current routine must be understood; and at the same time the sorts of novelty just entering into social effectiveness have got to be weighed against the old routine. In this way the type of modification and the type of persistence exhibited in the immediate future may be foreseen.

SECTION IV. It is now time to give some illustrations of assertions already made. Consider our main conclusions that our traditional doctrines of sociology, of political philosophy, of the practical conduct of large business, and of political economy are largely warped and vitiated by the implicit assumption of a stable unchanging social system. With this assumption it is comparatively safe to base reasoning upon a simplified edition of human nature. For well-known stimuli working under well-known conditions produce well-known reactions. It is safe then to assume that human nature, for the purpose in hand, is adequately described in terms of some of the major reactions to some of the major stimuli. For example, we can all remember our old friend, the economic man.

The beauty of the economic man was that we knew exactly what he was after. Whatever his wants were, he knew them and his neighbours knew them. His wants were those developed in a well-defined social system. His father and grandfather had the same wants, and satisfied them in the same way. So whenever there was a shortage, everyone— including the economic man himself—knew what was short, and knew the way to satisfy the consumer. In fact, the consumer knew what he wanted to consume. This was the demand. The producer knew how to produce the required articles, hence the supply. The men who got the goods onto the spot first, at the cheapest price, made their fortunes; the other producers were eliminated. This was healthy competition. This is beautifully simple and with proper elaboration is obviously true. It expresses the dominant truth exactly so far as there are stable well-tried conditions. But when we are concerned with a social system which in important ways is changing, this simplified conception of human relations requires severe qualification.

It is, of course, common knowledge that the whole trend of political economy during the last thirty or forty years has been away from these artificial simplifications. Such sharp-cut notions as 'the economic man', 'supply and demand', 'competition', are now in process of dilution by a close study of the actual re-actions of various populations to the stimuli which are relevant to modern commerce. This exactly illustrates the main thesis. The older political economy reigned supreme for about a hundred years from the time of Adam Smith, because in its main assumptions it did apply to the general circumstances of life as led, then and for innumerable centuries in the past. These circumstances were then already passing away. But it still remained a dominant truth that in commercial relations men were dominated by well-conditioned reactions to completely familiar stimuli.

In the present age, the element of novelty which life affords is too prominent to be omitted from our calculations. A deeper knowledge of the varieties of human nature is required to determine the reaction, in its character and its strength, to those elements of novelty which each decade of years introduces into social life. The possibility of this deeper knowledge constitutes the Foresight under discussion.

Another example which concerns sociological habits, and thence business relations and the shifting values of property, is to be seen in the history of cities. Throughout the whole span of civilization up to the present moment, the growth of condensed aggregates of humans, which we call cities, has been an inseparable accompaniment of the growth of civilization. There are many obvious reasons, the defence of accumulated wealth behind city walls, the concentration of materials requisite for manufacture, the concentration of power in the form of human muscles and, later, in the form of available heat energy, the ease of mutual intercourse required for business relations, the pleasure arising from a concentration of æsthetic and cultural opportunities, the advantages of a concentration of governmental and other directing agencies, administrative, legal, and military.

But there are disadvantages in cities. As yet no civilization has been self-supporting. Each civilization is born, it culminates, and it decays. There is a widespread testimony that this ominous fact is due to inherent biological defects in the crowded life of cities. Now, slowly and at first faintly, an opposite tendency is showing itself. Better roads and better vehicles at first induced the wealthier classes to live on the outskirts of the cities. The urgent need for defence had also vanished. This tendency is now spreading rapidly downwards. But a new set of conditions is just showing itself. Up to the present time, throughout the eighteenth and nineteenth centuries, this new tendency placed the homes in the immediate suburbs, but concentrated manufacturing activity, business relations, government, and pleasure, in the centres of the cities. Apart from the care of children, and periods of sheer rest, the active lives were spent in the cities. In some ways, the concentration of such activities was even more emphasized, and the homes were pushed outwards even at the cost of the discomfort of commuting. But, if we examine the trend of technology during the past generation, the reasons for this concentration are largely disappearing. Still more, the reasons for the choice of sites for cities are also altering. Mechanical power can be transmitted for hundreds of miles, men can communicate almost instantaneously by telephone, the chiefs of great organizations can be transported by airplanes, the cinemas can produce plays in every village, music, speeches, and sermons can be broadcast. Almost every reason for the growth of cities, concurrently with the growth of civilization, has been profoundly modified.

What then is to be the future of cities, three hundred years hence, a hundred years hence, or even thirty years hence? I do not know. But I venture a guess:—that those who are reasonably fortunate in this foresight will make their fortunes, and that others will be ruined by mistakes in calculation.

My second point that the reasons for the choice of sites for cities have also been modified is illustrated by recent

changes in my own country, England. The first effect of
the new industrial age of the eighteenth and nineteenth
centuries was to concentrate population round the coal-
fields. Thus the central portion of England on its northern
edge has become one huge city, disguised under different
names for its various regional parts. But the novel conditions are shifting population and manufactures to the south
of England, near to the great southern ports which look
towards the Mediterranean, the South Atlantic Ocean, and
the Panama Canal. They are the best ports, with the easiest
navigation, and with uncrowded land around them. At
present the transmission of electric power is one of the major
pre-occupations of the government of England.

The effect of new technologies on the sites of cities, and
on transformations of cities, is one of the fundamental problems which must enter into all sociological theories, including the forecasting of business relations. We must not exaggerate the importance of these particular examples. They
are just two examples selected from a whole situation which
can be analysed into innumerable examples with the same
moral. I mean nothing so absurd as that all industrialists
should meditate on the future of cities. The topic may be
quite irrelevant to the future activities of most of them.
Also I am ignorant as to how much Political Economy they
should study.

But we are faced with a fluid, shifting situation in the
immediate future. Rigid maxims, a rule-of-thumb routine,
and caste-iron particular doctrines will spell ruin. The
business of the future must be controlled by a somewhat different type of men to that of previous centuries. The type
is already changing, and has already changed so far as the
leaders are concerned. The Business Schools of Universities
are concerned with spreading this newer type throughout

the nations by aiming at the production of the requisite mentality.

SECTION V. I will conclude this chapter by a sketch of the Business Mind of the future. In the first place it is fundamental that there be a power of conforming to routine, of supervising routine, of constructing routine, and of understanding routine both as to its internal structure and as to its external purposes. Such a power is the bedrock of all practical efficiency. But for the production of the requisite Foresight, something more is wanted. This extra endowment can only be described as a philosophic power of understanding the complex flux of the varieties of human societies: for instance, the habit of noting varieties of demands on life, of serious purposes, of frivolous amusements. Such instinctive grasp of the relevant features of social currents is of supreme importance. For example, the time-span of various types of social behaviour is of the essence of their effect on policy. A widespread type of religious interest, with its consequent modes of behaviour, has a dominant life of about a hundred years, while a fashion of dress survives any time between three months and three years. Methods of agriculture change slowly. But the scientific world seems to be on the verge of far-reaching biological discoveries. The assumption of slow changes in agriculture must therefore be scanned vigilantly. This example of time-spans can be generalized. The quantitative aspect of social changes is of the essence of business relations. Thus the habit of transforming observation of qualitative changes into quantitative estimates should be a characteristic of business mentality.

I have said enough to show that the modern commercial mentality requires many elements of discipline, scientific and sociological. But the great fact remains that details of relevant knowledge cannot be foreseen. Thus even for mere success, and apart from any question of intrinsic quality of life, an unspecialized aptitude for eliciting generalizations from particulars and for seeing the divergent illustration of generalities in diverse circumstances is required. Such a reflective power is essentially a philosophic habit: it is the survey of society from the standpoint of generality. This habit of general thought, undaunted by novelty, is the gift of philosophy, in the widest sense of that term.

SECTION VI. But the motive of success is not enough. It produces a short-sighted world which destroys the sources of its own prosperity. The cycles of trade depression which afflict the world warn us that business relations are infected through and through with the disease of short-sighted motives. The robber barons did not conduce to the prosperity of Europe in the Middle Ages, though some of them died prosperously in their beds. Their example is a warning to our civilization. Also we must not fall into the fallacy of thinking of the business world in abstraction from the rest of the community. The business world is one main part of the very community which is the subject-matter of our study. The behaviour of the community is largely dominated by the business mind. A great society is a society in which its men of business think greatly of their functions. Low thoughts mean low behaviour, and after a brief orgy of exploitation low behaviour means a descending standard of life. The general greatness of the community, qualitatively as well as quantitatively, is the first condition for steady prosperity, buoyant, self-sustained, and commanding credit. The Greek philosopher who laid the foundation of all our finer thoughts ended his most marvellous dialogue with the reflection that the ideal state could never arrive till philosophers are kings. Today, in an age of democracy, the kings are the plain citizens pursuing their various avocations.

There can be no successful democratic society till general education conveys a philosophic outlook.

Philosophy is not a mere collection of noble sentiments. A deluge of such sentiments does more harm than good. Philosophy is at once general and concrete, critical and appreciative of direct intuition. It is not—or, at least, should not be—a ferocious debate between irritable professors. It is a survey of possibilities and their comparison with actualities. In philosophy, the fact, the theory, the alternatives, and the ideal, are weighed together. Its gifts are insight and foresight, and a sense of the worth of life, in short, that sense of importance which nerves all civilized effort. Mankind can flourish in the lower stages of life with merely barbaric flashes of thought. But when civilization culminates, the absence of a coördinating philosophy of life, spread throughout the community, spells decadence, boredom, and the slackening of effort.

Every epoch has its character determined by the way its populations re-act to the material events which they encounter. This reaction is determined by their basic beliefs—by their hopes, their fears, their judgments of what is worth while. They may rise to the greatness of an opportunity, seizing its drama, perfecting its art, exploiting its adventure, mastering intellectually and physically the network of relations that constitutes the very being of the epoch. On the other hand, they may collapse before the perplexities confronting them. How they act depends partly on their courage, partly on their intellectual grasp. Philosophy is an attempt to clarify those fundamental beliefs which finally determine the emphasis of attention that lies at the base of character.

Mankind is now in one of its rare moods of shifting its outlook. The mere compulsion of tradition has lost its force.

It is our business—philosophers, students, and practical men —to re-create and reënact a vision of the world, including those elements of reverence and order without which society lapses into riot, and penetrated through and through with unflinching rationality. Such a vision is the knowledge which Plato identified with virtue. Epochs for which, within the limits of their development, this vision has been widespread are the epochs unfading in the memory of mankind.

Our discussion has insensibly generalized itself. It has passed beyond the topic of Commercial Relations to the function of a properly concrete philosophy in guiding the purposes of mankind.

EPILOGUE TO PART I

At this stage we conclude the consideration of that group of ideas that most directly contributed to the civilization of the behaviour-systems of human beings in their intercourse with each other. This improvement depended on the slow growth of mutual respect, sympathy, and general kindliness. All these feelings can exist with the minimum of intellectuality. Their basis is emotional, and humanity acquired these emotions by reason of its unthinking activities amid the course of nature.

But mentality as it emerges into coördinated activity has a tremendous effect in selecting, emphasizing, and disintegrating. We have been considering the emergence of ideas from activities, and the effect of ideas in modifying the activities from which they emerge. Ideas arise as explanatory of customs and they end by founding novel methods and novel institutions. In the preceding chapters we have watched instances of their transition from one to other of these two modes of functioning.

PART II

COSMOLOGICAL

CHAPTER VII

LAWS OF NATURE

SECTION I. The previous part of this book dealt with the influence exerted by the Platonic and Christian doctrines of the human soul upon the sociological development of the European races. In this second part of the book, I shall deal with the influence of scientific ideas upon European culture, and with the more general cosmological ideas thus generated and presupposed.

It would be useless to attempt a history of science within this compass. Accordingly, I shall confine myself to the most general ideas at the base of the whole development of science. I mean the concepts of Speculation and of Scholarship, and the various notions of the Order of Nature, and of Nature itself. In short, my topic is 'Cosmologies, Ancient and Modern', together with the variety of methods, speculative and scholarly, employed in their production. Special developments of learning will only be cited in order to exemplify the specializations of general ideas amid changing epochs of Western Culture.

Modern Europe and America have derived their civilization from the races whose countries border the Eastern Mediterranean. In the earlier chapters, Greece and Palestine were the regions providing the initial formulations of the ideas concerning the essence of human nature. When we examine the history of science, to these two countries we must add Egypt. These three countries are the direct ancestors of our modern civilization.

Of course there is a long tale of civilization behind them. Mesopotamia, Crete, Phœnicia, and India, China, also contributed. But whatever of scientific or religious value has passed into modern life, finally reached us through the mediation of these three countries, Egypt, Greece, Palestine. Of these countries, Egypt provided the mature technology, arising from three thousand years of secure civilization, Palestine provided the final religious cosmology, Greece provided the clear-cut generalizations leading to philosophy and science. This logical lucidity also tinges the remaining legacy from Greece, its art and imaginative literature. Every Greek statue expresses the welding of beauty to regularity of geometrical form: every Greek play investigates the interweaving of physical circumstances arising from the Order of Nature with states of mind which issue from the urge of the Moral Order.

'Canst thou by searching find out God?' is good Hebrew, but it is bad Greek. The effort to comprehend the great fact which procures the order in the Universe urged Greek thinkers to that culmination when Plato and Aristotle defined the complex of general ideas forming the imperishable origin of Western thought. The work was only accomplished just in time. In the very lifetime of Aristotle the political and cultural barriers collapsed; and the subsequent Hellenistic development at Alexandria and elsewhere was the joint enterprise of Greeks, Egyptians, Semites, and the mixed races of Syria and Asia Minor. The untroubled faith in lucidity within the depths of things, to be captured by some happy glance of speculation, was lost forever. Duller men were content with limited accuracy and constructed special sciences: thicker intellects gloried in the notion that the foundations of the world were laid amid inpenetrable fog. They conceived God in their own image, and depicted him with a positive dislike of efforts after understanding beyond assigned methodologies. Satan acquired an intellectual character, and fell by reason of an indecent desire to understand his Creator. It was the downfall of Greece.

SECTION II. The progress of mankind proceeds by devious paths. The shift from the bright Hellenic age, whose final period was centred in Athens, to the Hellenistic age, with Alexandria as its intellectual capital, corresponds to a new direction of constructive genius. The special sciences were founded. Their principles were defined, their methods were determined, appropriate deductions were elicited. Learning was stabilized. It was furnished with methodologies, and was handed over to University professors of the modern type. Doctors of Medicine, Mathematicians, Astronomers, Grammarians, Theologians, for more than six hundred years dominated the schools of Alexandria, issuing text-books, treatises, controversies, and dogmatic definitions. Literature was replaced by Grammar, and Speculation by the Learned Tradition.

These men conventionalized learning. But they secured it. Their work survived two great religious revolutions, the rise of Christianity and the rise of Mahometanism. It provided both these religions with their philosophical theologies. It fitted them out with heresies and with orthodoxies.

In the Western Roman Empire, the Christian Church, armed with Hellenistic thought, captured the intellects of the victorious barbarians and civilized Western Europe up to the Arctic Ocean. Along the south of the Mediterranean the Mahometan conquerors carried Hellenistic thought, as coloured by the mentalities of Arabs, Jews, and Persians, through Africa into Spain. From Spain, the Mahometan

and Jewish versions made contact with the Christian version
of Alexandrian culture. This fusion produced the brilliant
culmination of Christian Scholasticism in the thirteenth
century; and, in the seventeenth century, Spinoza.

The note of Hellenism is delight, speculation, discoursive
literature: the note of Hellenistic Alexandria is concentration, thoroughness, investigation of the special types of order
appertaining to special topics. The great Alexandrians
were either right or wrong: Euclid either did, or did not
make his text-book of Geometry logically coherent: the
Ptolemaic doctrine of the heavens is true or false: Athanasius is directly opposed to Arius: and Cyril to Nestorius.
The nearest analogues to the Alexandrian theological debates are the modern debates among mathematical physicists
on the nature of the atom. The special topics differ slightly;
but the methods and the men are identical.

It is unmeaning bluntly to ask of Plato, whether he be
right or wrong, in the same exact sense in which we frame
the question about the Alexandrians. When any eminent
scholar has converted Plato into a respectable professor, by
providing him with a coherent system, we quickly find that
Plato in a series of Dialogues has written up most of the
heresies from his own doctrines. It is as though Ptolemy
had emitted the speculations of Aristarchus, and as though
Athanasius had suggested the profanities of Arius.

I am not alluding to the mere fact that men change their
opinions, with the advance of age, or with the advance or
decay of knowledge. The important point is the way in
which opinions are held, and the weight attached to particular modes of statement. St. Augustine changed his opinions. He not only published for all ages the tragic intensity
of feeling which the conversion involved, but also he devoted himself to exact statements of his new doctrines. He

remained a Platonist, and his interest in the doctrine of Grace was a Platonic interest in the exact expression how finite human life can participate in the Divine Perfections. He performed an immense service to civilization by providing Western Europe with accurate definitions on great topics just before the oncoming of the Barbarians. He secured that western Christianity should persist as a civilizing influence, and not degenerate into hereditary superstition of the Abyssinian type. But his attitude to his own doctrines was very different from that of Plato. Consider some of Plato's phrases about his own ideas: "If, then, Socrates, we find ourselves in many points unable to make our discourse of the generation of gods and the universe in every way wholly consistent and exact, you must not be surprised. Nay, we must be well content if we can provide an account not less likely than another's; we must remember that I who speak, and you who are my audience, are but men and should be satisfied to ask for no more than the likely story." [1]

Again:—"Perhaps they may be in a difficulty; and if this is the case, there is a possibility that they may accept a suggestion of ours respecting the nature of essence, having nothing of their own to offer." [2]

Can we imagine Augustine urbanely approaching Pelagius with 'a suggestion of ours respecting the nature of Grace'? It is quite true that passages can be quoted from Plato, more particularly from *The Laws,* which would justify all the persecution of atheists that has disgraced Europe. But the passages quoted above give the general tone of the *Dialogues* in their handling of the precise expression of speculative notions.

[1] The *Timæus,* A. E. Taylor's translation.
[2] The *Sophist,* Jowett's translation.

SECTION III. In many ways Aristotle and Epicurus fore-shadow the transition from Hellenic speculation to the exact scholarship of Alexandria. In both of them we find an effort towards system, explicitly stated and exactly phrased. Of course, Lucretius is our main authority for the Epicurean doctrines.

If we merely knew that great schools of exact scientific investigation had arisen in the succeeding generation, un-doubtedly modern critical scholarship would have assigned to Aristotle's influence the honour of their origination. We can imagine the contrast which would have been drawn between the barrenness of mere speculation and the fruit-fulness of Aristotle's power of detailed observation.

Unfortunately, cold fact points in exactly the opposite direction. In the first place Aristotle himself derived his own sources of thought from Plato's theoretical activity. He dissected fishes with Plato's thoughts in his head. He sys-tematized the welter of Platonic suggestions, and in the course of his work he modified, improved, and spoilt. But he did introduce into sciences other than Astronomy the much-needed systematic practice of passing beyond theory to direct observation of details. Unfortunately this was the one aspect of his life which never had any direct influence on any succeeding epoch.

Again, in point of fact the Alexandrian culture derived directly from Plato. Its thought was through and through Platonic both in science and theology. But it was not for nothing that Alexandria was situated in a land of old, secure technology. There were crafts and learned professions with traditions of detailed procedure stretching back for thou-sands of years. The schools of Alexandria were thronged with sons of priests, sons of metallurgists, sons of makers of implements for irrigation and agriculture, sons of land-surveyors. It is no wonder that the first emergence of modern scholarship studied in a modern university, took place when Platonic speculation was transferred to a land of old professional activity.

Undoubtedly the chasm between Hellenic mentality and mediæval scholastic learning was due to many influences accumulating their effects through a period of a thousand years. But the greatest gap in the transition is the first one, when the capital of Mediterranean learning was transferred from Athens to Alexandria. The general type of the cultural development of Western Civilization was then predetermined. How science should be developed: How mathematics should evolve: How religion, Jewish, Christian, Mahometan, should shape its various theologies. The modern world is primarily Alexandrian; and only for a short period of about a hundred years, to be placed somewhere between the Council of Constance and the Sack of Rome in 1527, did the Athenian tone of mind prevail: perhaps also earlier in the Italy of the Augustan epoch. The difference between the two, namely the Hellenic and the Hellenistic types of mentality, may be roughly described as that between speculation and scholarship. For progress, both are necessary. But, in fact, on the stage of history they are apt to appear as antagonists. Speculation, by entertaining alternative theories, is superficially sceptical, disturbing to established modes of prejudice. But it obtains its urge from a deep ultimate faith, that through and through the nature of things is penetrable by reason. Scholarship, by its strict attention to accepted methodologies, is superficially conservative of belief. But its tone of mind leans towards a fundamental negation. For scholars the reasonable topics in the world are penned in isolated regions, *this* subject-matter or *that* subject-matter. Your thorough-going scholar resents the airy speculation which connects his own patch of knowledge with that of his neighbour. He finds his fundamental concepts interpreted, twisted, modified. He has ceased to be king of his own castle, by reason of speculations of uncomfortable generality, violating the very grammar of his thoughts. Pope Adrian the Sixth exhibited himself as a typical scholar by remarking that in Luther's theological works so many errors could be found that any tyro could point them out.

New directions of thought arise from flashes of intuition bringing new material within the scope of scholarly learning. They commence as the sheer ventures of rash speculation. They may fortunately obtain quick acceptance, or they may initiate a quarrel of scholars from which all tinge of speculation has faded. Pope Leo the Tenth voiced the vanishing Athenian epoch when he characterized the Lutheran disputes as a quarrel of monks.

Pure speculation, undisciplined by the scholarship of detailed fact or the scholarship of exact logic, is on the whole more useless than pure scholarship, unrelieved by speculation. The proper balance of the two factors in progressive learning depends on the character of the epoch in question and on the capacities of particular individuals. Also it is a curious fact, somewhat lost sight of in Greek thought, that, notwithstanding the law of the Golden Mean between contrasted components, yet a certain excessiveness seems a necessary element in all greatness. In some direction or other we must devote ourselves beyond what would be warranted by the analysis of pure reason.

One aspect of the adventure of ideas is this story of the interplay of speculation and scholarship, a strife sustained through the ages of progress. This history discloses the happy balance attained in periods of culminating greatness, and it also exhibits the tinge of excessiveness in all such peaks of achievement. Thereby it gives the reason for the tragic transience of supreme moments in human life.

SECTION IV. The notion of Law, that is to say, of some measure of regularity or of persistence or of recurrence, is an essential element in the urge towards technology, methodology, scholarship, and speculation. Apart from a certain smoothness in the nature of things, there can be no knowledge, no useful method, no intelligent purpose. Lacking an element of Law, there remains a mere welter of details with no foothold for comparison with any other such welter, in the past, in the future, or circumambient in the present. But the expression of this notion of Law with due accuracy, and with due regard to what in fact is presupposed in human purposes, is a matter of extreme difficulty. Analogously to the histories of all the more general ideas, the notion of Law has entered into the explicit consciousness of various epochs under every variety of specialization, arising from its coalescence with other components in the popular cosmology.

The difficulty in all such notions of supreme generality is that conscious attention is not naturally directed to any factor which is a 'matter of course' in experience. Attention is rivetted upon 'news', and 'news' involves some aroma of capriciousness. It is useless to recur to periods of human history which lie beyond the reach of direct evidence. But anthropologists report the almost universal prevalence of tribal ceremonies having reference to the succession of the yearly seasons, more particularly to the Spring, the Harvest, and Mid-winter. Undoubtedly, as we view them now, there is a reference to agriculture in such celebrations. Now agriculture marks the first decisive step towards modern civilization. Its introduction marks the arrival of a stage of high

grade reflection upon the course of events. It requires a forecast of the course of nature months ahead. Many an ape-
man must have snatched up a stone wherewith to hit
somebody, either another man or other animal, on the head,
without any reflection upon the course of nature beyond the
next few minutes. Also he might notice that some stones
are better than others as lethal weapons, and he might even
help them out by chipping them. He is then approaching
civilization. But he—or more probably, she—has crossed
the great divide, when he puts seeds into a patch of earth
and waits for a season.

It is obvious that seasonal ceremonies must extend backwards in time far beyond the introduction of agriculture.
The differences between the seasons impose differences of
behaviour upon all living things, vegetables and animals
alike. The seasonal urge towards change of habit, hiberna-
tion or migration, must have begotten some expression of
emotional restlessness. The interest of agriculture comes in
when we consider the later interpretation of the seasonal
ceremonies in which the tribe had been indulging for countless ages. Civilization did not start with a social contract
determining modes of behaviour. Its earliest effort was the
slow introduction of ideas explanatory of modes of behaviour and of inrushes of emotion which already dominated
their lives. Undoubtedly ideas modified the practice. But
in the main practice precedes thought; and thought is
mainly concerned with the justification or the modification
of a pre-existing situation.

Now, apart from the practice of agriculture, animal habits
are mainly based on the massive recurrence of the seasons,
heat and frost, rain and drought, day and night. There
was stolid recurrent matter of fact, with accompanying
rhythms of emotion and ritual. Vagrant questions may have

disturbed exceptional minds. But there was little to provoke tribal interest in explanation. There must have been
some instances to provoke attention, because there was, in
fact, among some tribes of our ancestors, a drift towards
better ways of life. But I am seeking to determine the
dividing line after which the curiously quick acceleration
of civilized thought may conceivably have arisen. In the
earlier stage the convenient unit of time is of the order of
a hundred thousand years. In the later phases it shortens
up to ten thousand years, to five thousand years, to one
thousand years, to a hundred years.

Probably there was a concurrence of many causes. But
among such causes the introduction of agriculture must be
given a high place for its effectiveness in quickening progress. It at once introduced the capriciousness of the
weather as a major topic of tribal interest. Also it provoked
attention to the mystery of germination, and to the dependence of vegetable growth upon the seasonal phases. It compelled the tribe to descend from passive acquiescence in a
general matter of course towards active interest in the details. It led to a search for precautions, and discovery requires understanding. Of course, as we all know, the novel
situation did not require every tribe to advance. Also the
masses of mankind are always liable to reach some stable
level of custom, and to halt progress there. But human life
had then reached a stage at which obvious problems were
presented to the more active minds, wherever such existed.

We inherit legends, weird, horrible, beautiful, expressing
in curious, specialized ways the interweaving of law and
capriciousness in the mystery of things. It is the problem
of good and evil. Sometimes the law is good and the
capriciousness evil; sometimes the law is iron and evil and
the capriciousness is merciful and good. But from savage

legends up to Hume's civilized Dialogues on Natural religion, with the conversation between Job and his friends as an intermediate between the two, the same problem is discussed. Science and technology are based upon law. Human behaviour exhibits custom mitigated by impulse. What exactly do we mean by the notion of the Laws of Nature?

SECTION V. At the present time, there are prevalent four main doctrines concerning the Laws of Nature: the doctrine of Law as immanent, the doctrine of Law as imposed, and the doctrine of Law as observed order of succession, in other words, Law as mere description, and lastly the later doctrine of Law as conventional interpretation. It will be convenient first to discuss these four alternative doctrines from the standpoint of today. We shall then be in a better position to understand the chequered history of the notion in civilized thought.

By the doctrine of Law as immanent it is meant that the order of nature expresses the characters of the real things which jointly compose the existences to be found in nature. When we understand the essences of these things, we thereby know their mutual relations to each other. Thus, according as there are common elements in their various characters, there will necessarily be corresponding identities in their mutual relations. In other words, some partial identity of pattern in the various characters of natural things issues in some partial identity of pattern in the mutual relations of those things. These identities of pattern in the mutual relations are the Laws of Nature. Conversely, a Law is explanatory of some community in character pervading the things which constitute Nature. It is evident that the doctrine involves the negation of 'absolute being'. It presupposes the essential interdependence of things.

There are some consequences to this doctrine. In the first

place, it follows that scientists are seeking for explanations and not merely for simplified descriptions of their observations. In the second place the exact conformation of nature to any law is not to be expected. If all the things concerned have the requisite common character, then the pattern of mutual relevance which expresses that character will be exactly illustrated. But in general we may expect that a large proportion of things do possess the requisite character and a minority do not possess it. In such a case, the mutual relations of these things will exhibit lapses when the law fails to obtain illustration. In so far as we are merely interested in a confused result of many instances, then the law can be said to have a statistical character. It is now the opinion of physicists that most of the laws of physics, as known in the nineteenth century, are of this character.

Thirdly, since the laws of nature depend on the individual characters of the things constituting nature, as the things change, then correspondingly the laws will change. Thus the modern evolutionary view of the physical universe should conceive of the laws of nature as evolving concurrently with the things constituting the environment. Thus the conception of the Universe as evolving subject to fixed, eternal laws regulating all behaviour should be abandoned. Fourthly, a reason can now be produced why we should put some limited trust in induction. For if we assume an environment largely composed of a sort of existences whose natures we partly understand, then we have some knowledge of the laws of nature dominating that environment. But apart from that premise and apart from the doctrine of Immanent Law, we can have no knowledge of the future. We should then acknowledge blank ignorance, and not make pretences about probability.

Fifthly, the doctrine of Immanent Law is untenable unless

we can construct a plausible metaphysical doctrine according to which the characters of the relevant things in nature are the outcome of their interconnections, and their interconnections are the outcome of their characters. This involves some doctrine of Internal Relations.

Finally, the doctrine of Immanence is through and through a rationalistic doctrine. It is explanatory of the possibility of understanding nature.

Section VI. The doctrine of Imposed Law adopts the alternative metaphysical doctrine of External Relations between the existences which are the ultimate constituents of nature. The character of each of these ultimate things is thus conceived as its own private qualification. Such an existent is understandable in complete disconnection from any other such existent: the ultimate truth is that it requires nothing but itself in order to exist. But in fact there is imposed on each such existent the necessity of entering into relationships with the other ultimate constituents of nature. These imposed behaviour patterns are the Laws of Nature. But you cannot discover the natures of the relata by any study of the Laws of their relations. Nor, conversely, can you discover the laws by inspection of the natures.

The explanation of the doctrine of Imposition both suggests a certain type of Deism, and conversely it is the outcome of such a Deistic belief if already entertained. For example, we know from Newton's own statements that this was exactly how the Deistic problem presented itself to him. He definitely stated that the correlated modes of behaviour of the bodies forming the solar system required God for the imposition of the principles on which all depended. He was certainly doubtful, indeed more than doubtful, as to whether the Law of Gravity was the ultimate statement of principles imposed by God. But he certainly thought that the conception of the solar system exhibited in his *Principia* was sufficiently ultimate to make obvious the necessity of a God imposing Law. Newton was certainly right to this extent, that the whole doctrine of Imposition is without interest apart from the correlative doctrine of a transcendent' imposing Deity. This is also a Cartesian doctrine.

The doctrine of Imposition very naturally follows from Descartes' notion of 'substance'. Indeed the phrase 'requiring nothing but itself in order to exist' occurs in his *Principles of Philosophy*. The whole Cartesian apparatus of Deism, substantial materialism, and imposed law, in conjunction with the reduction of physical relations to the notion of correlated motions with mere spatio-temporal character, constitutes the simplified notion of Nature with which Galileo, Descartes, and Newton finally launched modern science on its triumphant career. If success be a guarantee of truth, no other system of thought has enjoyed a tithe of such success since mankind started on its job of thinking. Within three hundred years it has transformed human life, in its intimate thoughts, its technologies, its social behaviour, and its ambitions.

It follows from the Deism, which is part of the whole conception, that the Laws of Nature will be exactly obeyed. Certainly, what God meant he did. When he said, Let there be light, there was *light* and not a mere imitation or a statistical average. Thus the statistical notion, though it may explain some facts of our confused perception, is not applicable to the ultimate, imposed laws.

But even before Descartes, it was the implicit belief in some form of imposition, with its consequent exactness, that constituted the motive force in scientific research. Why should educated men have believed that there was anything to find out? Suppose that the doctrine of immanence had prevailed in Europe and in Mahometan Asia. Why should men assume that there were definite laws which even beyond the limits of meticulous observation underlie the apparent capriciousness of physical details? There are certain grand obvious uniformities, Day follows Night, and again relapses into Night, the Mountains endure, and Birth proceeds. But these grand regularities are shot through and through with details apparently capricious. The very savages saw that, and tremblingly worshipped malignant demons. But civilized men, who understand the doctrine of immanence, should draw the conclusion that the dominance of common traits of character throughout the constituents of nature is only very partial. There is no reason why it should be otherwise. A restless search for detailed explanation is futile, based upon no approach to probability. If in the past men had believed thus, today there would be no science. And even today, how little do we know about physiology. Also an individual electron is a rare bird whose behaviour is unpredictable: our information about electrons mostly concerns flocks numbering millions. What reason is there to expect success if we seek to push the reign of law one step further towards minute detail? Indeed, physicists in their recent researches have disclosed a novel illustration of capriciousness. These men, trained in the Positivist doctrine, have at once suggested the uselessness of further search for 'law'. Unless the psychology of mental behaviour still include some traces derived from the notion of Deistic imposition, even today the progress of science would cease by reason of the failure of hope. A considerable proportion of present-day philosophy is devoted to the endeavour by means of subtle argument to evade this plain inexorable conclusion.

Lastly apart from some notion of imposed Law, the doctrine of immanence provides absolutely no reason why the universe should not be steadily relapsing into lawless chaos. In fact, the Universe, as understood in accordance with the doctrine of Immanence, should exhibit itself as including a stable actuality whose mutual implication with the remainder of things secures an inevitable trend towards order. The Platonic 'persuasion' is required.

SECTION VII. Of the three earlier theories, there remains the Positivist doctrine concerning Law, namely, that a Law of Nature is merely an observed persistence of pattern in the observed succession of natural things: Law is then merely Description. There is an attractive simplicity about this doctrine. The two preceding doctrines lead us to the dubieties of metaphysics, such as the doctrine of internal relations or the existence and nature of God. But this third doctrine evades all such difficulties.

It presupposes that we have direct acquaintance with a succession of things. This acquaintance is analysable into a succession of things observed. But our direct acquaintance consists not only in distinct observations of the distinct things in succession, but also it includes a comparative knowledge of the successive observations. Acquaintance is thus cumulative and comparative. The laws of nature are nothing else than the observed identities of pattern persisting throughout the series of comparative observations. Thus a law of nature says something about things observed and nothing more.

The pre-occupation of science is then the search for simple statements which in their joint effect will express everything of interest concerning the observed recurrences. This is the whole tale of science, *that* and nothing more. It is the great Positivist doctrine, largely developed in the first half of the nineteenth century, and ever since growing in influence. It tells us to keep to things observed, and to describe them as simply as we can. This is all we can know. Laws are statements of observed facts. This doctrine dates back to Epicurus, and embodies his appeal to the plain man, away from metaphysics and mathematics. The observed facts of clear experience are understandable, and nothing else. Also 'understanding' means 'simplicity of description.'

Without doubt this Positivist doctrine contains a fundamental truth about scientific methodology. For example, consider the greatest of all scientific generalizations, Newton's Law of Gravitation:—Two particles of matter attract each other with a force directly proportional to the product of their masses and inversely proportional to the square of their distance. The notion of 'force' refers to the notion of the addition of a component to the vector acceleration of either particle. It also refers to the notion of the masses of the particles. Again the notion of mass is also explicitly referred to in the statement. Thus the mutual spatial relations of the particles, and their individual masses, are required for the Law. To this extent the Law is an expression of the presumed characters of the particles concerned. But the form of the Law, namely the product of the masses and the inverse square of the distance, is purely based upon description of observed fact. A large part of Newton's *Principia* is devoted to a mathematical investigation proving that the description is adequate for his purposes; it collects many details under one principle. Newton himself insisted upon this very point. He was not speculating: he was not explaining. Whatever your cosmological doctrines may be, the motions of the planets and the fall of the stones, so far as they have been directly measured, conform to his Law. He is enunciating a formula which expresses observed correlations of observed facts.

Without the shadow of a doubt, all science bases itself
upon this procedure. It is the first rule of scientific method,
—Enunciate observed correlations of observed fact. This is
the great Baconian doctrine, namely, Observe and observe,
until finally you detect a regularity of sequence. The scholastics had trusted to metaphysical dialectic giving them
secure knowledge about the nature of things, including the
physical world, the spiritual world, and the existence of
God. Thence they deduced the various laws, immanent
and imposed, which reigned throughout Nature.

Another difference between Scholasticism and the Moderns is in respect to criticism and reliance upon authority.
But this distinction has been overstressed and misunder-
stood. The Scholastics were intensely critical, but they were
critical within a different sphere of thought from that oc-
cupying the Moderns. Again modern scientists rely upon
authority, but they rely upon different authorities from those
to whom the Scholastics appealed. Undoubtedly the later
Scholastics were uncritical in their appeal to their chosen
authority, Aristotle, especially and most unfortunately in
regard to his physics. The moderns push their criticism
further. But the Scholastics and the modern Scientists are
alike scholars of the Alexandrian type. They have the same
sort of merit and the same sort of defect. Also, the sort of
person who was a scholastic doctor in a mediaeval university,
today is a scientific professor in a modern university. Again
the Scholastics differed among themselves in opinion widely.
The earlier set were not even Aristotelians, the later set were
not all Thomists. Analogously, modern scientists differ
among themselves, about details and about the general doctrine of the Laws of Nature.

Within the sphere of dialectic debate, the Scholastics
were supremely critical. They trusted Aristotle because they

could derive from him a coherent system of thought. It was a criticized trust. Unfortunately, they did not reflect that some of his main ideas depended upon his direct acquaintance with experienced fact. They trusted to the logical coherence of the system as a guarantee of the unrestricted relevance of his primary notions. They thus accepted his confusion—when there was confusion—of superficial aspects with fundamental principles of widest generality. Their method for the furtherance of natural knowledge was endless debate, unrelieved by recurrence to direct observation. Unfortunately also their instrument of debate, Aristotelian Logic, was a more superficial weapon than they deemed it. Automatically it kept in the background some of the more fundamental topics for thought. Such topics are the quantitative relations examined in mathematics, and the complex possibilities of multiple relationship within a system. All these topics, and others, were kept in the background by Aristotelian logic.

Fortunately the scholastic age of Alexandrian scholarship dominated Europe for centuries, and bestowed upon civilization priceless treasures of thought. It was an age of immense progress. But a scholarly age works within rigid limitations. Fortunately, a revival of Hellenism overwhelmed the Hellenistic unity of the Middle Age. Plato arose as if from his tomb. Vagrant speculation and direct observation broke up the scholarly system. New interests, new Gods, prevailed. The new basis for thought was the report upon facts, directly observed, directly employed. Fortunately, in the subsidence of the Italian Renaissance of the fifteenth century, the drama of the transference of culture from Athens to Alexandria was again repeated. Europe gradually entered upon a new scholarly age. The modern historian appeared, the modern critical literature appeared, the modern man of science appeared, modern technology appeared. The old Egyptian metallurgists, the Semitic mathematicians, and the mediaeval scholastics were avenged.

But modern scholarship and modern science reproduce the same limitations as dominated the bygone Hellenistic epoch, and the bygone Scholastic epoch. They canalize thought and observation within predetermined limits, based upon inadequate metaphysical assumptions dogmatically assumed. The modern assumptions differ from older assumptions, not wholly for the better. They exclude from rationalistic thought more of the final values of existence. The intimate timidity of professionalized scholarship circumscribes reason by reducing its topics to triviality, for example, to bare sensa and to tautologies. It then frees itself from criticism by dogmatically handing over the remainder of experience to an animal faith or a religious mysticism, incapable of rationalization. The world will again sink into the boredom of a drab detail of rational thought, unless we retain in the sky some reflection of light from the sun of Hellenism.

CHAPTER VIII

COSMOLOGIES

Section I. At the close of the previous chapter we were left with four antagonistic schools of thought regarding the analysis of the notion of Law, The School of Immanence, The School of Imposition, The Positivist School of Observation, that is to say, of mere Description, and finally the School of Conventional Interpretation. We find that each of these schools could produce grave reasons in confirmation of its own doctrine.

There is no greater hindrance to the progress of thought than an attitude of irritated party-spirit. Urbanity, the urbanity of Plato and, if we may trust his *Dialogues,* the urbanity of Athenian society, were part of the intellectual genius of those times. The vicious antagonisms of subsequent theologians, some centuries later, hid from them considerations which they ought never to have forgotten, and have hidden from us the metaphysical genius of their own contributions to thought.

We will recommence by scanning the history of these doctrines of Natural Law, with the view of determining their exact points of divergence, and the measure of conciliation of which they are capable. In the previous chapter Plato's urbane preface to a philosophical suggestion was quoted. The suggestion itself is now relevant to the present lecture:—

"My suggestion would be, that anything which possesses any sort of power to affect another, or to be affected by another even for a moment, however trifling the cause and however slight and momentary the effect, has real existence; and I hold that the definition of being is simply power." [1]

In the subsequent conduct of the dialogue Plato rises to the height of his genius as a metaphysician. But he also wrestles with the difficulty of making language express anything beyond the familiarities of daily life. It is misleading to study the history of ideas without constant remembrance of the struggle of novel thought with the obtuseness of language.

Also it is interesting to notice that, according to Plato, the distinguishing mark of the Philosopher in contrast to the Sophist is his resolute attempt to reconcile conflicting doctrines, each with its own solid ground of support. In the history of ideas the doctrine *of* Speculation is at least as important as the doctrines *for* Speculation.

Section II. But, to return to Plato's suggestion—"and I hold that the definition of being is simply power."

This statement can be construed in terms of the notion of imposed law, namely, that it is an external imposition on each existent, that it be correlated with determinate causal action on other such existents. But such an interpretation neglects the exact wording, Plato says that it is the *definition* of being that it exert power and be subject to the exertion of power. This means that the essence of being is to be implicated in causal action on other beings. It is the doctrine of Law as immanent. Further, a few sentences later he proceeds:—". . . being, as being known, is acted on by knowledge, and is therefore in motion, for that which is in a state of rest cannot be acted upon as we affirm. . . . Can we imagine being to be devoid of life and mind, and to remain in awful unmeaningness an everlasting fixture?"

[1] *Sophist,* 247, Jowett's translation.

Notice that in this argument, that which is not acted upon is a fixture. Plato denies that being can be conceived "in awful unmeaningness an everlasting fixture." It is therefore acted upon. This agrees with his primary definition, that 'being' is the agent in action, and the recipient of action. Thus, in these passages Plato enunciates the doctrine that 'action and reaction' belong to the essence of being: though the mediation of 'life and mind' is invoked to provide the medium of activity. This notion of a medium, connecting the eternality of being with the fluency of becoming, takes many shapes in Plato's *Dialogues*. Very probably, indeed almost certainly, passages inconsistent with this doctrine can be found in the *Dialogues*. For the moment, the interesting fact is that in these passages in this Dialogue we find a clear enunciation of the doctrine of Law as immanent.

The early, naïve trend of Semitic monotheism, Jewish and Mahometan, is towards the notion of Law imposed by the fiat of the One God. Subsequent speculation wavers between these two extremes, seeking their reconciliation. In this, as in most other matters, the history of Western thought consists in the attemped fusion of ideas which in their origin are predominantly Hellenic, with ideas which in their origin are predominantly Semitic. The modern scholar, with his tinge of speculation, is an Egyptian employing his wisdom upon his Hellenic and Semitic heritage.

In this instance, the extremes of the two doctrines of Law lead on the one hand to the extreme monotheistic doctrine of God, as essentially transcendent and only accidentally immanent, and on the other hand to the pantheistic doctrine of God, as essentially immanent and in no way transcendent.

Plato in the *Timæus* affords an early instance of this wavering between the two doctrines of Law, Immanence and Imposition. In the first place, Plato's cosmology in-

cludes an ultimate creator, shadowy and undefined, imposing his design upon the Universe. Secondly, the action and
reaction of the internal constituents is—for Plato—the self-
sufficient explanation of the flux of the world:—"Nothing
was given off from it, nothing entered it,—there was nothing but itself."

We have here been examining the basic notion of the
initial cosmology which dominated the world, Pagan, Christian, and Mahometan, before the rise of the modern period.
It was modified by Aristotle, by the Alexandrians, by the
Scholastics. But this fusion of the doctrines of Imposition
and Immanence, with adjustments this way or that way,
is the great conception which reigned supreme till the beginning of the seventeenth century.

SECTION III. But Greek thought provided a rival cosmology, in the shape of the Atomic theory, as adumbrated
by Democritus, systematized by Epicurus, and as finally
explained in Epic shape by Lucretius. According to Lucretius the world is an interminable shower of atomic particles,
streaming through space, swerving, intermingling, disen-
tangling their paths, recombining them. For this doctrine
qualitative differences are merely the statistical expression of
geometrical patterns of intermingled paths, the outcome of
swerving, combined with a finite number of diversities of
shape.

Plato and Lucretius both appeal to geometry, Plato to the
regular solids, and Lucretius to the shapes of paths, and
unspecified shapes of atoms. In this respect, their general
attitude has been sustained by modern science. It seems
necessary however for Epicurus to treat space and motion
with the metaphysical naïvety exhibited later in Newton's
Principia. Plato's doctrine of space, as stated in the *Timæus,*
has a superior metaphysical subtlety; although the Platonic

doctrine of a Receptacle, intrinsically devoid of any geometrical form, has some analogy to the doctrine of the
'Void' in Lucretius. It is probable however that if Lucretius
had possessed the penetration to explain Epicurus further,
he would have found it necessary to endow his Void with
exactly those geometrical forms which Plato denied to his
Receptacle considered in abstraction, and which Aristotle
denied to his Matter in abstraction.

Plato's cosmology tends to a fusion of the doctrines of
Imposition and Immanence; the Atomic Theory of Epicurus lends itself most readily to a fusion of the doctrines
of Imposition and of Description.

The reason for this distinction between the two cosmologies is that for Plato behaviour is a function of the various
characters of the things concerned—the intelligent activities
of indwelling souls, and the geometric necessities of the indwelling shapes. But for Epicurus the paths of the atoms
are derived from no necessities of their natures. It is intrinsic to their natures that they partake of spatial relations and
are moveable. But the special path of a special atom seems
to be a fact entirely extrinsic to its nature. The modern
wave-theory of the atom sides with Plato rather than with
Democritus: Newtonian dynamics sides with Democritus
against Plato. Some passages of Lucretius surreptitiously introduce the doctrine of immanence. What Lucretius mainly
cared about was the reign of law as opposed to the capricious
intervention of demons and gods, to be coaxed by superstition.

As to the paths of the atoms, two views are possible. One
theory can conceive them as imposed, and imposition requires a transcendent God as imposer. This is practically
the cosmology adopted by Newton. The Newtonian forces,
whatever their ultimate mathematical formulation, are

nothing else than the imposed conditions provided by God. This point of view was the working formula of the eighteenth century. God made his appearance in religion under the frigid title of the First Cause, and was appropriately worshipped in white-washed churches.

Another theory as to the paths can be adopted by the Positivist School of Mere Description. For this reason, the atomic theory, of the Lucretian type, has always been a favorite first principle of cosmology with this School of Thought. The paths of the molecules can be ascribed to mere chance. They are random distributions, each path being entirely disconnected from any other path, and each continuation of one path being unconditioned by the earlier portion of the same path.

Thus the world, as we know it, exhibits for our confused perception an involution of paths and a concatenation of circumstances which have arisen entirely by chance. We can describe what has happened, but with that description all possibility of knowledge ends.

Lucretius wavers between the notion of imposed law and the notion of chance. For example:—"This point too we wish you to apprehend: when bodies are borne downwards sheer through void by their own weights, at quite uncertain times and uncertain spots they push themselves a little from their course: you just and only just can call it a change of inclination. If they were not used to swerve, they would all fall down, like drops of rain, through the deep void, and no clashing would have been begotten nor blow produced among the first-beginnings [i.e. the atoms]: thus nature never would have produced aught." [2]

[2] Book II, lines 216-224. Translated by H. A. J. Monro, published separately in Bohn's series, by G. Bell and Sons, Ltd.: Cf. also Cyril Bailey's translation, *Lucretius on the Nature of Things*, Oxford University Press, 1929.

But he rigidly limits his suggestion of chance:—[3]

"But lest you haply suppose that living things alone are bound by these conditions, such a law keeps all things within their limits."

The objection to the extreme Positivist doctrine at once suggests itself, that the enormous aspect of regular evolution through vast regions embracing the remotest star-galaxies, and through vast periods of time, is an unlikely product of mere chance.

There are two answers to this objection. In the first place, there is plenty of time and plenty of space. We are dealing with all space, from infinity to infinity, we are dealing with all time from eternity to eternity, and we are dealing with the unbounded wealth of all existence, to be comprehended in terms of no finite number. In any finite region of space and time, with its finite cargo of atoms, any pre-conceived arrangement of paths, however simple or however complex, is equally unlikely, indeed there is an infinite probability against it. But we are not dealing with a pre-conceived concept, we observe what in fact is the case in a limited region. Something must be the case, and what we have observed is what in fact has been the case. There is nothing pre-conceived, and thus there is no question of infinite improbability. It is true that expectations float through our minds, but they are vague memories of what in fact has happened, combined with suggestions as to the more detailed analysis of past fact. The fact in the past is neither probable nor improbable, it is what in fact took place within the ambit of our observation.

The second answer takes the same point of view as that derived from the doctrine of immanence. There is no need —indeed there is not the slightest reason—to exaggerate the

[3] Cf. Book II, lines 718, 719.

order in the spatio-temporal region under our observation. In the remote regions and epochs we have only intelligence of very general aspects of order. That is all we know. In the present epoch we have more detail, but our observation is rough, inaccurate, and sporadic. Again, that is all we know. We must not ascribe, we must not expect, one step beyond our direct knowledge. The Positivist has no foothold on which he can rely for speculation beyond the region of direct observation.

SECTION IV. The great Positivist school of thought, whose epic is the poem of Lucretius, at the present time reigns supreme in the domain of science. Its aim is to con- fine itself to fact, with a discard of all speculation. Unfor- tunately, among all the variant schools of opinion, it is the one which can least bear confrontation with the facts. It has never been acted on. It can never be acted on, for it gives no foothold for any forecast of the future around which purpose can weave itself.

But before confronting Positivism with the practice of mankind, it is interesting to note that atomism has taken on a new form of modern thought. Epistemology has arisen, in its function of a critic of all pretensions to knowledge. Today, the question, How do we know, takes precedence of the question,—What do we know.

Again, the doctrine of atomism re-appears. The atomism of Democritus in the science of Cosmology is replaced by the atomism of Hume in the science of Epistemology. Epi- curus enunciates the doctrine that the ultimate elements of the physical universe are physical atoms, showering through space with paths associated in complexes. Hume enunciates the doctrine that the ultimate elements, subjec- tively given in the activity of knowing, are the impressions of sensation, showering through the stream of experience, associated as memories, provocative of emotions and reflexions, and expectations. But for Hume, each impression is a distinct existence arising in soul from unknown causes. Epicurus bases himself upon an epistemology closely allied to that of Hume.

Positivism has seized on Hume's atomism, with Hume himself as its leader. The task of science is explained to be merely the formulation of observed identities of pattern persistent and recurrent in each stream of experience. But since Hume is dealing with subjective experience, he can add a corollary not open to the more objective doctrine of Epicurus. Hume adds that we expect the recurrences observed in the past, also to recur in the future. At this stage, Hotspur's question arises in our mind, "But will they come, when you do call for them?" To this question Hume, following the example of Glendower, returns no answer. It is an observed fact in the past that expected recurrences have recurred. But Positivistic science is solely concerned with observed fact, and must hazard no conjecture as to the future. If observed fact be all we know, then there is no other knowledge. Probability is relative to knowledge. There is no probability as to the future within the doctrine of Positivism.

Of course most men of science, and many philosophers, use the Positivistic doctrine to avoid the necessity of considering perplexing fundamental questions—in short, to avoid metaphysics—, and then save the importance of science by an implicit recurrence to their metaphysical persuasion that the past does in fact condition the future.

Indeed, as Hume pointed out, human life cannot be carried on without this persuasion. In this way the Positivistic doctrine of today bases itself on some form of atomism, objective or subjective, and deduces that the sole occupation of science is to elaborate simple descriptions of things observed.

There is a curious misconception that somehow the mathematical mysteries of Statistics help Positivism to evade its proper limitation to the observed past. But statistics tell you nothing about the future unless you make the assumption of the permanence of statistical form. For example, in order to use statistics for prediction, assumptions are wanted as to the stability of the mean, the mode, the probable error, and the symmetry or skewness of the statistical expression of functional correlation. Mathematics can tell you the consequences of your beliefs. For example, if your apple is composed of a finite number of atoms, mathematics will tell you that the number is odd or even. But you must not ask mathematics to provide you with the apple, the atoms, and the finiteness of their number. There is no valid inference from mere possibility to matter of fact, or, in other words, from mere mathematics to concrete nature.

SECTION V. It is now time to confront the Positivist doctrine with the facts of the History of Science. We want to discover the type of purpose exhibited in the practices of men of science. In order to avoid the suspicion of biased selection, consider the last discovery, which at the time of writing this chapter, has occupied a leading position in American newspapers. I mean the discovery of the new planet by the Lowell Observatory in Arizona. The final interpretation of this discovery is irrelevant: Nature, even in the act of satisfying anticipation, often provides a surprise. The story is typical of the previous discovery of Neptune, and of many discoveries of the faint members of double stars, and of the famous empirical term in the formula for the moon's motion.

The recent discovery is based upon the observed deviations of the orbits of the planets Uranus and Neptune from the calculated order. This calculation embraces the effect produced by all the previously known bodies of the solar system upon the motions of these two planets, assuming the Law of Gravitation. But their observed motions deviate slightly from their orbits as thus calculated. There is however no difficulty in producing a mathematical formula which describes the observed deviation. Such a formula will be of the most elementary mathematical character. It will consist of a few terms involving trigonometrical sines and cosines, with certain numerical components defining their periods, with other numerical components defining their amplitudes, and other numerical components defining their epochs—or in modern popular phraseology, their 'zero times'. Altogether a description of charming simplicity, which would have delighted Plato by its exemplification of his most daring speculations as to the future of mathematics.

Every Positivist must have been completely satisfied. A simple description had been evolved which fitted the observed facts. They could now relapse into their unexplained persuasion that in the future these formulæ would continue to describe the motions of Uranus and Neptune. Positivism had exhausted its message. But astronomers were not satisfied. They remembered the law of Gravitation. Percy Lowell calculated the direction and magniture of the vector component of acceleration, directed to an imaginary point moving round the sun in an elliptic path, even more remote than the orbit of Neptune. He succeeded in choosing his assumed path, so that the magnitude of the acceleration varies as the inverse square of the distance between Neptune and the moving point. A new description had been discovered, requiring some complex mathematics to connect it with the successive positions of Uranus, but conforming to the general form of Newton's Law. There has been a gain in generality, pleasing if you cherish a virtuosity in descriptions. But we have forgotten the main interest:— We have only got to look in the sky, towards Percy Lowell's moving point, and we shall see a new planet. Certainly we shall not. All that any person has seen is a few faint dots on photographic plates, involving the intervention of photography, excellent telescopes, elaborate apparatus, long exposures and favourable nights. The new explanation is now involved in the speculative extension of a welter of physical laws, concerning telescopes, light, and photography, laws which merely claim to register observed facts. It is involved in the speculative application of such laws to particular circumstances within the observatories, for which circumstances these laws are not concurrently verified. The result of this maze of speculative extensions is to connect the deviations of Uranus and Neptune with the dots on the photographic plates.

This narrative, framed according to the strictest requirements of the Positivist Theory, is a travesty of the plain facts. The civilized world has been interested at the thought of the newly discovered planet, solitary and remote, for endless ages circling the sun and adding its faint influence to the tide of affairs. At last it is discovered by human reason, penetrating into the nature of things and laying bare the necessities of their interconnection. The speculative extensions of laws, baseless on the Positivist theory, are the obvious issue of speculative metaphysical trust in the material permanences, such as telescopes, observatories, mountains, planets, which are behaving towards each other according to the necessities of the universe, including theories of their own natures. The point is, that speculative extension beyond direct observation spells some trust in metaphysics, however vaguely these metaphysical notions may be entertained in explicit thought. Our metaphysical knowledge is slight, superficial, incomplete. Thus errors creep in. But, such as it is, metaphysical understanding guides imagination and justifies purpose. Apart from metaphysical presupposition there can be no civilization.

There is a moral to be drawn as to the method of science. All scientific progress depends on first framing a formula giving a general description of observed fact. Lowell worked with such a formula in front of him, namely, the simple mathematical expression for the deviations. At one stage, the method of all discovery conforms to the Positivist doctrine. There can be no doubt that, with this restriction of meaning, the Positivist doctrine is correct.

Certain branches of science halt for centuries in this stage. Then their votaries embrace the unguarded Positivist doctrine. There is however a motive of unrest which urges scientists beyond mere satisfaction with the simple description, beyond even the *general* description. It is the desire to obtain the *explanatory* description which may justify the speculative extension of Laws, beyond actual, particular instances of observation.

This urge towards explanatory description provides the interplay between science and metaphysics. The doctrines of metaphysics are modified, so as to be capable of providing the explanation, and the explanations of science are framed in terms of the popular metaphysics lingering in the imaginations of these scientists.

One aspect of the history of thought from the time of Plato to the present day is the struggle between metaphysicians and Positivists over the interpretation of the Laws of Nature. The Greeks, as distinguished from the Alexandrians, are to be looked on as the discoverers of ideas, rather than their systematizers. Thus it is not surprising, that the attitude of Plato on this topic is not as clearly defined as the preceding quotations might imply. In some of his Dialogues his attention is fixed on the distinction between the eternal world of ideas, completely open to the understanding, and the fluent world disclosed by the senses which fails to participate with any exact clarity in the eternal forms. To that extent the sensible world is closed to the understanding. Its history is reduced to matter of fact, incapable of complete rationalization. It is but a short step from the Plato who composed the myth of the shadows on the wall of the cave to the full Positivist doctrine of Hume [i.e. the 'Hume' of the *Treatise*], Mill, Comte and Huxley. The main distinction between Plato in this mood and the Moderns—and it is a great distinction—is that the Platonic emphasis on the eminent reality of the eternal world of ideas must be replaced by the nominalism of most of these moderns.

But in his later Dialogues Plato's interest is concentrated on cosmology; and, as the quotations show, his final judgment, or the decay of his old age, leads him to an intermediate position between the doctrines of Immanent Law, and of Imposed Law.

SECTION VI. It was Plato in his later mood who put forward the suggestion, "and I hold that the definition of being is simply power." This suggestion is the charter of the doctrine of Immanent Law.

The next important landmark in the history of this doctrine is provided by the theological Alexandrians, some four to six hundred years later. It is customary to undervalue theology in a secular history of philosophical thought. This is a mistake, since for a period of about thirteen hundred years the ablest thinkers were mostly theologians.

The theologians of Alexandria were greatly exercised over the immanence of God in the world. They considered the general question, how the primordial Being, who is the source of the inevitable recurrence of the world towards order, shares his nature with the world. In some sense he is a component in the natures of all fugitive things. Thus, an understanding of the nature of temporal things involves a comprehension of the immanence of the Eternal Being. This doctrine effects an important reconciliation between the doctrines of Imposed Law and Immanent Law. For, with this doctrine, the necessity of the trend towards order does not arise from the imposed will of a transcendent God. It arises from the fact, that the existents in nature are sharing in the nature of the immanent God.

This doctrine, in any clear form, is not Platonic, though it is a natural modification from Plato's own doctrine. But in the *Timæus,* Plato provides a soul of this world who definitely is not the ultimate creator. By this notion, Plato prepared the way for the Gnostics with their fantastic machinery of emanations, and for the Arians. In the *Timæus* the doctrine can be read as an allegory. In that case it was Plato's most unfortunate essay in mythology. The World-Soul, as an emanation, has been the parent of puerile metaphysics, which only obscures the ultimate question of the relation of reality as permanent with reality as fluent: the mediator must be a component in common, and not a transcendent emanation.

The Western doctrine of Grace, derived from St. Augustine, leans heavily towards the notion of a wholly transcendent God imposing his partial favours on the world. Indeed, Calvin's rigid version of the same doctrine suggests the Manichean doctrine of a wholly evil material world partially rescued by God's arbitrary selection. For Calvinistic thought the physical order of the world was an arbitrary imposition of God's will. Indeed the Augustinian doctrine takes on diverse aspects according as it is derived from the will of a transcendent God, or the nature of an immanent God.

This unquestioned belief in order, with this chequered history,—Plato and Epicurus, the Gnostics, the Alexandrian theologians, the rationalists of Antioch and Mopsuetia, the Manicheans, Augustine, Calvin,—finally started the first phase of the modern world in the sixteenth century with the unquestioning presupposition that there is an order of nature which lies open in every detail to human understanding.

This belief can be traced back to the initiation of Plato and the Jewish prophets. But, in all probability, it is more than any of them clearly formulated or consistently believed. Lucretius gives the clearest formulation of the doctrine of an exact detailed order of nature. But even he has to make everything depend upon swervings of atoms which take place "at no fixed part of space and no fixed time."

SECTION VII. The conclusion of the seventeenth century marks a new stabilization of cosmological doctrine for the next two hundred years. For the moment the extreme Positivistic doctrine was eliminated. But, curiously enough, the three great figures, Newton, Leibniz, Locke, then dominating the world of thought, gave three diverse interpretations of the Platonic and Lucretian problems.

Newton's position was the more useful as a justification of the methodology required for the state of science, then and in the immediate future. He held the most simple-minded version of the Lucretian doctrine of the Void, the most simple-minded version of the Lucretian doctrine of material atoms, and the most simple-minded version of Law imposed by Divine decree. His only approach to any metaphysical penetration arises from his way of connecting the Void with the Sensorium of the Divine Nature. His cosmology is very easy to understand and very hard to believe. Pragmatically it experienced a supreme justification, for two centuries. Thus its truth was pragmatically established, for the same period. His doctrine will stand for all time as a clear and distinct system of ideas, with large applications. Any cosmology must be capable of interpreting this system and of expressing its limitations.

The monads of Leibniz constitute another version of an atomic doctrine of the universe. It is true that Newton adopted without question some of the main positions of the Cartesian physics. But Newton was entirely innocent of the subjectivist bias of thought introduced by Descartes. Newton found himself knowing a lot of things, as interpreted in Cartesian fashion; and he successfully introduced a systematization of this knowledge, thus interpreted. But Descartes, before he attacked the problem of physics, asked the momentous questions,—How do I know, and How can I divest my knowledge of doubtful interpretation? The final issue of this subjective train of thought after a century of philosophizing is given by Hume's mental atomism, already mentioned in this chapter.

Leibniz was acutely conscious of this problem of the criticism of knowledge. Thus he approached the problem of cosmology from the subjective side, whereas Lucretius and Newton approach it from the objective point of view. They implicitly ask the question, What does the world of atoms look like to an intellect surveying it? What would such an intellect say about the spectacle of an atomic universe? The answer is contained in the Epic of Lucretius and the *Principia* of Newton, immortal works.

But Leibniz answered another question. He explained what it must be like to be an atom. Lucretius tells us what an atom looks like to others, and Leibniz tells us how an atom is feeling about itself. In this account Leibniz wrestles with a difficulty which infects modern cosmologies, a difficulty which Plato, Aristotle, Lucretius, and Newton entirely ignore—perhaps because they would have declared it to be founded upon a mistake. Descartes, as is usual with the founders of new schools of thought, exactly balanced himself between the old way and the new way of which he was the founder. The modern outlook arises from the slow influence of Aristotle's Logic, during a period of two thousand years. Also Aristotle's Logic is founded upon an analysis of the simplest form of a verbal sentence. For example, the sentence 'This water is hot' attributes the character of high temperature to the particular mass of water in the particular bathtub. The quality of 'being hot' is an abstraction. Many different things can be hot, and we can think of being hot without thinking of any particular thing in a bathtub which is hot. But in the real physical world, the quality of 'being hot' can only appear as a characteristic of concrete things which *are* hot.

Again, still keeping to the point of view derived from Aristotelian Logic, if we ask for a complete account of a real particular thing in the physical world, the adequate answer is expressed in terms of a set of these abstract characteristics, which are united into an individualized togetherness which is the real thing in question.

This answer is beautifully simple. But it entirely leaves out of account the interconnections between real things. Each substantial thing is thus conceived as complete in itself, without any reference to any other substantial thing. Such an account of the ultimate atoms, or of the ultimate monads, or of the ultimate subjects enjoying experience, renders an interconnected world of real individuals unintelligible. The universe is shivered into a multitude of disconnected substantial things, each thing in its own way exemplifying its private bundle of abstract characters which have found a common home in its own substantial individuality. But substantial thing cannot call unto substantial thing. A substantial thing can acquire a quality, a credit— but real landed estate, never. In this way, Aristotle's doctrines of Predication and of Primary Substance have issued into a doctrine of the conjunction of attributes and of the disjunction of primary substances.

All modern epistemologies, all modern cosmologies, wrestle with this problem. There is, for their doctrine, a mysterious reality in the background, intrinsically unknowable by any direct intercourse. In the foreground of direct enjoyment, there is the play and interplay of various qualities diversifying the surface of the substantial unity of the solitary individual in question.

But one characteristic of each experiencing subject is a mysterious impulse to interpret its private world of enjoyed qualifications as indicating and symbolically defining a complex of communication between ultimate realities. Yet, according to the doctrine of these modern cosmologies, the how, or the why, of such communication must for ever lie beyond reason: for reason can only discern the set of qualities constituting the nature of an individual substance.

Such has been the long slow influence of Aristotelian Logic upon cosmological theory. Leibniz was the first, and by far the greatest philosopher, who both accepted the modern doctrine and frankly faced its difficulty. He boldly excepted God from the scope of the doctrine. God and each individual monad were in communication. Thus there is,

on his doctrine, an indirect communication between monads
by the mediation of God. But each monad independently
develops its own experience according to its character which
is imposed on it aboriginally by communication with God.
This Leibnizian doctrine of Law by pre-established harmony
is an extreme example of the doctrine of imposition, capable
in some ways of being mitigated by the notion of the immanence of God. But no reason can be given why the
supreme monad, God, is exempted from the common fate of
isolation. Monads, according to this doctrine, are window-
less for each other. Why have they windows towards God,
and Why has God windows towards them?

It is interesting to enquire how the ancient cosmologists
—Plato and Lucretius—evaded this difficulty.

In the first place it must be acknowledged that in Plato's
Dialogues many unguarded statements, and many trains of
thought, can be found which in themselves would lead
straight to the modern difficulty. In fact, in this respect
Aristotle's Logic can be found in germ in Plato. But in the
ancient cosmologies, including Aristotle's own doctrine of
matter, another train of thought can be found, which is in
fact an emphatic doctrine of real communication. Plato's
doctrine of the real Receptacle [ὑποδοχή and χώρα], and
Epicurus' doctrine of the real Void [τό κενόν], differ in
some details. But both doctrines are emphatic assertions of a
real communication between ultimate realities. This communication is not accidental. It is part of the essential nature
of each physical actuality that it is itself an element qualifying the Receptacle, and that the qualifications of the Receptacle enter into its own nature. In itself, with the various
actualities abstracted from it, the Receptacle participates in
no forms, according to Plato. But he designates it as 'the fos-
termother of all becoming'. Later in the same Dialogue he

calls it 'a natural matrix for all things'. It receives its forms
by reason of its inclusion of actualities, and in a way not to
be abstracted from those actualities. The Receptacle, as discussed in the *Timæus,* is the way in which Plato conceived
the many actualities of the physical world as components in
each other's natures. It is the doctrine of the immanence of
Law, derived from the mutual immanence of actualities. It
is Plato's doctrine of the medium of intercommunication.[4]

Thus finally we can understand that the Receptacle, according to Plato, the Void, according to Lucretius, and God,
according to Leibniz, play the same part in cosmological
theory. Also in his general scholium, Newton definitely connects the Lucretian Void with the Leibnizian God. For he
calls Empty space the 'sensorium of God'. We have here a
formidable display of men of diverse genius, Plato and
Aristotle, Epicurus and Lucretius, Newton and Leibniz.
The modern cosmologies are all detailed variations of the
great types which we have discussed. They revolve round
the diverse notions of Law, the diverse notions of the communication between real individuals, the diverse notions of
the mediating basis in virtue of which such communication
is attained. One other problem, derivative from these general principles, but of major importance for human life is
the doctrine of the status of the spirit of man in the scheme
of things.

This more special problem of cosmological theory was the
theme of the former part of this book. Its important influ-

   [4] On this topic, it is interesting to note the extreme difficulty of determining,
whether or no Descartes held to the doctrine of *one* individual corporeal substance with many modal diversities of motion, or to the doctrine of *many* diverse
individual corporeal substances essentially connected by extensive relations. Almost all his phrases are ambiguous on this point, with the exception of Principle
LX, Part I, of his *Principles of Philosophy.* Here he unambiguously speaks of
every corporeal substance, thus—at least in this place—deciding for a multiplicity
of such substances. Either alternative leads him into difficulties.

ence upon the course of human history was illustrated. But it must not be thought that the more general problem of cosmology lies outside the scope of practical interest. The directions of human activities in various epochs, and the clashings of such directions in the same epoch, are the outcome of rough and ready solutions of the problem of cosmology, popularized throughout masses of mankind. Millions of men have marched to battle fiercely nerved by intense faith in Law imposed by the will of inflexible Allah, Law sharing out to each human his inevitable fate, Law sharing out to each faithful Mahometan either victory, or death and Paradise. Millions of Buddhists have shunned the intrinsic evils of such fierce Mahometan emotion relying on the impersonal immanence of Law, made clear to them by the doctrines of the Buddha. Millions of humans have shaped their lives according to the compromise between these two doctrines due to the Platonism of Christianity.

Finally, the restless modern search for increased accuracy of observation and for increased detailed explanation is based upon unquestioning faith in the reign of Law. Apart from such faith, the enterprise of science is foolish, hopeless.

SECTION VIII. The most recent of the four doctrines of the Laws of Nature still remains for discussion—The Doctrine of Conventional Interpretation. This doctrine certainly expresses the procedure by which free speculation passes into an interpretation of Nature. We elaborate a system of ideas, in detachment from any direct, detailed observation of matter of fact. For example, such detachment from detailed observation seems, on the surface, to be characteristic of Plato's *Dialogues*. They do not bear the aspect of patient induction from the facts. They are dominated by speculation and dialectics. Also Mathematics has developed, especially in recent years, by a speculative interest in types of order, without any determination of particular entities illustrative of those types. But Nature has subsequently been interpreted in terms of such mathematical laws. The conclusion seems to be, that Nature is patient of interpretation in terms of Laws which happen to interest us.

Yet another consideration supports this point of view. There is an element of arbitrary choice in our interpretation of the geometrical character of the physical world. Mathematicians have proved that any region which exemplifies metrical geometry of the Euclidean type, also exemplifies metrical geometry of the Elliptic type, and also metrical geometry of the Hyperbolic type. Further, if we start with any one of the three types, we can prove that both the remaining types are severally exemplified in the same subject-matter.

But it is an entire misconception, which has been entertained even by some mathematicians, to deduce that this mathematical truth has any bearing upon the notion of the Laws of Nature as arbitrary convention. For in the three metrical geometries as applying to the same subject-matter, the definitions of distance are different. Thus mathematicians have proved that if there be a metrical geometry of the Euclidean type, then with another definition of distance, and hence with another definition of congruence, there is a metrical geometry of the elliptic type also applying to the same subject-matter. There are three diverse systems of relationship within the subject-matter, so related that if one be present then the others are present. Also, of course, the description of one set of relationships can be achieved, though very clumsily, in terms of any one of the other two sets. There is nothing 'conventional' in this, except the obvious fact that we can direct attention to any selected group of facts. Of course the question remains, What set of geometrical relationships are we referring to, when we say that we have walked thirty miles and are tired? Are they thirty Euclidean miles, or thirty Elliptic miles, or thirty Hyperbolic miles? Here the standard of reference can be the same in both cases, namely, the interval between two assigned marks fixed securely in Washington, D. C.

Again there is yet another geometrical ambiguity. For keeping to the same type of geometry—Euclidean, say, but either of the other two would serve equally well—keeping to Euclidean geometry, there are an infinite number of different alternative ways of defining distance so as to produce alternative systems of Euclidean geometry. Thus granting that one Euclidean system holds, an infinite number of other Euclidean systems also hold. Thus when a friend says that he has motored a hundred miles to see us, we should enquire what particular geometrical system of metrics he has adopted. And he had not settled the question by merely answering Euclidean. Also the differences are not necessarily slight. A thousand miles between particular towns on one system may be two miles on another system. It follows that every legislature should anxiously settle the metric system that it means to adopt. This question has nothing to do with the difference between miles and kilometers, or with mere imperfections of measurement. That is a much slighter point.

It is fairly obvious that, apart from minor inaccuracies of perception, we all do in fact adopt the same system. It is a fact of nature that a distance of thirty miles is a long walk for any one. There is no convention about that. Thus the appeal to geometry can be dismissed when we are discussing the question of the conventionality of the Laws of Nature.

SECTION IX. But the analogy of Geometry suggests an important reflection. It is well-known that Geometry can be developed without any reference to measurement,—and thus without any reference to distance, and without any reference to numerical coördinates for the indication of points. Geometry, developed in this fashion has been termed 'Non-metrical Projective Geometry'. Elsewhere [5] I have termed it, 'the science of cross-classification'. Aristotle's science of classification into genera, and species, and sub-species, is the science of mutually exclusive classification. It develops Plato's suggestion of a science of 'Division'.

Projective Geometry is only one example of a science of cross-classification. Other such sciences have not been developed, partly because no obvious applications have obtruded themselves, and partly because the abstract interest of such sciences have not engaged the interest of any large group of mathematicians. For example, in *Principia Mathematica,* [6] Section 93, 'On the Inductive Analysis of the Field of a Relation', is a suggestion for another science of that type. Indeed the whole of Vol. I is devoted to the initiation of non-numerical quasi-geometrical sciences, together with a technique for their elaboration. The subsequent parts of the book specialize on those more special mathematical sciences which involve number and quantity.

This reference to *Principia Mathematica* has been made to remind ourselves that numerical relations derived from measurements constitute the subject-matter of a very special development of mathematics. This development has as yet constituted the only really important part of mathematics, except for the impressive disclosure of the extent to which

[5] *The Axioms of Projective Geometry,* Cambridge Tracts in Mathematics, No. 4, Cambridge University Press, 1906. The reference is to Chapter I, Section 3.
[6] Cambridge University Press, 1910.

ordinary Geometry is independent of measurement and number.

It follows that there are an indefinite number of purely abstract sciences, with their laws, their regularities, and their complexities of theorems—all as yet undeveloped. We can hardly avoid the conclusion that Nature in her procedures illustrates many such sciences. We are blind to such illustration because we are ignorant of the type of regularities to look for. In such cases, we may dimly sense a sort of familiarity attached to novel circumstances, without any notion how to proceed in the analysis of the vague feeling.

There is thus a certain amount of convention as to the emergence into human consciousness of sorts of Laws of Natures. The order of emergence depends upon the abstract sciences which civilized mankind have in fact chosen to develop.

But such 'convention' should not be twisted to mean that any facts of nature can be interpreted as illustrating any laws that we like to assign.

SECTION X. This discussion of the possible variety of types of Laws of Nature draws attention to a three-fold distinction which it is important to keep in mind during philosophic discussion. There are: (i) our direct intuitions which we enjoy prior to all verbalization: (ii) our literary modes of verbal expression of such intuitions, together with the dialectic deductions from such verbal formulæ: (iii) the set of purely deductive sciences, which have been developed so that the network of possible relations with which they deal are familiar in civilized consciousness.

The sciences under the heading (iii) direct attention for the exploration of the recesses of experience, and also assist in providing the verbal formulæ belonging to the heading (ii). The chief danger in philosophy is that the dialectic deductions from inadequate formulæ should exclude direct intuitions from explicit attentions. In fact the abstract sciences tend to correct the evil effects of the inadequacy of language, and the consequent dangers of a logic which presupposes linguistic adequacy.

CHAPTER IX

SCIENCE AND PHILOSOPHY

SECTION I. In one sense, Science and Philosophy are merely different aspects of one great enterprise of the human mind. We will dwell upon their coöperation in the task of raising humanity above the general level of animal life. At this low, animal level, flashes of æsthetic insight, of technological attainment, of sociological organization, of affectionate feeling, display themselves. Nightingales, beavers, ants, the kindly nurture of the young, all witness to the existence of this level of life in the animal world. Of course all these modes of functioning are carried to an immeasurably higher level among mankind. In human beings these various modes of functioning exhibit more variety of adaptation to special circumstances, they are more complex, and they are more interwoven with each other. But without question, among animals they are there, plainly demonstrated to our observation.

Among living things on this planet, so far as direct evidence reaches, Science and Philosophy belong to men alone. They are both concerned with the understanding of individual facts as illustrations of general principles. The principles are understood in the abstract, and the facts are understood in respect to their embodiment of the principles.

For example, animals seem quite familiar with the habit of bodies to fall down. They show no surprise at such an occurrence, and they often knock things over. But quite

early in the history of modern European science we find
Aristotle formulating the law that there is a tendency for
material bodies to seek the centre of the Earth. This law
was almost certainly not a discovery of Aristotle's. It was
a reigning commonplace of Greek thought, although not accepted unanimously. But it is plainly set forth in his writings, and it is beside our point to indulge further in archæological conjectures. This scientific law seems rather anti-
quated to us, and in fact not quite true. It is over special,
and yet requires severe limitation before the quantitative
measurements bear out its statements with any exactness.
We shall find that the subsequent history of this law and of
its successive modifications throws great light upon the relative functions of Science and Philosophy.

But let us first examine Aristotle's Law, which is one of
the earlier doctrines of that Western Science whose history
stretches from Thales of Miletus, alive at the date 600 B.C.,
to the present day. Roughly speaking, it is a history of about
twenty-five hundred years. Of course there were anticipations in Egypt, Mesopotamia, India, and China. But modern
science, urged onward by the curiosity of the human spirit,
permeated with criticism, and divorced from hereditary
superstitions, had its birth with the Greeks; and among the
Greeks Thales was the earliest exponent known to us.

In this general characterization science and philosophy are
not discriminated. But the word 'curiosity' somewhat triv-
ializes that inward motive which has driven men. In the
greater sense, in which it is here used, 'curiosity' means the
craving of reason that the facts discriminated in experience
be understood. It means the refusal to be satisfied with the
bare welter of fact, or even with the bare habit of routine.
The first step in science and philosophy has been made
when it is grasped that every routine exemplifies a principle

which is capable of statement in abstraction from its particular exemplifications. The curiosity, which is the gadfly driving civilization from its ancient safeties, is this desire to state the principles in their abstraction. In this curiosity there is a ruthless element which in the end disturbs. We are American, or French, or English; and we love our modes of life, with their beauties and tendernesses. But curiosity drives us to an attempt to define civilization; and in this generalization we soon find that we have lost our beloved America, our beloved France, and our beloved England. The generality stands with a cold impartiality, where our affections cling to one or other of the particulars.

An examination of Aristotle's Law of Gravitation exemplifies this abstractive process inherent in science. The Law involves a classification of the things around us. There are the heavy bodies with the property of tending downwards, and there are the other elements such as flames, with the intrinsic nature that they tend upwards though they are component things on the Earth's surface. These upward moving things tend to their proper place which is the heavens. The stars and planets form yet a third class of things which by their own nature are in the heavens, things which are ingenerable and incorruptible. In this classification of the components of physical nature yet a fourth component remains over, in its character unique and thus the only member of its class. This component is the Earth, the centre of the Universe, by reference to which all these other types of being are defined.

In this classification of the various components of physical nature Aristotle has given to Science and Philosophy its first sweeping analysis of the facts of physical nature. You will notice that the classification proceeds entirely by reference to function, quite in the modern spirit. In the place of an uninterpreted swamp, pestilential with mystery and magic, he sets before our understanding a majestic, coördinated scheme, lucid to the understanding and based upon the obvious, persistent facts of our experience. In the generality of its scope, it is equally philosophic and scientific, and later on it provided the physical background for the Christian scheme of salvation. Its overthrow, eighteen hundred years later, was resisted equally by Luther and the Church of Rome. As an example of a majestic inductive generalization, appealing to the obvious facts, and neglecting the welter of minor differences, Aristotle's general conception of the physical universe remains unsurpassed. For every feature in it, there is an appeal to observation; and for every observation to which appeal is made, there is the possibility of its indefinite repetition. With Aristotle and Epicurus, the science of modern civilization reached adolescence.

SECTION II. There is a clear-act obviousness about Aristotle's doctrines which is entirely lacking to Plato's cosmology. Of course neither Plato, nor Aristotle, originated his own particular line of thought. There was a history behind them of three or four generations of thinkers, back to the dim figures of Thales and Pythagoras, and even beyond them. Also Aristotle worked for twenty years in the Academy of Plato, and derived ideas from that active, speculative group of thinkers, to whom the modern world owes its speculation, its criticism, its deductive and inductive sciences, and the civilization of its religious concepts. They were the narrow channel through which passed the confused traditions of Egypt, Mesopotamia, Syria, and of the sea-borne Greek civilization. From this Academy and its Aristotelian off-shoot, there emerged the various lines of thought which the subsequent schools of Alexandria turned into the first phase of

modern science, natural and humane. Undoubtedly the
world then lost picturesqueness. For prophets were super-
seded by professors. In other words, as the movement has
penetrated into habits of thought, intuitive conviction has
wilted in the face of criticism. But amid all the limitations
of humanity, wandering dazed in the abundant universe,
knowledge has re-conditioned human life, and has made
possible that virtue which requires such measure of intellectual analysis.

Between them, Plato and Aristotle succeed in illustrating
the chief connections between science and philosophy. The
emphasis of science is upon observation of particular occurrences, and upon inductive generalization, issuing in wide
classifications of things according to their modes of functioning, in other words according to the laws of nature
which they illustrate. The emphasis of philosophy is upon
generalizations which almost fail to classify by reason of
their universal application. For example, all things are involved in the creative advance of the Universe, that is, in the
general temporality which affects all things, even if at all
times they remain self-identical. Thus the consideration of
time does not lead to classification in the same direct way
in which the consideration of weight led Aristotle to his
four-fold classification.

Now Plato had already emphasized the importance of this
Aristotelian notion of classification, that is to say, of 'division' as he called it. Perhaps indeed he invented the method.
It would have been quite in accordance with his clear-cut
intellectual subtlety to have done so. We find in his dialogues the first explicit formulations of the science of Logic.
But his applications of the method are feeble in the extreme,
from the point of view of the advancement of natural
science. Whereas Aristotle in his life's work seized upon

the general notion of classification, he gave a masterly analysis of the complexities inherent in the mutual relation of classes. He also applied his theoretical doctrine to the immense material to be collected by direct observation in the fields of zoölogy, physics, sociology. Indeed we must trace to him nearly all our special sciences, both the natural sciences, and those concerning the activities of the spirit of mankind. He is the origin of the striving towards an accurate analysis of each given situation which in the end has created modern European Science. We can see in the labours of his life, the first clear example of a philosophic intuition passing into a scientific method.

SECTION III. This transition from philosophic intuitions to scientific methods is in fact the whole topic of this chapter. A philosophic system, viewed as an attempt to coördinate all such intuitions, is rarely of any direct importance for particular sciences. Each such science in tracing its ideas backward to their basic notions stops at a half-way house. It finds a resting place amid notions which for its immediate purposes and for its immediate methods it need not analyse any further. These basic notions are a specialization from the philosophic intuitions which form the background of the civilized thought of the epoch in question. They are intuitions which, apart from their use in science, ordinary language rarely expresses in any defined accuracy, but habitually presupposes in its current words and expressions. For example, the words 'tables', 'chairs', 'rocks', presuppose the scientific notion of material bodies, which has governed natural science from the seventeenth century to the end of the nineteenth.

But, even from the point of view of the special sciences, philosophic systems with their ambitious aims at full comprehensiveness, are not useless. They are the way in which the human spirit cultivates its deeper intuitions. Such systems give life and motion to detached thoughts. Apart from these efforts at coördination, detached thoughts would flash out in idle moments, illuminate a passing phase of reflection, and would then perish and be forgotten. The scope of an intuition can only be defined by its coördination with other notions of equal generality. Even the discordance of competing philosophic systems is a factor essential for progress. The history of European thought, even to the present day, has been tainted by a fatal misunderstanding. It may be termed The Dogmatic Fallacy. The error consists in the persuasion that we are capable of producing notions which are adequately defined in respect to the complexity of relationship required for their illustration in the real world. Canst thou by searching describe the Universe? Except perhaps for the simpler notions of arithmetic, even our more familiar ideas, seemingly obvious, are infected with this incurable vagueness. Our right understanding of the methods of intellectual progress depends on keeping in mind this characteristic of our thoughts. The notions employed in every systematic topic require enlightenment from the perspective of every standpoint. They must be criticized from the standpoint of their own internal consistency within that topic, and from the standpoint of other topics of analogous generality, and from the standpoint of so-called philosophic topics with a wider range. During the mediaeval epoch in Europe, the theologians were the chief sinners in respect to dogmatic finality. During the last three centuries, their bad preëminence in this habit passed to the men of science. Our task is to understand how in fact the human mind can successfully set to work for the gradual definition of its habitual ideas. It is a step by step process, achieving no triumphs of finality. We cannot produce that final adjustment of well-defined generalities which constitute a complete meta-physics. But we can produce a variety of partial systems of limited generality. The concordance of ideas within any one such system shows the scope and virility of the basic notions of that scheme of thought. Also the discordance of system with system, and success of each system as a partial mode of illumination, warns us of the limitations within which our intuitions are hedged. These undiscovered limitations are the topics for philosophic research.

This doctrine of the limitations to which our best ideas are subject is illustrated by that very notion of material bodies which has just been mentioned. That notion is so obvious that it has haunted language so far as we can trace history backwards. Finally in the seventeenth century it was given a new precision for the purposes of physical science. Also physical science, thus re-conditioned, proved an overwhelming success for three centuries. It has transformed thought, and has transformed the physical activities of mankind. It seemed that at last mankind had achieved the fundamental notion for all practical purposes, and that beyond it in the way of generality there lay mere aimless speculation. But in the twentieth century this great notion, as shaped for use by Galileo and Newton, has completely collapsed so far as concerns its use as a fundamental notion for physical science. In the modern science, it is a limited notion confined to special purposes.

This collapse of nineteenth century dogmatism is a warning that the special sciences require that the imaginations of men be stored with imaginative possibilities as yet un-utilized in the service of scientific explanation. The nearest analogy is to be seen in the history of some species of animal, or plant, or microbe, which lurks for ages as an obscure by-product of nature in some lonely jungle, or morass, or island. Then by some trick of circumstance it escapes into the outer world and transforms a civilization, or destroys an empire or the forests of a continent. Such is the potential power of the ideas which live in the various systems of philosophy.

Of course in this action, and reaction, between science and philosophy either helps the other. It is the task of philosophy to work at the concordance of ideas conceived as illustrated in the concrete facts of the real world. It seeks those generalities which characterize the complete reality of fact, and apart from which any fact must sink into an abstraction. But science makes the abstraction, and is content to understand the complete fact in respect to only some of its essential aspects. Science and Philosophy mutually criticize each other, and provide imaginative material for each other. A philosophic system should present an elucidation of concrete fact from which the sciences abstract. Also the sciences should find their principles in the concrete facts which a philosophic system presents. The history of thought is the story of the measure of failure and success in this joint enterprise.

SECTION IV. Plato's contribution to the basic notions connecting Science and Philosophy, as finally settled in the later portion of his life, has virtues entirely different from that of Aristotle, although of equal use for the progress of thought. It is to be found by reading together the *Theætetus,* the *Sophist,* the *Timæus,* and the fifth and tenth books of the *Laws;* and then by recurrence to his earlier work, the *Symposium.* He is never entirely self-consistent, and rarely explicit and devoid of ambiguity. He feels the difficulties, and expresses his perplexities. No one could be perplexed over

Aristotle's classifications; whereas Plato moves about amid a fragmentary system like a man dazed by his own penetration.

A few main doctrines stand out and they are of priceless importance for science, in the largest sense of that term. As to their coördination into a system, he is undogmatic and can only tell 'the most likely tale'. Indeed, in his seventh Epistle [1] he denounces the notion that a final system can be verbally expressed. His later thought circles round the interweaving of seven main notions namely, The Ideas, The Physical Elements, The Psyche, The Eros, The Harmony, The Mathematical Relations, The Receptacle. These notions are as important for us now, as they were then at the dawn of the modern world, when civilizations of the old type were dying. From their point of view the Athenians were right to condemn Socrates. After the coalescence of Greek and Semitic thought the old order of life was doomed. Western Civilization acquired a new intellectuality, clarified, humanized, moralized.

Considering the Ideas by themselves, Plato points out that any selections are either compatible for joint exemplification, or are incompatible. It thus follows, as he notes, that the determinations of compatibilities and incompatibilities are the key to coherent thought, and to the understanding of the world in its function as the theatre for the temporal realization of ideas. The Aristotelian Logic is only a specialized derivative from this general notion.

Plato then passes on to the agency whereby ideas obtain efficiency in the creative advance. As he conceives them in abstraction, he finds ideas to be static, frozen, and lifeless. They obtain 'life and motion' by their entertainment in a living intelligence. Such a living intelligence with its 'gaze

[1] Cf. 341, C.

fixed upon ideas' was what Plato termed a Psyche, a word
we can translate as 'soul'. We must, however, be careful to
divest the associations of the English word from the accre-
tions due to centuries of Christianity. He conceives of a
basic Psyche whose active grasp of ideas conditions impar-
tially the whole process of the Universe. This is the Supreme
Craftsman, on whom depends that degree of orderliness
which the world exhibits. There is a perfection in this
Psyche, which Plato finds out of his power to explain. There
are also finite souls of varying grades, including human
souls, all playing their part in conditioning nature by the
inherent persuasiveness of ideas.

But the notion of mere knowledge, that is to say, of mere
understanding, is quite alien to Plato's thought. The age of
professors had not yet arrived. In his view, the entertainment of ideas is intrinsically associated with an inward ferment, an activity of subjective feeling, which is at once immediate enjoyment, and also an appetition which melts into
action. This is Plato's Eros, which he sublimates into the
notion of the soul in the enjoyment of its creative function,
arising from its entertainment of ideas. The word Eros
means 'Love', and in *The Symposium* Plato gradually elicits
his final conception of the urge towards ideal perfection.
It is obvious that he should have written a companion
dialogue which might have been named The Furies,
dwelling on the horrors lurking within imperfect realization.

Plato, although he neglected to write this missing dialogue, did not overlook the confusion and disorder in
Nature. He expressly denies omnipotence to his Supreme
Craftsman. The influence of the entertainment of ideas is
always persuasive, and can only produce such order as is
possible. However, on this point he wavers, and sometimes

writes as if the Craftsman were disposing the world according to his supreme will.

This notion of an excellence, partly attained and partly missed, raises another problem which greatly exercised Greek thought at the time of Plato. The problem can take many special forms. In what does beauty consist, for example, the beauty of a musical melody, the beauty of a statue, or of a building such as the Parthenon? Also, there is that other form of beauty, which is rightness of conduct. Probably, in this naïve shape, the question has no answer; since 'The Good' is an ultimate qualification not to be analysed in terms of any things more final than itself. But an analogous question can be asked, to which Greek thought was unanimous as to its answer. To what sort of things does the concept apply, and in particular what sort of conditions are requisite for its evocation? The Greek answer to this latter pair of questions was that beauty belonged to composite things, and that the composition is beautiful when the many components have obtained in some sense their proper proportions. This was the Greek doctrine of Harmony, in respect to which neither Plato nor Aristotle ever waver.

In respect to Harmony, the Greeks made a discovery which is a landmark in the history of thought. They found out that exact Mathematical Relationships, as they exist in Geometry and in the numerical proportions of measurements, are realized in various outstanding examples of beautiful composition. For instance Archytas discovered that, other circumstances being equal, the note given out by a stretched string depends on the length of the string, and that beautiful compositions of notes correspond to certain simple laws as to the proportional lengths of the strings. Also they investigated the dependence of the beauty of architecture upon the preservation of the proper proportions in the various dimensions. This was an immense discovery, the dependence of the qualitative elements in the world upon mathematical relations. The facts had gradually accumulated through thousands of years. The early Babylonians knew that the qualitative fact of the succession of seasons depended upon the lapse of definite numbers of days. In fact, they constructed very creditable calendars. But the Greeks, with their power of generalization, grasped the full law of the interweaving of qualitative fact with geometrical and quantitative composition. They had the genius to be astonished.

Plato drew the conclusion that the key to the understanding of the natural world, and in particular of the physical elements, was the study of mathematics. There is good reason to believe that the greater part of the studies of his Academy was devoted to mathematics. The mathematicians of the succeeding generation, and indeed of the next two hundred years, ending with the astronomers Ptolemy and Hipparchus, are the product of the systematic tradition shaped by the example and the doctrine of Plato. Of course the Academy inherited the Pythagorean tradition of Mathematics.

Thus with Plato and Aristotle, a new epoch commences. Science acquires the cleansing of logical and mathematical lucidity. Aristotle established the importance of scientific classification into species and genera; Plato divined the future scope of applied mathematics. Unfortunately, later on, the explicit development of Plato's doctrines has been exclusively in the hands of religious mystics, of literary scholars, and of literary artists. Plato, the mathematician, for long intervals disappeared from the explicit Platonic tradition.

The notions of Harmony and of Mathematical Relations are only special exemplifications of a yet more general philosophic concept, namely, that of the general interconnectedness of things, which transforms the manifoldness of the many into the unity of the one. We speak in the singular of *The* Universe, of Nature, of φύσις which can be translated as Process. There is the one all-embracing fact which is the advancing history of the one Universe. This community of the world, which is the matrix for all begetting, and whose essence is process with retention of connectedness,—this community is what Plato terms The Receptacle [ὑποδοχή]. In our effort to divine his meaning, we must remember that Plato says that it is an obscure and difficult concept, and that in its own essence the Receptacle is devoid of all forms. It is thus certainly not the ordinary geometrical space with its mathematical relations. Plato calls his Receptacle, 'The foster-mother of all becoming'. He evidently conceived it as a necessary notion without which our analysis of Nature is defective. It is dangerous to neglect Plato's intuitions. He carefully varies his phrases in referring to it, and implies that what he says is to be taken in its most abstract sense. The Receptacle imposes a common relationship on all that happens, but does not impose what that relationship shall be. It seems to be a somewhat more subtle notion than Aristotle's 'matter' which, of course, is not the 'matter' of Galileo and Newton. Plato's Receptacle may be conceived as the necessary community within which the course of history is set, in abstraction from all the particular historical facts. I have directed attention to Plato's doctrine of The Receptacle because, at the present moment, physical science is nearer to it than at any period since Plato's death. The space-time of modern mathematical physics, conceived in abstraction from the particular mathematical formulæ which applies to the happenings in it, is almost exactly Plato's Receptacle. It is to be noted that mathematical physicists are extremely uncertain as to what these formulæ are exactly, nor do they believe that any such formulæ can be derived from the mere notion of space-time. Thus, as Plato declares, space-time in itself is bare of all forms.

SECTION V. In the preceding sketch only one incidental generalization, selected from one topic comprised in the enormous labours of Aristotle's life, has been brought forward. Aristotle was at once a man of science, a philosopher, a literary critic, and a student of political theory. This particular classification of the things constitutive of the visible universe has been dwelt upon because it is an almost perfect example of a scientific induction satisfying all the conditions insisted on by the modern philosophy of science. It was a generalization from observed fact, and could be confirmed by repeated observation. In its day—and its day lasted for eighteen hundred years—it was extremely useful; and now that it is dead, it is stone-dead, an archæological curiosity. This is the fate of scientific generalizations, so long as they are considered in relation to their strict scientific purpose. Towards the end of its long life, the doctrine lost its utility and turned into an obstructive agency.

The Platonic group of notions which have been considered have none of the merits of the Aristotelian set. In fact, they are philosophic, and in the narrow sense are not scientific. They suggest no detailed observation. Indeed it has always been a reproach to Plato that he diverted interest from observation of the particular facts. So far as concerns political theory, and in particular jurisprudence, this accusation is certainly untrue, and arises from the habit of concentrating interest on his Dialogues in proportion to their literary brilliance. Nevertheless the assertion is undoubtedly true in respect to physical science. But Plato had another message. Where Aristotle said 'observe' and 'classify', the moral of Plato's teaching is the importance of the study of mathematics. Of course, neither of them was so stupid as to dissuade from observation or, on the other hand, to deny the utility of mathematics. Probably Aristotle thought that the mathematical knowledge of his day was about as much as was wanted for the purposes of physical science. Any further progress could only minister to an unpractical curiosity about subtle abstractions.

An intense belief that a knowledge of mathematical relations would prove the key to unlock the mysteries of the relatedness within Nature was ever at the back of Plato's cosmological speculations. In one passage he reprobates the swinish [2] ignorance of those who have failed to study the doctrine of proportions incapable of expression as numerical ratios. He evidently feels that the chance of some subtle elucidation of the nature of Harmony is being crassly lost. His own speculations as to the course of nature are all founded upon the conjectural application of some mathematical construction. So far as I can remember, in every case he made a sensible shot which, in fact, went wide of the mark.

Although the *Timæus* was widely influential, yet for about eighteen hundred years after their epoch, it seemed that Aristotle was right and Plato wrong. Some mathematical formulæ were interwoven with scientific ideas, but no more than would have been perfectly familiar to Aristotle apart from what were in his day the latest refinements. The cosmological scheme of the active scientists was in fact that of Aristotle. But Plato's divination exemplifies another im-

[2] ὑηνός cf. *Laws*, Bk. VII, 819 D

portant function for philosophy. It evokes interest in topics as yet remote from our crude understanding of the interplay of natural forces. The science of the future depends for its ready progress upon the antecedent elucidation of hypothetical complexities of connection, as yet unobserved in nature. Plato's mathematical speculations have been treated as sheer mysticism by scholars who follow the literary traditions of the Italian Renaissance. In truth, they are the products of genius brooding on the future of intellect exploring a world of mystery.

Greeks, Egyptians, Arabs, Jews, and Mesopotamians advanced the science of mathematics beyond the wildest dreams of Plato. Unfortunately this side of Plato's interest was notably absent among the Christian populations. I believe it to be true that no Christian made any original contribution to mathematical science before the revival of science at the time of the Renaissance. Pope Silvester II—Gerbert, who reigned in the year 1000 A.D.—studied mathematics. But he added nothing. Roger Bacon proclaimed the importance of mathematics and named contemporary mathematicians. In the thirteenth and fourteenth centuries the University of Oxford cherished mathematics. But none of these mediaeval Europeans advanced the subject. An exception must be made in favour of Leonardo of Pisa who flourished at the beginning of the thirteenth century. He was the first Christian to make an advance in the science which in its early history illustrates the cultural union of the Hellenistic Greeks with the Near East. But, subject to this qualification, sixteenth-century mathematics was entirely based upon non-Christian sources. Among the Christians mathematics and magic were confused. The Pope himself hardly escaped. We can hardly hope for a better illustration of the curious limitations of epochs and schools of civilization. It is especially interesting in view of the dominant influence of Plato upon Christian thought.

But the Platonic doctrine of the interweaving of Harmony with mathematical relations has been triumphantly vindicated. The Aristotelian classifications based upon qualitative predicates have a very restricted application apart from the introduction of mathematical formulæ. Indeed, Aristotelian Logic, by its neglect of mathematical notions, has done almost as much harm as good for the advancement of science. We can never get away from the questions:—How much,— In what proportions,—and In what pattern of arrangement with other things. The exact laws of chemical proportions make all the difference; CO will kill you, when CO_2 will only give you a headache. Also CO_2 is a necessary element for the dilution of oxygen in the atmosphere; but too much or too little is equally harmful. Arsenic deals out either health or death, according to its proportions amid a pattern of circumstances. Also when the health-giving proportion of CO_2 to free oxygen has been obtained, a rearrangement of these proportional quantities of carbon and oxygen into carbon monoxide and free oxygen will provide a poisonous mixture. In Political Economy, the Law of Diminishing Returns points to the conditions for the maximum efficiency of a dose of capital. In fact, there is hardly a question to be asked which should not be fenced round with qualifications as to how much, and as to what pattern of circumstances. Aristotelian Logic, apart from the guardianship of mathematics, is the fertile matrix of fallacies. It deals with propositional forms only adapted for the expression of high abstractions, the sort of abstractions usual in current conversation where the presupposed background is ignored.

But it is evident that even the appeal to mathematics is too narrow, at least if mathematics is taken to mean those branches hitherto developed. The general science of mathematics is concerned with the investigation of patterns of connectedness, in abstraction from the particular relata and the particular modes of connection. It is only in some special branches of mathematics that notions of quantity and number are dominant themes. The real point is that the essential connectedness of things can never be safely omitted. This is the doctrine of the thoroughgoing relativity which infects the universe and which makes the totality of things as it were a Receptacle uniting all that happens.

The Greek doctrine of Composition and Harmony has been vindicated by the progress of thought. Yet the vivid fancy of the Greeks was also apt to invest each factor in the Universe with an independent individuality, for example, the self-sufficient realm of ideas which dominated Plato's earlier thought, and which intermittently intrudes into his later Dialogues. But we must not blame the Greeks for this excess of individualization. All language witnesses to the same error. We habitually speak of stones, and planets, and animals, as though each individual thing could exist, even for a passing moment, in separation from an environment which is in truth a necessary factor in its own nature. Such an abstraction is a necessity of thought, and the requisite background of systematic environment can be presupposed. That is true. But it also follows that, in the absence of some understanding of the final nature of things, and thus of the sorts of backgrounds presupposed in such abstract statements, all science suffers from the vice that it may be combining various propositions which tacitly presuppose inconsistent backgrounds. No science can be more secure than the unconscious metaphysics which tacitly it presupposes. The individual thing is necessarily a modification of its environment, and cannot be understood in disjunction. All reasoning, apart from some metaphysical reference, is vicious.

SECTION VI. Thus the Certainties of Science are a delusion. They are hedged around with unexplored limitations. Our handling of scientific doctrines is controlled by the diffused metaphysical concepts of our epoch. Even so, we are continually led into errors of expectation. Also, whenever some new mode of observational experience is obtained the old doctrines crumble into a fog of inaccuracies.

Our coördinated knowledge, which in the general sense of the term is Science, is formed by the meeting of two orders of experience. One order is constituted by the direct, immediate discriminations of particular observations. The other order is constituted by our general way of conceiving the Universe. They will be called, the Observational Order, and the Conceptual Order. The first point to remember is that the observational order is invariably interpreted in terms of the concepts supplied by the conceptual order. The question as to the priority of one or the other is, for the purpose of this discussion, academic. We inherit an observational order, namely types of things which we do in fact discriminate; and we inherit a conceptual order, namely a rough system of ideas in terms of which we do in fact interpret. We can point to no epoch in human history, or even in animal history, at which this interplay began. Also it is true that novel observations modify the conceptual order. But equally, novel concepts suggest novel possibilities of observational discrimination.

The history of thought cannot be understood unless we take account of a grave weakness in the observational order. Observational discrimination is not dictated by the impartial facts. It selects and discards, and what it retains is rearranged in a subjective order of prominence. This order of prominence in observation is in fact a distortion of the facts. Thus we have to rescue the facts as they are from the facts as they appear. We have to rescue the facts in the discard, and we have to discard the subjective order of prominence which is itself a fact of observation. For example, consider the observed facts in early stages of civilization. The observed fact was a flat Earth with the arched dome of the Sky. Even to the contemporaries of Pope Silvester the antipodes were inconceivable, and his reputed belief in them did no credit to the old wizard of a Pope.

Again we view the sky at noon on a fine day. It is blue, flooded by the light of the Sun. The direct fact of observation is the sun as the sole origin of light, and the bare heavens. Conceive the myth of Adam and Eve in the Garden on the first day of human life. They watch the sunset, the stars appear:—

'And, Lo!, creation widened to man's view'.

The excess of light discloses facts and also conceals them. It distorts the facts for human observation. It is one task of speculation to urge observation beyond the boundaries of its delusive completeness, and to urge the doctrines of science beyond their delusive air of finality.

We can now briefly characterize the history of the transformation of mediaeval cosmology into our modern standpoint. The effective agency in this transformation has a history of about eighteen hundred years entirely divorced from physical observation. It is a history of abstract thought, namely, of the development of mathematics. The interest, which was the motive in its development, was the interest in the coördination of theoretical notions and in the theoretical constructions arising from the domination of such notions. Yet, if many modern philosophers and men of science could have had their way, they would have been dissuading

Greeks, Jews, and Mahommedans from such useless studies, from such pure abstractions for which no foresight could divine the ghost of an application. Luckily they could not get at their ancestors.

SECTION VII. The services to mankind rendered by the Newtonian System of Nature are incalculable. It combines ideas derived from Plato, Aristotle, and Epicurus, into a consistent scheme of thought which elucidates an incredible number of observed facts. Thereby it has enabled men to obtain a new command over Nature. Where we formerly obeyed, we now direct. But at last the Newton cosmology has broken down.

The story of the breakdown extends over more than a century. For by far the greater part of that period men of science were quite unaware that the ideas which they were introducing, slowly, one after the other, were finally to accumulate into a body of thought inconsistent with the Newtonian ideas dominating their thoughts and shaping their modes of expression. The story commences with the wave-theory of light and ends with the wave-theory of matter. It finally leaves us with the philosophic question, What are the concrete facts which exhibit this mathematical attribute of wave-vibration?

The story in detail is the history of modern physics, which lies beyond the scope of this discussion. We merely require to understand the contrast between the most general notions respectively underlying Newtonian physics and modern physics. Newtonian physics is based upon the independent individuality of each bit of matter. Each stone is conceived as fully describable apart from any reference to any other portion of matter. It might be alone in the Universe, the sole occupant of uniform space. But it would still be that stone which it is. Also the stone could be adequately described without any reference to past or future. It is to be conceived fully and adequately as wholly constituted within the present moment.

This is the full Newtonian concept, which bit by bit was given away, or dissolved, by the advance of modern physics. It is the thorough-going doctrine of 'simple location' and of 'external relations'. There was some divergence of opinion as to the external relations. Newton himself was inclined to construe them in terms of shock and of stress between contiguous bodies. But his immediate followers, such as Roger Cotes, added the notion of force at a distance. But either alternative was wholly and completely a fact in the present, namely, the fact of that external relation between two bits of matter either contiguous or distant. The opposed doctrine of internal relations has been distorted by reason of its description in terms of language adapted to the presupposition of external relations of the Newtonian type. Even its adherents, such as F. H. Bradley for instance, fall into this pitfall. It must be remembered that just as the relations modify the natures of the relata, so the relata modify the nature of the relation. The relationship is not a universal. It is a concrete fact with the same concreteness as the relata. The notion of the immanence of the cause in the effect illustrates this truth. We have to discover a doctrine of nature which expresses the concrete relatedness of physical functionings and mental functionings, of the past with the present, and also expresses the concrete composition of physical realities which are individually diverse.

Modern physics has abandoned the doctrine of Simple Location. The physical things which we term stars, planets, lumps of matter, molecules, electrons, protons, quanta of energy, are each to be conceived as modifications of conditions within space-time, extending throughout its whole range. There is a focal region, which in common speech is where the thing is. But its influence streams away from it with finite velocity throughout the utmost recesses of space and time. Of course, it is natural, and for certain purposes entirely proper, to speak of the focal region, thus modified, as the thing itself situated there. But difficulties arise if we press this way of thought too far. For physics, the thing itself is what it does, and what it does is this divergent stream of influence. Again the focal region cannot be separated from the external stream. It obstinately refuses to be conceived as an instantaneous fact. It is a state of agitation, only differing from the so-called external stream by its superior dominance within the focal region. Also we are puzzled how to express exactly the existence of these physical things at any definite moment of time. For at every instantaneous point-event, within or without the focal region, the modification to be ascribed to this thing is antecedent to, or successive to, the corresponding modification introduced by that thing at another point-event. Thus if we endeavor to conceive a complete instance of the existence of the physical thing in question, we cannot confine ourselves to one part of space or to one moment of time. The physical thing is a certain coördination of spaces and times and of conditions in those spaces at those times, this coördination illustrating one exemplification of a certain general rule, expressible in terms of mathematical relations. Here we have returned to a fundamental Platonic doctrine.

Again, with the denial of simple location we must admit that within any region of space-time the innumerable multitude of these physical things are in a sense superposed. Thus the physical fact at each region of space-time is a composition of what the physical entities throughout the Universe mean for that region. But a complete existence is not a composition of mathematical formulæ, mere formulæ. It is a concrete composition of things illustrating formulæ. There is an interweaving of qualitative and quantitative elements. For example, when a living body assimilates food, the fact cannot be *merely* that one mathematical formula assimilates another mathematical formula. The fact cannot be merely that the equality of two and three with five assimilates the fact of the equality of thrice three with nine, nor can the number eleven assimilate the number sixteen. Any of these mathematical notions may be illustrated, but the fact is more than the formulæ illustrated.

SECTION VIII. The final problem is to conceive a complete [παντελής] fact.[3] We can only form such a conception in terms of fundamental notions concerning the nature of reality. We are thrown back upon philosophy. Centuries ago Plato divined the seven main factors interwoven in fact:— The Ideas, The Physical Elements, The Psyche, The Eros, The Harmony, The Mathematical Relations, The Receptacle. All philosophical systems are endeavours to express the interweaving of these components. Of course, it is most unscholarly to identify our modern notions with these archaic thoughts of Plato. For us everything has a subtle difference. But for all these differences, human thought is now endeavouring to express analogous elements in the composition of nature. It only dimly discerns, it misdescribes, and it wrongly associates. But always there remain the same beacons that lure. Systems, scientific and philosophic, come and go. Each method of limited understanding is at length exhausted. In its prime each system is a triumphant success: in its decay it is an obstructive nuisance. The transitions to new fruitful-

---

[3] Cf. *Sophist*, 248 E, τῷ παντελῶς ὄντι. Here παντελῶς is often wrongly translated by 'absolute'. For Plato's reference to 'absolute' and 'relative' cf. *Sophist*, 255 C.

ness of understanding are achieved by recurrence to the utmost depths of intuition for the refreshment of imagination. In the end—though there is no end—what is being achieved, is width of view, issuing in greater opportunities. But opportunity leads upwards or downwards. In unthinking Nature 'natural selection' is a synonym for 'waste'. Philosophy should now perform its final service. It should seek the insight, dim though it be, to escape the wide wreckage of a race of beings sensitive to values beyond those of mere animal enjoyment.

CHAPTER X

THE NEW REFORMATION

Section I. The theme of this chapter can be introduced by directing attention to a contrast. Protestant Christianity, so far as concerns the institutional and dogmatic forms in which it flourished for three hundred years as derived from Luther, Calvin, and the Anglican Settlement, is shewing all the signs of a steady decay. Its dogmas no longer dominate: its divisions no longer interest: its institutions no longer direct the patterns of life. That is one side of the contrast.

The other side is that the religious spirit as an effective element in the affairs of men has just [April, 1931] obtained one of its most signal triumphs. In India the forces of violence and strife, between rulers and people, between races, between religions, between social grades,—forces threatening to overwhelm with violence hundreds of millions of mankind—these forces have for the moment been halted by two men acting with the moral authority of religious conviction, the Mahatma Gandhi and the Viceroy of India [Lord Irwin].

They may fail. More than two thousand years ago, the wisest of men proclaimed that the divine persuasion is the foundation of the order of the world, but that it could only produce such a measure of harmony as amid brute forces it was possible to accomplish. This, I suggest, is a plain anticipation by Plato of a doctrine of Grace, seven hundred years before the age of Pelagius and Augustine.

But the dramatic halt effected by Gandhi and the Viceroy, requiring as it does an effective response from uncounted millions in India, in England, in Europe, and America, witnesses that the religious motive, I mean the response to the divine persuasion, still holds its old power, even more than its old power, over the minds and the consciences of men. In this response the protestant populations of the British Empire, and importantly, though more remotely, that of the United States, have sustained their part. We stand at a moment when the course of history depends upon the calm reasonableness arising from a religious public opinion. An initial triumph has already been gained.

There is the contrast, decay and survival. We have to estimate what has decayed, and what has survived. My thesis is that a new Reformation is in full progress. It is a re-formation; but whether its issue be fortunate or unfortunate depends largely on the actions of comparatively few men, and notably upon the leaders of the protestant clergy.

I do not hold it to be possible, or even desirable, that identity of detailed belief can be attained. But it is possible that amid diversities of belief, arising from differences of stress exhibited in metaphysical insight and from differences of sympathetic intuition respecting historical events,—that it is possible, amid these differences, to reach a general agreement as to those elements, in intimate human experience and in general history, which we select to exemplify that ultimate theme of the divine immanence, as a completion required by our cosmological outlook. In other words, we may agree as to the qualitative aspects of religious facts, and as to their general way of coördination in metaphysical theory, while disagreeing in various explanatory formulations.

The problem, however, is not nearly so simple as this exordium suggests. We are dealing with a topic, complex and many-sided. It comprises the deliverances of the understanding as it harmonizes our deepest intuitions. It comprises emotional responses to formulations of thought and to modes of behaviour. It comprises the direction of purposes and the modifications of behaviour. It cuts into every aspect of human existence. So far as concerns religious problems, simple solutions are bogus solutions. It is written, that he who runs, may read. But it is not said, that he provides the writing.

For religion is concerned with our reactions of purpose and emotion due to our personal measure of intuition into the ultimate mystery of the universe. We must not postulate simplicity. The witness of history and of common sense tells us that systematic formulations are potent engines of emphasis, of purification, and of stability. Christianity would long ago have sunk into a noxious superstition, apart from the Levantine and European intellectual movement, sustained from the very beginning until now. This movement is the effort of Reason to provide an accurate system of theology. Indeed, in outlying districts where this effort at rationalization died away, the religion has in fact sunk into the decrepitude of failure.

SECTION II. Thus the attack of the liberal clergy and laymen, during the eighteenth and nineteenth centuries, upon systematic theology was entirely misconceived. They were throwing away the chief safeguard against the wild emotions of superstition. A civilized religion should aim at the training of such emotions as naturally arise from a civilized rational criticism of the metaphysical intuitions powerfully influential in great epochs of human history. The appeal to history is the appeal to summits of attainment beyond any immediate clarity in our own individual existence. It is an appeal to authority. The appeal to reason is the appeal to that ultimate judge, universal and yet individual to each, to which all authority must bow. History has authority so far, and exactly so far, as it admits of some measure of rational interpretation.

Thus an attack upon systematic thought is treason to civilization. Yet the great minds who laid the foundations of our modern mentality—John Locke, for example—had reason for their dissatisfaction with the traditional dogmatic theology, though they partially misconceived the grounds upon which they should base their attitude. Their true enemy was the doctrine of dogmatic finality, a doctrine which flourished and is flourishing with equal vigour throughout Theology, Science, and Metaphysics. The methodology of rational thought from the Greeks to our own times has been vitiated by this fundamental misconception. These errors are not confined to religious thought. They have infected all departments. Their total effect has been to introduce in each age a dogmatic sense of finality. The emphasis of certainty has been wrongly placed, and with equal error dogmatic rejection.

From the very beginning of critical thought, we find the distinction between topics susceptible of certain knowledge, and topics about which only uncertain opinions are available. The dawn of this distinction, explicitly entertained, is the dawn of modern mentality. It introduces criticism. Such a notion hardly enters into any book of the Bible, either in the mind of Jehovah, or of any of his worshippers. The first effect of this new distinction was very unfortunate. For it was much too simple-minded, and the area of certainty was misconceived. For example, we find Plato in his old age advocating religious persecution, and justifying himself by the importance of the topic and the certainty of his own demonstrations.[1]

I suggest that the development of systematic theology should be accompanied by a critical understanding of the relation of linguistic expression to our deepest and most persistent intuitions. Language was developed in response to the excitements of practical actions. It is concerned with the prominent facts. Such facts are those seized upon by consciousness for detailed examination, with the view of emotional response leading to immediate purposeful action. These prominent facts are the variable facts,—the appearance of a tiger, of a clap of thunder, or of a spasm of pain. They are the facts entering into experience by the medium of our sense-organs. Hence the sensationalist doctrine concerning the data which are the origin of experience.

But the prominent facts are the superficial facts. They vary because they are superficial; and they enter into conscious discrimination because they vary. There are other elements in our experience, on the fringe of consciousness, and yet massively qualifying our experience. In regard to these other facts, it is our consciousness that flickers, and not the facts themselves. They are always securely there, barely discriminated, and yet inescapable. For example, consider our derivation from our immediate past of a quarter of a second ago. We are continuous with it, we are the same as it, prolonging its affective tone, enjoying its data. And yet we are modifying it, deflecting it, changing its purposes, altering its tone, re-conditioning its data with new elements.

We reduce this past to a perspective, and yet retain it as the basis of our present moment of realization. We are different from it, and yet we retain our individual identity with

[1] Cf. Plato's *Laws*, Book X.

it. This is the mystery of personal identity, the mystery of the immanence of the past in the present, the mystery of transience. All our science, all our explanations require concepts originating in this experience of derivation. In respect to such intuitions, language is peculiarly inadequate. Our powers of analysis, and of expression, flicker with our consciousness. It is not true that there is a definite area of human consciousness, within which there is clear discrimination and beyond which mere darkness. Nor is it true that elements of experience are important in proportion to their clarity in consciousness.

The appeal to history gains its importance by reason of this complex character of human experience. Metaphysics and theology alike require it. The requisite evidence cannot be gained by mere acts of direct introspection conducted at one epoch by a few clear-sighted individuals. If a flood of oblivion should overwhelm human memory, we could in this way of introspection recover the multiplication table. But not much else. In each age of the world, the actions of men and their interpretations of feelings, motives, and purposes, throw light upon the recesses of their experience. In this elucidation of what it means to live, to act, and feel, age differs from age. In the discrimination of this historical evidence, there is required a criticism founded upon taste, and a criticism founded upon logical analysis and inductive probability.

The two grounds of criticism, æsthetic and logical, are welded together in the final judgment of reason as to the comparison of historical periods, one with the other. Each age deposits its message as to the secret character of the nature of things. Civilizations can only be understood by those who are civilized. And they have this property, that the appropriation of them in the understanding unveils

truths concerning our own natures. It has been said that
the great dramatic tragedies in their representations before
audiences act as a purification of the passions. In the same
way, the great periods of history act as an enlightenment.
They reveal ourselves to ourselves.

SECTION III. Christianity bases itself upon an intensive
study of the significance of certain historical occasions scattered irregularly within a period of about twelve hundred
years, from the earlier Hebrew prophets and historians to
the stabilization of western theology by Augustine. The
story wanders around the shores of the Eastern Mediterranean, from the Palestine of the prophets to the Athens of
Plato: it culminates in Galilee and Jerusalem: the main interest then fluctuates uncertainly backwards and forwards
between Antioch, Ephesus, Egypt, Rome, Constantinople
and Africa. When Augustine died at Hippo in the year
430, the religion of the European races was in its main outlines settled. All its capacities for variant forms were already
inherent in it. The Papal Church, the Eastern Church,
Wycliffe and Huss, Luther and Calvin, Archbishop Cran-
mer, Jonathan Edwards and John Wesley, Erasmus, Igna-
tius Loyola, the Socinians, George Fox, and the Vatican
Council could with equal right appeal to history. The conclusion to be drawn from the appeal entirely depends upon
the value-judgments guiding your selection, and upon the
metaphysical presuppositions dictating your notions of a
coherent theology. The appeal is to the actions, thoughts,
emotions, and institutions, which great persons and great
occasions had made effective on the shores of the Mediterranean within that earlier period of time.

In this appeal to history we must remember the gaps in
time between the extant written Gospels and the events
which they relate: the discordances in accounts, the transla-

tions of tradition from language to language, the suspicious passages: also the seeming indifference to direct historical evidence, notably in the case of St. Paul, who retired to Arabia when we should have expected him to have recourse to the disciples who had seen his Lord. I mention these latter points, upon which whole libraries have been written, merely to draw the unquestioned conclusion that any modern re-formation of the religion must first concentrate upon the moral and metaphysical intuitions scattered throughout the whole epoch. This conclusion is a commonplace of modern thought.

I suggest, with the diffidence due to my entire lack of expertness in the literature of this immense stretch of history, that even now there is room for a new appeal to the lesson to be derived from it. In this chapter I shall deal wholly in general principles. My personal conclusions as to the details of reconstruction have none of the importance to be ascribed to scholarship. Also to speak with complete candour, I cannot place any of the events within that period as out of scale in type of happenings with analogous occurrences elsewhere. I do hold, however, that the culminating points of the period embody the greatest advances in the expression of moral and intellectual intuitions which mark the growth of recent civilization.

The period as a whole begins in barbarism and ends in failure. The failure consisted in the fact that barbaric elements and the defects in intellectual comprehension had not been discarded, but remained as essential elements in the various formulations of Christian theology, orthodox and heretical alike. Also the later Protestant Reformation was, in this respect, an even more complete failure, in no way improving Catholic theology. The Quakers perhaps form a minor exception to this statement. But George Fox lived a hundred years after the age of Luther. The issue of these failures is the tragic history of Christianity.

SECTION IV. I suggest that in the whole period there are three culminating phases which, in theological language, constitute its threefold revelation. The first and the last phases were primarily intellectual with a sufficient background of moral insight. The middle phase, which forms the driving power of the religion, is primarily an exhibition in life of moral intuition, with a sufficiency of intellectual insight to give an articulate expression of singular beauty. The three phases are bound together as intellectual discovery,—then exemplification,—finally metaphysical interpretation. The discovery and the exemplification are historically independent.

The first phase is constituted by Plato's publication of his final conviction, towards the end of his life,[2] that the divine element in the world is to be conceived as a persuasive agency and not as a coercive agency. This doctrine should be looked upon as one of the greatest intellectual discoveries in the history of religion. It is plainly enunciated by Plato, though he failed to coördinate it systematically with the rest of his metaphysical theory. Indeed, Plato always failed in his attempts at systematization, and always succeeded in displaying depth of metaphysical intuition—the greatest metaphysician, the poorest systematic thinker. The alternative doctrine, prevalent then and now, sees either in the many gods or in the one God, the final coercive forces wielding the thunder. By a metaphysical sublimation of this doctrine of God as the supreme agency of compulsion. he is transformed into the one supreme reality, omnipotently disposing a wholly derivative world. Plato wavered inconsistently between these diverse conceptions. But he does finally enun-

[2] Cf. The *Sophist* and *the Timæus*.

ciate without qualification the doctrine of the divine persuasion, by reason of which ideals are effective in the world and forms of order evolve.

The second phase is the supreme moment in religious history, according to the Christian religion. The essence of Christianity is the appeal to the life of Christ as a revelation of the nature of God and of his agency in the world. The record is fragmentary, inconsistent, and uncertain. It is not necessary for me to express any opinion as to the proper reconstruction of the most likely tale of historic fact. Such a procedure would be useless, without value, and entirely out of place in this book. But there can be no doubt as to what elements in the record have evoked a response from all that is best in human nature. The Mother, the Child, and the bare manger: the lowly man, homeless and self-forgetful, with his message of peace, love, and sympathy: the suffering, the agony, the tender words as life ebbed, the final despair: and the whole with the authority of supreme victory.

I need not elaborate. Can there be any doubt that the power of Christianity lies in its revelation in act, of that which Plato divined in theory?

The third phase is again intellectual. It is the first period in the formation of Christian theology by the schools of thought mainly associated with Alexandria and Antioch. The originality and value of their contribution to the thought of the world has been greatly underestimated. This is partly their own fault. For they persisted in declaring that they were only stating the faith once delivered to the saints; whereas in fact they were groping after the solution of a fundamental metaphysical problem, although presented to them in a highly special form.

These Christian theologians have the distinction of being

stood in the same relation to the whole World as early Egyptian or Mesopotamian kings stood to their subject populations. Also the moral characters were very analogous. In the final metaphysical sublimation, he became the one absolute, omnipotent, omniscient source of all being, for his own existence requiring no relations to anything beyond himself. He was internally complete. Such a conception fitted on very well to the Platonic doctrine of subordinate derivations. The final insistence, after much wavering, on the immanence of God was therefore all the more a fine effort of metaphysical imagination on the part of the theologians of the early Christian ages. But their general concept of the Deity stopped all further generalization. They made no effort to conceive the World in terms of the metaphysical categories by means of which they interpreted God, and they made no effort to conceive God in terms of the metaphysical categories which they applied to the World. For them, God was eminently real, and the World was derivatively real. God was necessary to the World, but the World was not necessary to God. There was a gulf between them.

The worst of a gulf is, that it is very difficult to know what is happening on the further side of it. This has been the fate of the God of traditional theology. It is only by drawing the long bow of mysticism that evidences for his existence can be collected from our temporal World. Also the worst of unqualified omnipotence is that it is accompanied by responsibility for every detail of every happening. This whole topic is discussed by Hume in his famous Dialogues.

SECTION V. I am suggesting that Protestant theology should develop as its foundation an interpretation of the Universe which grasps its unity amid its many diversities.

The interpretation to be achieved is a reconciliation of seeming incompatibilities. But these incompatibilities are not
hypothetical. They are there on the stage of history, undoubted and claiming interpretation. There stand in the
public view the persuasiveness of the eternal ideals, the same
today as when realized in the Founder of Christianity, and
the compulsoriness of physical nature, which passes and yet
remains, and the compulsoriness of that realized urge toward
social union, such as the Roman Empire, which was then,
and is now as it were a dream. Nature changes and yet remains. The ideals declare themselves as timeless; and yet
they pass on, as it were the flicker of a brightness.

It is the business of philosophical theology to provide a
rational understanding of the rise of civilization, and of
the tendernesses of mere life itself, in a world which superficially is founded upon the clashings of senseless compulsion. I am not disguising my belief that in this task, theology has largely failed. The notion of the absolute despot
has stood in the way. The doctrine of Grace has been de-
graded, and the doctrines of the Atonement are mostly
crude. The defect of the liberal theology of the last two hundred years is that it has confined itself to the suggestion of
minor, vapid reasons why people should continue to go to
church in the traditional fashion.

The last book in the Bible illustrates the barbaric elements
which have been retained to the undoing of Christian intuition. In itself and apart from its bearing upon religious
sentiment, it is one of the finest examples of imaginative
literature as it stands translated in King James's Bible. Also,
as an historical document, whether its origin be Christian or
Jewish, it is of priceless value for the understanding of
strains of thought prevalent when the Christian religion was
in process of formation. Finally, the book only states, more

pointedly and more vividly, ideas spread throughout the Old Testament and the New Testament, even in the Gospels themselves. Yet it is shocking to think that this book has been retained for the formation of religious sentiment, while the speech of Pericles, descriptive of the Athenian ideal of civilization, has remained neglected in this connection. What I am advocating can be symbolized by this shift in the final book of the authoritative collection of religious literature, namely, the replacement of the book of the Revelation of St. John the Divine by the imaginative account given by Thucydides of the Speech of Pericles to the Athenians. Neither of them is history: St. John never received just that revelation, nor did Pericles ever make just that speech.

SECTION VI. There remains for discussion one final question. I wish to emphasize the importance that, amid many divergencies of interpretation, the leaders of religious thought should today concentrate upon the Christian tradition and more particularly upon its historical origins. In the case of the more conservative schools of thought such advice is, of course, unnecessary, and indeed impertinent. But it is a question for discussion why the more radical schools should not cut entirely free from any appeal to the past, and concentrate entirely upon the contemporary world and contemporary examples. The summary answer is that in so far as such an appeal to tradition can be made with complete honesty, without any shadow of evasion, there is an enormous gain in popular effectiveness.

Civilization is constituted out of four elements, (1) Patterns of Behaviour, (2) Patterns of Emotion, (3) Patterns of Belief, and (4) Technologies. We can at once dismiss Technologies as beyond our topic, though all four constitutive elements interact upon each other. Also patterns of behaviour are in the long run sustained or modified by patterns of emotion and patterns of belief. It is the primary business of religion to concentrate upon emotion and belief.

Now, so far as concerns beliefs of a general character, it is much easier for them to destroy emotion than to generate it. In any survey of the adventure of ideas nothing is more surprising than the ineffectiveness of novel general ideas to acquire for themselves an appropriate emotional pattern of any intensity. Profound flashes of insight remain ineffective for centuries, not because they are unknown, but by reason of dominant interests which inhibit reaction to that type of generality. The history of religion is the history of the countless generations required for interest to attach itself to profound ideas. For this reason religions are so often more barbarous than the civilizations in which they flourish.

This faintness of impress of general ideas upon the human mind has another effect. It is difficult even for acute thinkers to understand the analogies between ideas expressed in diverse phraseologies and illustrated by different sorts of examples. Desperate intellectual battles have been fought by philosophers who have expressed the same idea in different ways. For both these reasons, if you want to make a new start in religion, based upon ideas of profound generality, you must be content to wait a thousand years. Religions are like species of animals: they do not originate from special creations.

Finally, if there be any truth in the contention that dogmatic finality of verbal expression is a mistaken notion, there is an enormous advantage in keeping together, with common modes of procedure, religious opinions of analogous types. They can learn from each other, borrow from each other, and individuals can make imperceptible transitions. Above all, they can learn to understand each other and to love.

Must 'religion' always remain as a synonym for 'hatred'? The great social ideal for religion is that it should be the common basis for the unity of civilization. In that way it justifies its insight beyond the transient clash of brute forces.

This discussion has concentrated upon three culminating phases, the thought of Plato, the life of Christ, and the first formative period of Christian theology. But this whole period of twelve centuries, with its legendary antecedents and its modern successors, is required to complete the tale of the Christian religion. The story is wholly concerned with the interplay of ideas belonging to different levels of insight. The religious spirit is always in process of being explained away, distorted, buried. Yet, since the travel of mankind toward civilization, it is always there.

The task of Theology is to show how the World is founded on something beyond mere transient fact, and how it issues in something beyond the perishing of occasions. The temporal World is the stage of finite accomplishment. We ask of Theology to express that element in perishing lives which is undying by reason of its expression of perfections proper to our finite natures. In this way we shall understand how life includes a mode of satisfaction deeper than joy or sorrow.

PART III
PHILOSOPHICAL

CHAPTER XI

OBJECTS AND SUBJECTS

. . . Τὸ παρὸν ἑκάστῳ πάθος, ἐξ ὧν αἱ αἰσθήσεις καὶ αἱ κατὰ ταύτας δόξαι γίγνονται, . . . *Theaetetus*, 179 C.

§1. *Prefatory.*—When Descartes, Locke, and Hume undertake the analysis of experience, they utilize those elements in their own experience which lie clear and distinct, fit for the exactitude of intellectual discourse. It is tacitly assumed, except by Plato, that the more fundamental factors will ever lend themselves for discrimination with peculiar clarity. This assumption is here directly challenged.

§2. *Structure of Experience.*—No topic has suffered more from this tendency of philosophers than their account of the object-subject structure of experience. In the first place, this structure has been identified with the bare relation of knower to known. The subject is the knower, the object is the known. Thus, with this interpretation, the object-subject relation is the known-knower relation. It then follows that the more clearly any instance of this relation stands out for discrimination, the more safely we can utilize it for the interpretation of the status of experience in the universe of things. Hence Descartes' appeal to clarity and distinctness.

This deduction presupposes that the subject-object relation is the fundamental structural pattern of experience. I agree with this presupposition, but not in the sense in which subject-object is identified with knower-known. I contend that the notion of mere knowledge is a high abstraction, and that

225

conscious discrimination itself is a variable factor only present in the more elaborate examples of occasions of experience. The basis of experience is emotional. Stated more generally, the basic fact is the rise of an affective tone originating from things whose relevance is given.

§3. *Phraseology.*—Thus the Quaker word 'concern', divested of any suggestion of knowledge, is more fitted to express this fundamental structure. The occasion as subject has a 'concern' for the object. And the 'concern' at once places the object as a component in the experience of the subject, with an affective tone drawn from this object and directed towards it. With this interpretation the subject-object relation is the fundamental structure of experience.

Quaker usages of language are not widely spread. Also each phraseology leads to a crop of misunderstandings. The subject-object relation can be conceived as Recipient and Provoker, where the fact provoked is an affective tone about the status of the provoker in the provoked experience. Also the total provoked occasion is a totality involving many such examples of provocation. Again this phraseology is unfortunate; for the word 'recipient' suggests a passivity which is erroneous.

§4. *Prehensions.*—A more formal explanation is as follows. An occasion of experience is an activity, analysable into modes of functioning which jointly constitute its process of becoming. Each mode is analysable into the total experience as active subject, and into the thing or object with which the special activity is concerned. This thing is a datum, that is to say, is describable without reference to its entertainment in that occasion. An object is anything performing this function of a datum provoking some special activity of the occasion in question. Thus subject and object are relative terms. An occasion is a subject in respect to its special activity concerning an object; and anything is an object in respect to its provocation of some special activity within a subject. Such a mode of activity is termed a 'prehension'. Thus a prehension involves three factors. There is the occasion of experience within which the prehension is a detail of activity; there is the datum whose relevance provokes the origination of this prehension; this datum is the prehended object; there is the subjective form, which is the affective tone determining the effectiveness of that prehension in that occasion of experience. How the experience constitutes itself depends on its complex of subjective forms.

§5. *Individuality*.—The individual immediacy of an occasion is the final unity of subjective form, which is the occasion as an absolute reality. This immediacy is its moment of sheer individuality, bounded on either side by essential relativity. The occasion arises from relevant objects, and perishes into the status of an object for other occasions. But it enjoys its decisive moment of absolute self-attainment as emotional unity. As used here the words 'individual' and 'atom' have the same meaning, that they apply to composite things with an absolute reality which their components lack. These words properly apply to an actual entity in its immediacy of self-attainment when it stands out as for itself alone, with its own affective self-enjoyment. The term 'monad' also expresses this essential unity at the decisive moment, which stands between its birth and its perishing. The creativity of the world is the throbbing emotion of the past hurling itself into a new transcendent fact. It is the flying dart, of which Lucretius speaks, hurled beyond the bounds of the world.

§6. *Knowledge*.—All knowledge is conscious discrimination of objects experienced. But this conscious discrimination, which is knowledge, is nothing more than an additional factor in the subjective form of the interplay of subject with object. This interplay is the stuff constituting those individual things which make up the sole reality of the Universe. These individual things are the individual occasions of experience, the actual entities.

But we do not so easily get rid of knowledge. After all, it is knowledge that philosophers seek. And all knowledge is derived from, and verified by, direct intuitive observation. I accept this axiom of empiricism as stated in this general form. The question then arises how the structure of experience outlined above is directly observed. In answering this challenge I remind myself of the old advice that the doctrines which best repay critical examination are those which for the longest period have remained unquestioned.

§7. *Sense-Perception.*—The particular agelong group of doctrines which I have in mind is: (1) that all perception is by the mediation of our bodily sense-organs, such as eyes, palates, noses, ears, and the diffused bodily organization furnishing touches, aches, and other bodily sensations; (2) that all percepta are bare sensa, in patterned connections, given in the immediate present; (3) that our experience of a social world is an interpretative reaction wholly derivative from this perception; (4) that our emotional and purposive experience is a reflective reaction derived from the original perception, and intertwined with the interpretative reaction and partly shaping it. Thus the two reactions are different aspects of one process, involving interpretative, emotional, and purposive factors. Of course, we are all aware that there are powerful schools of philosophy which explicitly reject this doctrine. Yet I cannot persuade myself that this rejection has been taken seriously by writers be-

longing to the schools in question. When the direct question
as to things perceived arises, it seems to me that the answer
is always returned in terms of sensa perceived.

§8. *Perceptive Functions.*—In the examination of the sensationalist doctrine, the first question to be asked concerns
the general definition of what we mean by those functions
of experience which we term 'perceptions'. If we define
them as those experiential functions which arise directly
from the stimulation of the various bodily sense-organs, then
argument ceases. The traditional doctrine then becomes a
mere matter of definition of the use of the word 'perception'.
Indeed, having regard to long-standing usage, I am inclined
to agree that it may be advisable for philosophers to confine
the word 'perception' to this limited meaning. But the point
on which I am insisting is that this meaning *is* limited, and
that there is a wider meaning with which this limited use
of the term 'perception' has been tacitly identified.

§9. *Objects.*—The process of experiencing is constituted
by the reception of entities, whose being is antecedent to that
process, into the complex fact which is that process itself.
These antecedent entities, thus received as factors into the
process of experiencing, are termed 'objects' for that experiential occasion. Thus primarily the term 'object' expresses
the relation of the entity, thus denoted, to one or more occasions of experiencing. Two conditions must be fulfilled in
order that an entity may function as an object in a process
of experiencing: (1) the entity must be *antecedent,* and
(2) the entity must be experienced in virtue of its antecedence; it must be *given.* Thus an object must be a thing
received, and must not be either a *mode* of reception or
a thing *generated* in that occasion. Thus the process of
experiencing is constituted by the reception of objects into

the unity of that complex occasion which is the process itself. The process creates itself, but it does not create the objects which it receives as factors in its own nature.

'Objects' for an occasion can also be termed the 'data' for that occasion. The choice of terms entirely depends on the metaphor which you prefer. One word carries the literal meaning of 'lying in the way of', and the other word carries the literal meaning of 'being given to'. But both words suffer from the defect of suggesting that an occasion of experiencing arises out of a passive situation which is a mere welter of many data.

§10. *Creativity*.—The exact contrary is the case. The initial situation includes a factor of activity which is the reason for the origin of that occasion of experience. This factor of activity is what I have called 'Creativity'. The initial situation with its creativity can be termed the initial phase of the new occasion. It can equally well be termed the 'actual world' relative to that occasion. It has a certain unity of its own, expressive of its capacity for providing the objects requisite for a new occasion, and also expressive of its conjoint activity whereby it is essentially the primary phase of a new occasion. It can thus be termed a 'real potentiality'. The 'potentiality' refers to the passive capacity, the term 'real' refers to the creative activity, where the Platonic definition of 'real' in the *Sophist* is referred to. This basic situation, this actual world, this primary phase, this real potentiality—however you characterize it—as a whole is active with its inherent creativity, but in its details it provides the passive objects which derive their activity from the creativity of the whole. The creativity is the actualization of potentiality, and the process of actualization is an occasion of experiencing. Thus viewed in abstraction objects are passive, but viewed in conjunction they carry the creativity which drives the world. The process of creation is the form of unity of the Universe.

§11. *Perception.*—In the preceding sections, the discovery of objects as factors in experience was explained. The discussion was phrased in terms of an ontology which goes beyond the immediate purpose, although the status of objects cannot be understood in the absence of some such ontology explaining their function in experience, that is to say, explaining why an occasion of experience by reason of its nature requires objects.

The objects are the factors in experience which function so as to express that that occasion originates by including a transcendent universe of other things. Thus it belongs to the essence of each occasion of experience that it is concerned with an otherness transcending itself. The occasion is one among others, and including the others which it is among. Consciousness is an emphasis upon a selection of these objects. Thus perception is consciousness analysed in respect to those objects selected for this emphasis. Consciousness is the acme of emphasis.

It is evident that this definition of perception is wider than the narrow definition based upon sense-perception, sensa, and the bodily sense-organs.

§12. *Non-Sensuous Perception.*—This wider definition of perception can be of no importance unless we can detect occasions of experience exhibiting modes of functioning which fall within its wider scope. If we discover such instances of non-sensuous perception, then the tacit identification of perception with sense-perception must be a fatal error barring the advance of systematic metaphysics.

Our first step must involve the clear recognition of the limitations inherent in the scope of sense-perception. This special mode of functioning essentially exhibits percepta as *here, now, immediate,* and *discrete.* Every impression of sensation is a distinct existence, declares Hume; and there can be no reasonable doubt of this doctrine. But even Hume clothes each impression with force and liveliness. It must be distinctly understood that no prehension, even of bare sensa, can be divested of its affective tone, that is to say, of its character of a 'concern' in the Quaker sense. Concernedness is of the essence of perception.

Gaze at a patch of red. In itself as an object, and apart from other factors of concern, this patch of red, as the mere object of that present act of perception, is silent as to the past or the future. How it originates, how it will vanish, whether indeed there was a past, and whether there will be a future, are not disclosed by its own nature. No material for the interpretation of sensa is provided by the sensa themselves, as they stand starkly, barely, present and immediate. We *do* interpret them; but no thanks for the feat is due to them. The epistemologies of the last two hundred years are employed in the tacit introduction of alien considerations by the uncritical use of current forms of speech. A copious use of simple literary forms can thus provide a philosophy delightful to read, easy to understand, and entirely fallacious. Yet the usages of language do prove that our habitual interpretations of these barren sensa are in the main satisfying to common sense, though in particular instances liable to error. But the evidence on which these interpretations are based is entirely drawn from the vast background and foreground of non-sensuous perception with which sense-perception is fused, and without which it can never be. We can discern no clean-cut sense-perception wholly concerned with present fact.

In human experience, the most compelling example of non-sensuous perception is our knowledge of our own immediate past. I am not referring to our memories of a day past, or of an hour past, or of a minute past. Such memories are blurred and confused by the intervening occasions of our personal existence. But our immediate past is constituted by that occasion, or by that group of fused occasions, which enters into experience devoid of any perceptible medium intervening between it and the present immediate fact. Roughly speaking, it is that portion of our past lying between a tenth of a second and half a second ago. It is gone, and yet it is here. It is our indubitable self, the foundation of our present existence. Yet the present occasion while claiming self-identity, while sharing the very nature of the byegone occasion in all its living activities, nevertheless is engaged in modifying it, in adjusting it to *other* influences, in completing it with *other* values, in deflecting it to *other* purposes. The present moment is constituted by the influx of *the other* into that self-identity which is the continued life of the immediate past within the immediacy of the present.

§13. *Illustration.*—Consider a reasonably rapid speaker enunciating the proper name 'United States'. There are four syllables here. When the third syllable is reached, probably the first is in the immediate past; and certainly during the word 'States' the first syllable of the phrase lies beyond the immediacy of the present. Consider the speaker's own occasions of existence. Each occasion achieves for him the immediate sense-presentation of sounds, the earlier syllables in the earlier occasions, the word 'States' in the final occasion. As mere sensuous perception, Hume is right in saying that the sound 'United' as a mere sensum has nothing in its nature referent to the sound 'States', yet the speaker is carried from 'United' to 'States', and the two conjointly live in the present, by the energizing of the past occasion as it claims its self-identical existence as a living issue in the present. The immediate past as surviving to be again lived through in the present is the palmary instance of non-sensuous perception.

The Humian explanation, involving the 'association of ideas', has its importance for this topic. But it is not to the point for this example. The speaker, a citizen of the United States and therefore dominated by an immense familiarity with that phrase, may in fact have been enunciating the phrase 'United Fruit Company'—a corporation which, for all its importance, he may not have heard of till half a minute earlier. In his experience the relation of the later to the earlier parts of this phrase is entirely the same as that described above for the phrase 'United States'. In this latter example it is to be noted that while association would have led him to 'States', the fact of the energizing of the immediate past compelled him to conjoin 'Fruit' in the immediacy of the present. He uttered the word 'United' with the non-sensuous anticipation of an immediate future with the sensum 'Fruit', and he then uttered the word 'Fruit' with the non-sensuous perception of the immediate past with the sensum 'United'. But, unfamiliar as he was with the United Fruit Company, he had no association connecting the various words in the phrase 'United Fruit Company'; while, patriot as he was, the orator had the strongest association connecting the words 'United' and 'States'. Perhaps, indeed, he was the founder of the Company, and also invented the name. He then uttered the mere sounds 'United Fruit Company' for the first time in the history of the English language. There could not have been the vestige of an association to help him along. The final occasion of his experience which drove his body to the utterance of the sound 'Company' is only explicable by his concern with the earlier occasions with their subjective forms of intention to procure the utterance of the complete phrase. Also, in so far as there was consciousness, there was direct observation of the past with its intention finding its completion in the present fact. This is an instance of direct intuitive observation which is incapable of reduction to the sensationalist formula. Such observations have not the clear sharp-cut precision of sense-perception. But surely there can be no doubt about them. For instance, if the speaker had been interrupted after the words 'United Fruit', he might have resumed his speech with the words 'I meant to add the word Company'. Thus during the interruption, the past was energizing in his experience as carrying in itself an unfulfilled intention.

§14. *Conformation of Feeling.*—Another point emerges in this explanation, namely, the doctrine of the continuity of nature. This doctrine balances and limits the doctrine of the absolute individuality of each occasion of experience. There is a continuity between the subjective form of the immediate past occasion and the subjective form of its primary prehension in the origination of the new occasion. In the process of synthesis of the many basic prehensions modifications enter. But the subjective forms of the immediate past are continuous with those of the present. I will term this doctrine of continuity, the Doctrine of Conformation of Feeling.

Suppose that for some period of time some circumstance of his life has aroused anger in a man. How does he now know that a quarter of a second ago he was angry? Of course, he remembers it; we all know that. But I am enquiring about this very curious fact of memory, and have chosen an overwhelmingly vivid instance. The mere word 'memory' explains nothing. The first phase in the immediacy of the new occasion is that of the conformation of feelings. The feeling as enjoyed by the past occasion is present in the new occasion as datum felt, with a subjective form conformal to that of the datum. Thus if A be the past occasion, D the datum felt by A with subjective form describable as A angry, then this feeling—namely, A feeling D with subjective form of anger—is initially felt by the new occasion B with the same subjective form of anger. The anger is continuous throughout the successive occasions of experience. This continuity of subjective form is the initial sympathy of B for A. It is the primary ground for the continuity of nature.

Let us elaborate the consideration of the angry man. His anger is the subjective form of his feeling some datum D. A quarter of a second later he is, consciously, or unconsciously, embodying his past as a datum in the present, and maintaining in the present the anger which is a datum from the past. In so far as that feeling has fallen within the illumination of consciousness, he enjoys a non-sensuous perception of the past emotion. He enjoys this emotion both objectively, as belonging to the past, and also formally as continued in the present. This continuation is the continuity of nature. I have labored this point, because traditional doctrines involve its denial.

Thus non-sensuous perception is one aspect of the continuity of nature.

§15. *Hume's Doctrine of Custom.*—Hume appeals to a doctrine of force and liveliness as an essential factor in an impression of sensation. This doctrine is nothing but a special case of the doctrine of subjective forms. Again he holds that the force and liveliness of one occasion of experience enter into the character of succeeding occasions. The whole doctrine of 'custom' depends on this assumption. If the occasions be entirely separate, as Hume contends, this transition of character is without any basis in the nature of things. What Hume, in his appeal to memory, is really doing is to appeal to an observed immanence of the past in the future, involving a continuity of subjective form.

With this addition, every argument of Part III of Hume's *Treatise* can be accepted. But the conclusion follows that there is an observed relation of causation between such occasions. The general character of this observed relation explains at once memory and personal identity. They are all different aspects of the doctrine of the immanence of occasions of experience. The additional conclusion can also be derived, that in so far as we apply notions of causation to the understanding of events in nature, we must conceive these events under the general notions which apply to occasions of experience. For we can only understand causation in terms of our observations of these occasions. This appeal to Hume has the sole purpose of illustrating the common-sense obviousness of the present thesis.

§16. *The Flux of Energy.*—An occasion of experience which includes a human mentality is an extreme instance, at one end of the scale, of those happenings which constitute nature. As yet this discussion has fixed attention upon this extreme. But any doctrine which refuses to place human experience outside nature, must find in descriptions of human experience factors which also enter into the descriptions of less specialized natural occurrences. If there be no such factors, then the doctrine of human experience as a fact within nature is mere bluff, founded upon vague phrases whose sole merit is a comforting familiarity. We should either admit dualism, at least as a provisional doctrine, or we should point out the identical elements connecting human experience with physical science.

The science of physics conceives a natural occasion as a

locus of energy. Whatever else that occasion may be, it is an individual fact harboring that energy. The words electron, proton, photon, wave-motion, velocity, hard and soft radiation, chemical elements, matter, empty space, temperature, degradation of energy, all point to the fact that physical science recognizes qualitative differences between occasions in respect to the way in which each occasion entertains its energy.

These differences are entirely constituted by the flux of energy, that is to say, by the way in which the occasions in question have inherited their energy from the past of nature, and in which they are about to transmit their energy to the future. The discussion of the Poynting Flux of Energy is one of the most fascinating chapters of Electrodynamics. Forty-seven years ago, when a young graduate student, I first heard of it in a lecture delivered by Sir J. J. Thomson. It was then a new discovery recently published by Poynting. But its father was the great Clerk-Maxwell who had expounded all the requisite principles. The sole conclusion with which we are concerned is that energy has recognizable paths through time and space. Energy passes from particular occasion to particular occasion. At each point there is a flux, with a quantitative flow and a definite direction.

This is a conception of physical nature in terms of continuity. In fact, the concept of continuity was dominant in Clerk-Maxwell's thought. But the alternative concept of distinguishable individualities has again emerged into importance in the more recent physics. Electrons and protons and photons are unit charges of electricity; also there are the quanta of the flux of energy. These contrasted aspects of nature, continuity and atomicity, have a long history in European thought, reaching back to the origin of science among the Greeks. The more probable conclusion is that

neither can be dispensed with, and that we are only wit-
nessing that modern phase of the contrast which is relevant
to the present stage of science.

§17. *Mind and Nature Compared.*—The doctrine of human experience which I have outlined above, also for its
own purposes preserves a doctrine of distinguishable individualities which are the separate occasions of experience,
and a doctrine of continuity expressed by the identity of subjective form inherited conformally from one occasion to the
other. The physical flux corresponds to the conformal inheritance at the base of each occasion of experience. This
inheritance, in spite of its continuity of subjective form, is
nevertheless an inheritance from definite individual occasions. Thus, if the analogy is to hold, in the account of the
general system of relations binding the past to the present,
we should expect a doctrine of quanta, where the individualities of the occasions are relevant, and a doctrine of continuity where the conformal transference of subjective form
is the dominating fact.

The notion of physical energy, which is at the base of
physics, must then be conceived as an abstraction from the
complex energy, emotional and purposeful, inherent in the
subjective form of the final synthesis in which each occasion
completes itself. It is the total vigor of each activity of experience. The mere phrase that 'physical science is an abstraction', is a confession of philosophic failure. It is the
business of rational thought to describe the more concrete
fact from which that abstraction is derivable.

§18. *Personality.*—In our account of human experience
we have attenuated human personality into a genetic relation between occasions of human experience. Yet personal
unity is an inescapable fact. The Platonic and Christian doctrines of the Soul, the Epicurean doctrine of a Concilium of

subtle atoms, the Cartesian doctrine of Thinking Substance, the Humanitarian doctrine of the Rights of man, the general Common Sense of civilized mankind,—these doctrines between them dominate the whole span of Western thought. Evidently there is a fact to be accounted for. Any philosophy must provide some doctrine of personal identity. In some sense there is a unity in the life of each man, from birth to death. The two modern philosophers who most consistently reject the notion of a self-identical Soul-Substance are Hume and William James. But the problem remains for them, as it does for the philosophy of organism, to provide an adequate account of this undoubted personal unity, maintaining itself amidst the welter of circumstance.

§19. *Plato's Receptacle.*—In mathematical studies, where there is a problem to be solved it is a sound method to generalize, so as to divest the problem of details irrelevant to the solution. Let us therefore give a general description of this personal unity, divesting it of minor details of humanity. For this purpose it is impossible to improve upon a passage from one of Plato's Dialogues. I summarize it with the insertion of such terms as 'personal unity', 'events', 'experience', and 'personal identity', for two or three of its own phrases:—"In addition to the notions of the welter of events and of the forms which they illustrate, we require a third term, personal unity. It is a perplexed and obscure concept. We must conceive it the receptacle, the foster-mother as I might say, of the becoming of our occasions of experience. This personal identity is the thing which receives all occasions of the man's existence. It is there as a natural matrix for all transitions of life, and is changed and variously figured by the things that enter it; so that it differs in its character at different times. Since it receives all manner of experiences into its own unity, it must itself be bare of all forms. We shall not be far wrong if we describe it as invisible, formless, and all-receptive. It is a locus which persists, and provides an emplacement for all the occasions of experience. That which happens in it is conditioned by the compulsion of its own past, and by the persuasion of its immanent ideals."

You will have recognized that in this description I have been adapting from Plato's *Timæus,*[1] with the slightest of changes. But this is not Plato's description of the Soul. It is his doctrine of the Receptacle [ὑποδοχή] or Locus [χώρα] whose sole function is the imposition of a unity upon the events of Nature. These events are together by reason of their community of locus, and they obtain their actuality by reason of emplacement within this community.

§20. *Immanence.*—This is at once the doctrine of the unity of nature, and of the unity of each human life. The conclusion follows that our consciousness of the self-identity pervading our life-thread of occasions, is nothing other than knowledge of a special strand of unity within the general unity of nature. It is a locus within the whole, marked out by its own peculiarities, but otherwise exhibiting the general principle which guides the constitution of the whole. This general principle is the object-to-subject structure of experience. It can be otherwise stated as the vector-structure of nature. Or otherwise, it can be conceived as the doctrine of the immanence of the past energizing in the present.

This doctrine of immanence is practically that doctrine adumbrated by the Hellenistic Christian theologians of Egypt. But they applied the doctrine only to the relation of God to the World, and not to all actualities.

§21. *Space and Time.*—The notion of Space-Time repre-

[1] I have used A. E. Taylor's translation, with compression and changes of phrase.

sents a compromise between Plato's basic Receptacle, imposing no forms, and the Actual World imposing its own variety of forms. This imposition of forms is subject to the perspective elimination required by incompatibilities of affective tone. Geometry is the doctrine of loci of intermediaries imposing perspective in the process of inheritance. In geometry this doctrine is restricted to its barest generalities of coördination prevailing for this epoch of the Universe. These generalities solely concern the complex of serial relations persistently illustrated in the connection of events.

Our perception of this geometrical order of the Universe brings with it the denial of the restriction of inheritance to mere personal order. For personal order means one-dimensional serial order. And space is many-dimensional. Spatiality involves separation by reason of the diversity of intermediate occasions, and also it involves connection by reason of the immanence involved in the derivation of present from past. There is thus an analogy between the transference of energy from particular occasion to particular occasion in physical nature and the transference of affective tone, with its emotional energy, from one occasion to another in any human personality. The object-to-subject structure of human experience is reproduced in physical nature by this vector relation of particular to particular. It was the defect of the Greek analysis of generation that it conceived it in terms of the bare incoming of novel abstract form. This ancient analysis failed to grasp the real operation of the antecedent particulars imposing themselves on the novel particular in process of creation. Thus the geometry exemplified in fact was disjoined from their account of the generation of fact.

§22. *The Human Body.*—But this analogy of physical

nature to human experience is limited by the fact of the linear seriality of human occasions within any one personality and of the many-dimensional seriality of the occasions in physical Space-Time.

In order to prove that this discrepancy is only superficial, it now remains for discussion whether the human experience of direct inheritance provides any analogy to this many-dimensional character of space. If human occasions of experience essentially inherit in one-dimensional personal order, there is a gap between human occasions and the physical occasions of nature.

The peculiar status of the human body at once presents itself as negating this notion of strict personal order for human inheritance. Our dominant inheritance from our immediately past occasion is broken into by innumerable inheritances through other avenues. Sensitive nerves, the functionings of our viscera, disturbances in the composition of our blood, break in upon the dominant line of inheritance. In this way, emotions, hopes, fears, inhibitions, sense-perceptions arise, which physiologists confidently ascribe to the bodily functionings. So intimately obvious is this bodily inheritance that common speech does not discriminate the human body from the human person. Soul and body are fused together. Also this common identification has survived the scientific investigation of physiologists, who are apt to see more body than soul in human beings.

But the human body is indubitably a complex of occasions which are part of spatial nature. It is a set of occasions miraculously coördinated so as to pour its inheritance into various regions within the brain. There is thus every reason to believe that our sense of unity with the body has the same original as our sense of unity with our immediate past of personal experience. It is another case of non-sensuous perception, only now devoid of the strict personal order.

But physiologists and physicists are equally agreed that the body inherits physical conditions from the physical environment according to the physical laws. There is thus a general continuity between human experience and physical occasions. The elaboration of such a continuity is one most obvious task for philosophy.

§23. *Dualism.*—This discussion has begged attention to a complex argument. I will conclude it by drawing attention to a general question which is relevant.

Is this discussion to be looked upon as another example of *The Revolt against Dualism?* We have all read with high appreciation Professor Lovejoy's brilliant book in criticism of this revolt. Now superficially the position which I have here put forward is certainly an instance of the revolt which he criticizes. But in another sense, I have endeavored to put forward a defence of dualism, differently interpreted. Plato, Descartes, Locke, prepared the way for Hume; and Kant followed upon Hume. The point of this discussion is to show an alternative line of thought which evades Hume's deduction from philosophical tradition, and at the same time preserves the general trend of thought received from his three great predecessors. The dualism in the later Platonic dialogues between the Platonic 'souls' and the Platonic 'physical' nature, the dualism between the Cartesian 'thinking substances' and the Cartesian 'extended substances', the dualism between the Lockian 'human understanding' and the Lockian 'external things' described for him by Galileo and Newton—all these kindred dualisms are here found within each occasion of actuality. Each occasion has its physical inheritance and its mental reaction which drives it on to its self-completion. The world is not merely physical, nor is it merely mental. Nor is it merely *one* with many subordinate phases. Nor is it merely a complete fact, in its essence static with the illusion of change. Wherever a vicious dualism appears, it is by reason of mistaking an abstraction for a final concrete fact.

The universe is dual because, in the fullest sense, it is both transient and eternal. The universe is dual because each final actuality is both physical and mental. The universe is dual because each actuality requires abstract character. The universe is dual because each occasion unites its formal immediacy with objective otherness. The universe is *many* because it is wholly and completely to be analysed into many final actualities—or in Cartesian language, into many *res verae*. The Universe is *one*, because of the universal immanence. There is thus a dualism in this contrast between the unity and multiplicity. Throughout the universe there reigns the union of opposites which is the ground of dualism.

CHAPTER XII

PAST, PRESENT, FUTURE

SECTION I. The doctrine of the immanence of past occa-sions in the occasions which are future, relatively to them, has been sufficiently discussed in the previous chapter. The past has an objective existence in the present which lies in the future beyond itself. But the sense in which the future can be said to be immanent in occasions antecedent to itself, and the sense in which contemporary occasions are imma-nent in each other, are not so evident in terms of the doc-trine of the subject-object structure of experience. It will be simpler first to concentrate upon the relation of the future to the present. It is evident that the future certainly is something for the present. The most familiar habits of mankind witness to this fact. Legal contracts, social under-standings of every type, ambitions, anxieties, railway time-tables, are futile gestures of consciousness apart from the fact that the present bears in its own realized constitution relationships to a future beyond itself. Cut away the future, and the present collapses, emptied of its proper content. Immediate existence requires the insertion of the future in the crannies of the present.

Here again the habits of a literary training with its long-range forecast and back-cast of critical thought exercise an unfortunate effect upon philosophy. We think of the future in time-spans of centuries, or of decades, or of years, or of days. We dwell critically upon the mass of fables termed history. As a result we conceive ourselves as related to past or to future by a mere effort of purely abstract imagination, devoid of direct observation of particular fact. If we admit this conclusion, there is no real evidence that there was a past, or that there will be a future. Our ignorance on this point is complete. All that we can observe consists of conceptual persuasions in the present. Such is the outcome of the literary habit of dwelling upon the long future or upon the long past. Literature preserves the wisdom of the human race; but in this way it enfeebles the emphasis of first-hand intuition. In considering our direct observation of past, or of future, we should confine ourselves to time-spans of the order of magnitude of a second, or even of fractions of a second.

Section II. If we keep ourselves to this short-range intuition, assuredly the future is not nothing. It lives actively in its antecedent world. Each moment of experience confesses itself to be a transition between two worlds, the immediate past and the immediate future. This is the persistent delivery of common-sense. Also this immediate future is immanent in the present with some degree of structural definition. The difficulty lies in the explanation of this immanence in terms of the subject-object structure of experience. In the present, the future occasions, as individual realities with their measure of absolute completeness, are non-existent. Thus the future must be immanent in the present in some different sense to the objective immortality of the individual occasions of the past. In the present there are no individual occasions belonging to the future. The present contains the utmost verge of such realized individuality. The whole doctrine of the future is to be understood in terms of the account of the process of self-completion of each individual actual occasion.

This process can be shortly characterized as a passage from re-enaction to anticipation. The intermediate stage in this transition is constituted by the acquisition of novel content, which is the individual contribution of the immediate subject for the re-shaping of its primary phase of re-enaction into its final phase of anticipation. This final phase is otherwise termed the 'satisfaction,' since it marks the exhaustion of the creative urge for that individuality. This novel content is composed of positive conceptual prehensions, that is to say, of conceptual feelings. These conceptual feelings become integrated with the physical prehensions of antecedent occasions, and thus yield propositions concerning the past. These propositions are again integrated and re-integrated with each other and with conceptual feelings, and yield other propositions.

Finally propositions emerge concerning the constitution of the immediate subject. It belongs to the essence of this subject that it pass into objective immortality. Thus its own constitution involves that its own activity in *self*-formation passes into its activity of *other*-formation. It is by reason of the constitution of the present subject that the future will embody the present subject and will re-enact its patterns of activity. But the future individual occasions are non-existent. The sole immediate actuality is the constitution of the present subject which embodies its own necessity for objective immortality beyond its own immediacy of self-formation. This objective immortality is a stubborn fact for the future, involving its pattern of perspective re-enaction.

The final phase of anticipation is a propositional realization of the essence of the present-subject, in respect to the necessities which it lays upon the future to embody it and to re-enact it so far as compatibility may permit. Thus the self-enjoyment of an occasion of experience is initiated by an enjoyment of the past as alive in itself and is terminated by an enjoyment of itself as alive in the future. This is the account of the creative urge of the universe as it functions in each single individual occasion. In this sense, the future is immanent in each present occasion, with its particular relations to the present settled in various degrees of dominance. But no future individual occasion is in existence. The anticipatory propositions all concern the constitution of the present occasion and the necessities inherent in it. This constitution necessitates that there be a future, and necessitates a quota of contribution for re-enaction in the primary phases of future occasions.

The point to remember is that the fact that each individual occasion is transcended by the creative urge, belongs to the essential constitution of each such occasion. It is not an accident which is irrelevant to the completed constitution of any such occasion.

In the formation of each occasion of actuality the swing over from re-enaction to anticipation is due to the intervening touch of mentality. Whether the ideas thus introduced by the novel conceptual prehensions be old or new, they have this decisive result, that the occasion arises as an effect facing its past and ends as a cause facing its future. In between there lies the teleology of the Universe.

If the mental activity involves no introduction of ideal novelty, the data of the conceptual feelings are merely eternal objects already illustrated in the initial phase of re-enaction. In that case, the reintegration with the primary phase merely converts the initial conformal reception into the anticipation of preservation of types of order and of patterns of feeling already dominant in the inheritance. There is a reign of acquiescence. In this way, a region of such occasions assumes the aspect of passive submission to imposed laws of nature. But when there is conceptual novelty made effective by its re-iteration and by the added emphasis on it throughout a chain of coördinated occasions, we have the aspect of an enduring person with a sustained purpose originated by that person and made effective in that person's environment. Thus in this case the anticipation of kinship with the future assumes the form of purpose to transform concept into fact. In either case, whether or no there be conceptual novelty, the subjective forms of the conceptual prehensions constitute the drive of the Universe, whereby each occasion precipitates itself into the future.

SECTION III. It is now possible to determine the sense in which the future is immanent in the present. The future is immanent in the present by reason of the fact that the present bears in its own essence the relationships which it will have to the future. It thereby includes in its essence the necessities to which the future must conform. The future is there in the present, as a general fact belonging to the nature of things. It is also there with such general determinations as it lies in the nature of the particular present to impose on the particular future which must succeed it. All this belongs to the essence of the present, and constitutes the future, as thus determined, an object for prehension in the subjective immediacy of the present. In this way each present occasion prehends the general metaphysical character of the universe, and thereby it prehends its own share in that character. Thus the future is to the present as an object for a subject. It has an objective existence in the present. But the objective existence of the future in the present differs from the objective existence of the past in the present. The various particular occasions of the past are in existence, and are severally functioning as objects for prehension in the present. This individual objective existence of the actual occasions of the past, each functioning in each present occasion, constitutes the causal relationship which is efficient causation. But there are no actual occasions in the future, already constituted. Thus there are no actual occasions in the future to exercise efficient causation in the present. What is objective in the present is the necessity of a future of actual occasions, and the necessity that these future occasions conform to the conditions inherent in the essence of the present occasion. The future belongs to the essence of present fact, and has no actuality other than the actuality of present fact. But its particular relationships to present fact are already realized in the nature of present fact.

SECTION IV. It is the definition of contemporary events that they happen in causal independence of each other. Thus two contemporary occasions are such that neither belongs to the past of the other. The two occasions are not in any direct relation of efficient causation. The vast causal independence of contemporary occasions is the preservative of the elbow-room within the Universe. It provides each actuality with a welcome environment for irresponsibility. 'Am I my brother's keeper?' expresses one of the earliest gestures of self-consciousness. Our claim for freedom is rooted in our relationship to our contemporary environment. Nature does provide a field for independent activities. The understanding of the Universe requires that we conceive in their proper relations to each other the various rôles, of efficient causation, of teleological self-creation, and of contemporary independence. This adequate conception requires also understanding of perspective elimination, and of types of order dominating vast epochs, and of minor endurances with their own additional modes of order diversifying each larger epoch within which they find themselves.

The mutual independence of contemporary occasions lies strictly within the sphere of their teleological self-creation. The occasions originate from a common past and their objective immortality operates within a common future. Thus indirectly, *via* the immanence of the past and the immanence of the future, the occasions are connected. But the immediate activity of self-creation is separate and private, so far as contemporaries are concerned.

There is thus a certain indirect immanence of contemporary occasions in each other. For if A and B be contemporaries, and C be in the past of both of them, then A and B are each in a sense immanent in C, in the way in which the future can be immanent in its past. But C is objectively immortal in both A and B. Thus, in this indirect sense, A is immanent in B, and B is immanent in A. But the objective immortality of A does not operate in B, nor does that of B operate in A. As individual complete actualities, A is shrouded from B, and B is shrouded from A. It is not wholly true that two contemporaries A and B enjoy a common past. In the first place, even if the occasions in the past of A be identical with the occasions in the past of B, yet A and B by reason of their difference of status, enjoy that past under a difference of perspective elimination. Thus the objective immortality of the past in A differs from the objective immortality of that same past in B. Thus two contemporary occasions, greatly remote from each other, are in effect derived from different pasts.

Again, according to the notions of time recently developed in modern physics, if A and B are contemporaries and P is contemporary with A, then it is not necessarily true that P is contemporary with B. It is possible that P may be earlier than B, or that it may be later than B. Thus even the occasions in the past of A are not wholly identical with those in the past of B. When A and B are neighbouring, then this distinction between their pasts may be negligible. But when they are remote from each other, the distinction may be of major importance.

It follows from this discussion that in so far as the relevant environment is dominated by any uniform type of coördination, any occasion will experience its past as 'anticipating' the prolongation of that type of order into the future beyond that past. But this future includes the occasion in question and its contemporary environment. In this way there is an indirect immanence of its contemporary world in that occasion; not in respect to its particular individual occasions, but as the general substratum for that relation of order. This type of order will both relate the various parts of the contemporary world among themselves, and will also relate these parts to the occasion in question. But the parts of the contemporary world will only belong to the experience of the occasion in their function of relata for this type of order. This is the general explanation why the contemporary world should be perceived as the field of the uniform spatial relations. It gives no reason why any special system of relationships should dominate this epoch. But the explanation does give a reason why some system of uniform relations should dominate our perceptions of the contemporary world. Also the intrinsic activity has been lost. The contemporary world enters into experience as the passive subject of relations and qualities.

SECTION V. The actualities of the Universe are processes of experience, each process an individual fact. The whole Universe is the advancing assemblage of these processes. The Aristotelian doctrine, that all agency is confined to actuality, is accepted. So also is the Platonic dictum that the very meaning of existence is 'to be a factor in agency', or in other words 'to make a difference'. Thus, 'to be something' is to be discoverable as a factor in the analysis of some actuality. It follows that in one sense everything is 'real', according to its own category of being. In this sense the word 'real' can only mean that some sound or mark is a word with a denotation. But the term 'realization' refers to the actual entities which include the entity in question as a positive factor in their constitutions. Thus though everything is real, it is not necessarily realized in some particular set of actual occasions. But it is necessary that it be discoverable somewhere, realized in some actual entity. There is not anything which has failed in some sense to be realized, physically or conceptually. The term 'real' can also mark the differences arising in the contrast between physical and conceptual realization.

SECTION VI. Any set of actual occasions are united by the mutual immanence of occasions, each in the other. To the extent that they are united they mutually constrain each other. Evidently this mutual immanence and constraint of a pair of occasions is not in general a symmetric relation. For, apart from contemporaries, one occasion will be in the future of the other. Thus the earlier will be immanent in the later according to the mode of efficient causality, and the later in the earlier according to the mode of anticipation, as explained above. Any set of occasions, conceived as thus combined into a unity, will be termed a nexus. The unity of such a nexus may be of a trivial description, if the various occasions are dispersed through the Universe, each with a widely different status from the other. When the unity of the nexus is of dominating importance, nexus of different types emerge, which may be respectively termed Regions,

Societies, Persons, Enduring Objects, Corporal Substances, Living Organisms, Events, with other analogous terms for the various shades of complexity of which Nature is capable. It will be sufficient in the next chapter to indicate a few of these special types of nexūs.

SECTION VII. We think of Constraint and Freedom in terms of the values realized in connection with them, and also in terms of the antithesis between them. But there is another way of considering them. We can ask what there is in the physical nature of things constituting the physical realization either of freedom, or of constraint, or of a compatible association of both in a suitable pattern.

In fact we do habitually interpret human history in terms of freedom and constraint. Apart from the realization of this antithesis in physical occurrences, the history of civilized humanity is a meaningless succession of events, involving a play of emotions concerned with concepts entirely irrelevant to the physical facts.

The causal independence of contemporary occasions is the ground for the freedom within the Universe. The novelties which face the contemporary world are solved in isolation by the contemporary occasions. There is complete contemporary freedom. It is not true that whatever happens is immediately a condition laid upon everything else. Such a conception of complete mutual determination is an exaggeration of the community of the Universe. The notions of 'sporadic occurrences' and of 'mutual irrelevance' have a real application to the nature of things. Again the perspective imposed by incompatibilities of subjective form in another way provides for freedom. The antecedent environment is not wholly efficacious in determining the initial phase of the occasion which springs from it. There are factors in the environment which are eliminated from any function as explicit facts in the new creation. The running stream purifies itself, or perhaps loses some virtue which in happier circumstances might have been retained. The initial phase of each fresh occasion represents the issue of a struggle within the past for objective existence beyond itself. The determinant of the struggle is the supreme Eros incarnating itself as the first phase of the individual subjective aim in the new process of actuality. Thus in any two occasions of the Universe there are elements in either one which are irrelevant to the constitution of the other. The forgetfulness of this doctrine leads to an over-moralization in the view of the nature of things. Fortunately there are a great many things which do not much matter, and we can have them how we will. The opposite point of view has been the nursery of fanaticism, and has tinged history with ferocity.

SECTION VIII. The understanding of the Universe, in terms of the type of metaphysic here put forward, requires that the various rôles of efficient causation, of teleological self-creation, of perspective elimination, of contemporary independence, of the laws of order dominating vast epochs, and of the minor endurances within each epoch, be conceived in their various relations to each other. Another summary expression of this type of understanding is contained in the phrases, Constraint and Freedom, Survival and Destruction, Depth of Feeling and Triviality of Feeling, Conceptual realization and physical realization, Appearance and Reality. Any account of the Adventure of Ideas is concerned with Ideas threading their way among the alternatives presented by these various phrases.

When we examine the structure of the epoch of the Universe in which we find ourselves, this structure exhibits successive layers of types of order, each layer introducing some additional type of order within some limited region which shares in the more general type of order of some larger environment. Also this larger environment in its turn is a specialized region within the general epoch of creation as we know it. Each one of these regions, with its dominant set of ordering relations, can either be considered from the point of view of the mutual relations of its parts to each other, or it can be considered from the point of view of its impact, as a unity, upon the experience of an external percipient. There is yet a third mode of consideration which combines the other two. The percipient may be an occasion within the region, and may yet grasp the region as one, including the percipient itself as a member of it.

A region, analysed in the first way, is thereby conceived as subject to certain Laws of Nature, which laws are its dominant set of ordering relations. In the second mode of consideration, synthesis replaces analysis. The region in question assumes the guise of an enduring unity, of which the essence is a certain complex internal character. This essential character, as it appears in the second approach, is nothing other than the set of Laws of Nature reigning within the region, as they appear in the first approach. Either mode of approach simply lays stress upon the dominant identity of character pervading the concrete connexity of the many occasions constituting the region. The unity of the region is two-fold:—first, by reason of the sheer connexity arising from the mutual immanence of the various occasions included in it, and secondly, by reason of a pervasive identity of character whereby the various parts play an analogous rôle in any external occasion. Thus the region with its Laws of Nature is a synonym for the enduring substance with its Essential Character.

CHAPTER XIII

THE GROUPING OF OCCASIONS

SECTION I. The Grouping of Occasions is the outcome of some common function performed by those occasions in the percipient experience. The grouped occasions then acquire a unity; they become, for the experience of the percipient, one thing which is complex by reason of its divisibility into many occasions, or into many subordinate groups of occasions. The subordinate groups are then complex unities, each belonging to the same metaphysical category of existence as the total group. This characteristic, namely divisibility into groups of analogous type of being, is the general notion of extensiveness. The peculiar relationships (if any) diffused systematically between the extensive groups of an epoch constitute the system of geometry prevalent in that epoch.

The general common function exhibited by any group of actual occasions is that of mutual immanence. In Platonic language, this is the function of belonging to a common Receptacle. If the group be considered merely in respect to this basic property of mutual immanence, however otherwise lacking in common relevance, then—conceived as exemplifying this general connectedness—the group is termed a Nexus.

Thus the term Nexus does not presuppose any special type of order, nor does it presuppose any order at all pervading its members other than the general metaphysical obligation of mutual immanence. But in fact the teleology of the Universe, with its aim at intensity and variety, produces epochs with various types of order dominating subordinate nexūs interwoven with each other. A nexus can spread itself both spatially and temporally. In other words, it can include sets of occasions which are contemporary with each other, and it can include sets which are relatively past and future. If the nexus be purely spatial, then it will include no pair of occasions such that one of the pair is antecedent to the other. The mutual immanence between the occasions of the nexus will then be of the indirect type proper to contemporary occasions. It is for this reason that the notion of externality dominates our intuition of space. If the nexus be purely temporal, then it will include no pair of contemporary occasions. It is to be a mere thread of temporal transition from occasion to occasion. The idea of temporal transition can never be wholly disengaged from that of 'causation'. This latter notion is merely a special way of considering direct immanence of the past in its future.

SECTION II. The notion of the contiguity of occasions is important. Two occasions, which are not contemporary, are contiguous in time when there is no occasion which is antecedent to one of them and subsequent to the other. A purely temporal nexus of occasions is continuous when, with the exception of the earliest and the latest occasions, each occasion is contiguous with an earlier occasion and a later occasion. The nexus will then form an unbroken thread in temporal or serial order. The first and the last occasions of the thread will, of course, only enjoy a one-sided contiguity with the thread.

Spatial contiguity is more difficult to define. It requires a reference to the temporal dimension. It can be defined by the aid of the doctrine that no two contemporary occasions are derived from a past wholly in common. Thus if A and B be two contemporary occasions, the past of A includes some occasions not belonging to the past of B, and that of B includes occasions not belonging to the past of A. Then A and B are contiguous when there is no occasion (i) contemporary with both A and B, and (ii) such that its past includes all occasions, each belonging both to the past of A and the past of B. The particular form of this definition is of no great importance. But the principle that the inter-relations of the present are derived from a reference to the past is fundamental. It gives the reason why the contemporary world is experienced as a display of lifeless substances passively illustrating imposed characters.

Anyhow contiguity, temporal and spatial, is definable in terms of the doctrine of immanence. By the aid of the notion of contiguity, the notion of a region can be defined as denoting a nexus in which certain conditions of contiguity are preserved. The logical details of such a definition are irrelevant to this discussion.

So far we have been considering various species of nexus, whose sole principle of unity is derived from the bare fact of mutual immanence. We will term this genus of nexus, the genus whose species are discriminated by differences of bare extensive pattern. More briefly, it will be termed the *Genus* of *Patterned Nexūs*. Every nexus belongs to some species of this genus, if we abstract from the qualitative factors which are interwoven in its patterns.

SECTION III. We now pass on to the general notion of a *Society*. This notion introduces the general consideration of types of order, and the genetic propagation of order. The definition depends upon taking into account factors which are omitted in the analysis of the Genus of Patterned Nexūs.

A Society is a nexus which 'illustrates' or 'shares in', some type of 'Social Order'. 'Social Order' can be defined [1] as follows:—'A nexus enjoys "social order" when (i) there is a common element of form illustrated in the definiteness of each of its included actual entities, and (ii) this common element of form arises in each member of the nexus by reason of the conditions imposed upon it by its prehensions of some other members of the nexus, and (iii) these prehensions impose that condition of reproduction by reason of their inclusion of positive feelings involving [2] that common form. Such a nexus is called a "society", and the common form is the "defining characteristic" of that society'.

Another rendering [3] of the same definition is as follows: —'The point of a "society" as the term is here used, is that it is self-sustaining; in other words, that it is its own reason. Thus a society is more than a set of [actual] entities to which the same class-name applies: that is to say, it involves more than a merely mathematical conception of 'order'. To constitute a society, the class-name has got to apply to each member, by reason of genetic derivation from other members of that same society. The members of the society are alike because, by reason of their common character, they impose on other members of the society the conditions which lead to that likeness.'

It is evident from this description of the notion of a 'Society', as here employed, that a set of mutually contemporary occasions cannot form a complete society. For the genetic condition cannot be satisfied by such a set of contemporaries. Of course a set of contemporaries may belong to a society. But the society, as such, must involve antecedents and subsequents. In other words, a society must exhibit the

---

[1] Cf. *Process and Reality*, Part I, Ch. III, Sect. II.

[2] In the original, *Process and Reality*, 'of that' in place of 'involving'.

[3] Cf. *Process and Reality*, Part II, Ch. III, Sect. II.

peculiar quality of endurance. The real actual things that endure are all societies. They are not actual occasions. It is the mistake that has thwarted European metaphysics from the time of the Greeks, namely, to confuse societies with the completely real things which are the actual occasions. A society has an essential character, whereby it is the society that it is, and it has also accidental qualities which vary as circumstances alter. Thus a society, as a complete existence and as retaining the same metaphysical status, enjoys a history expressing its changing reactions to changing circumstances.⁴ But an actual occasion has no such history. It never changes. It only becomes and perishes. Its perishing is its assumption of a new metaphysical function in the creative advance of the universe.

The self-identity of a society is founded upon the self-identity of its defining characteristic, and upon the mutual immanence of its occasions. But there is no definite nexus which is the nexus underlying that society, except when the society belongs wholly to the past. For the realized nexus which underlies the society is always adding to itself, with the creative advance into the future. For example, the man adds another day to his life, and the earth adds another millennium to the period of its existence. But until the death of the man and the destruction of the earth, there is no determinate nexus which in an unqualified sense is either the man or the earth.

Section IV. Though there is no one nexus which can claim to be the society, so long as that society is in existence, there is a succession of nexūs each of which is the whole realized society up to that stage of its existence. The extensive patterns of various members of such a succession for a

⁴ This notion of 'society' has analogies to Descartes' notion of 'substance', cf. Descartes' *Principles of Philosophy*, Part I, Principles LI-LVII.

given society may be different. In such a case the extensive patterns, so far as they differ, cannot be any element in the defining characteristic of the society. But the extensive patterns of the various nexūs of the succession may be identical, or at least they may have in common some feature of their pattern. In this case the common pattern, or the common feature, can be one element in the defining characteristic of the society in question.

The simplest example of a society in which the successive nexus of its progressive realization have a common extensive pattern is when each such nexus is purely temporal and continuous. The society, in each stage of realization, then consists of a set of contiguous occasions in serial order. A man, defined as an enduring percipient, is such a society. This definition of a man is exactly what Descartes means by a thinking substance. It will be remembered that in his *Principles of Philosophy* [Part I, Principle XXI; also *Meditation* III] Descartes states that endurance is nothing else than successive re-creation by God. Thus the Cartesian conception of the human soul and that here put forward differ only in the function assigned to God. Both conceptions involve a succession of occasions, each with its measure of immediate completeness.

Societies of the general type, that their realized nexūs are purely temporal and continuous, will be termed 'personal'. Any society of this type may be termed a 'person'. Thus, as defined above, a man is a person.

But a man is more than a serial succession of occasions of experience. Such a definition may satisfy philosophers—Descartes, for example. It is not the ordinary meaning of the term 'man'. There are animal bodies as well as animal minds; and in our experience such minds always occur incorporated. Now an animal body is a society involving a vast number of occasions, spatially and temporally co-ordinated. It follows that a 'man', in the full sense of ordinary usage, is not a 'person' as here defined. He has the unity of a wider society, in which the social coördination is a dominant factor in the behaviours of the various parts.

Also, when we survey the living world, animal and vegetable, there are bodies of all types. Each living body is a society, which is not personal. But most of the animals, including all the vertebrates, seem to have their social system dominated by a subordinate society which is 'personal'. This subordinate society is of the same type as 'man', according to the personal definition given above, though of course the mental poles in the occasions of the dominant personal society do not rise to the height of human mentality. Thus in one sense a dog is a 'person', and in another sense he is a non-personal society. But the lower forms of animal life, and all vegetation, seem to lack the dominance of any included personal society. A tree is a democracy. Thus living bodies are not to be identified with living bodies under personal dominance. There is no necessary connection between 'life' and 'personality'. A 'personal' society need not be 'living', in the general sense of the term; and a 'living' society need not be 'personal'.

SECTION V. The Universe achieves its values by reason of its coördination into societies of societies, and into societies of societies of societies. Thus an army is a society of regiments, and regiments are societies of men, and men are societies of cells, and of blood, and of bones, together with the dominant society of personal human experience, and cells are societies of smaller physical entities such as protons, and so on, and so on. Also all of these societies presuppose the circumambient space of social physical activity.

It is evident that the previous definition of 'society' has

been phrased so as to suggest an over-simplified concept of the meaning. For the notion of a defining characteristic must be construed to include the notion of the coördination of societies. Thus there are societies at different levels. For instance, the army is a society at a level different from that of a regiment, and similarly for a regiment and a man. Nature is a complex of enduring objects, functioning as subordinate elements in a larger spatial-physical society. This larger society is for us the natural universe. There is however no reason to identify it with the boundless totality of actual things.

Also each of these enduring objects, such as tables, animal bodies, and stars, is itself a subordinate universe including subordinate enduring objects. The only strictly personal society of which we have direct discriminative intuition is the society of our own personal experiences. We also have a direct, though vaguer, intuition of our derivation of experience from the antecedent functioning of our bodies, and a still vaguer intuition of our bodily derivation from external nature.

Nature suggests for our observation gaps, and then as it were withdraws them upon challenge. For example, ordinary physical bodies suggest solidity. But solids turn to liquids, and liquids to gases. And from the gas the solid can again be recovered. Also the most solid of solids is for certain purposes a viscous fluid. Again impenetrability is a difficult notion. Salt dissolves in water, and can be recovered from it. Gases interfuse in liquids. Molecules arise from a patterned interfusion of atoms. Food interfuses with the body, and produces an immediate sense of diffused bodily vigour. This is especially the case with liquid stimulants. Thus the direct immediate experience of impenetrability loses upon challenge its sharp-cut status.

Section VI. Another gap is that between lifeless bodies and living bodies. Yet the living bodies can be pursued down to the edge of lifelessness. Also the functionings of inorganic matter remain intact amid the functionings of living matter. It seems that, in bodies that are obviously living, a coördination has been achieved that raises into prominence some functionings inherent in the ultimate occasions. For lifeless matter these functionings thwart each other, and average out so as to produce a negligible total effect. In the case of living bodies the coördination intervenes, and the average effect of these intimate functionings has to be taken into account.

Those activities in the self-formation of actual occasions which, if coördinated, yield living societies are the intermediate mental functionings transforming the initial phase of reception into the final phase of anticipation. In so far as the mental spontaneities of occasions do not thwart each other, but are directed to a common objective amid varying circumstances, there is life. The essence of life is the teleological introduction of novelty, with some conformation of objectives. Thus novelty of circumstance is met with novelty of functioning adapted to steadiness of purpose.

Life may characterize a set of occasions diffused throughout a society, though not necessarily including all, or even a majority of, the occasions of that society. The common element of purpose which characterizes these various occasions must be reckoned as one element of the determining characteristic of the society. It is evident that according to this definition no single occasion can be called living. Life is the coördination of the mental spontaneities throughout the occasions of a society.

But apart from life a high grade of mentality in individual occasions seems to be impossible. A personal society, itself living and dominantly influencing a living society wider than itself, is the only type of organization which provides occasions of high-grade mentality. Thus in a man, the living body is permeated by living societies of low-grade occasions so far as mentality is concerned. But the whole is coördinated so as to support a personal living society of high-grade occasions. This personal society is the man defined as a person. It is the soul of which Plato spoke.

How far this soul finds a support for its existence beyond the body is:—another question. The everlasting nature of God, which in a sense is non-temporal and in another sense is temporal, may establish with the soul a peculiarly intense relationship of mutual immanence. Thus in some important sense the existence of the soul may be freed from its complete dependence upon the bodily organization.

But it is to be noticed that the personality of an animal organism may be more or less. It is not a mere question of having a soul or of not having a soul. The question is, How much, if any? Any tendency to a high-grade multiple personality would be self-destructive by the antagonism of divergent aims. In other words, such multiple personality is destructive of the very essence of life, which is conformation of purpose.

CHAPTER XIV

APPEARANCE AND REALITY

SECTION I. The objective content of an occasion of experience sorts itself out under two contrasted characters—Appearance and Reality. It is to be noticed that this is not the only dichotomy exhibited in experience. There are the physical and the mental poles, and there are the objects prehended and the subjective forms of the prehensions. In fact this final pair of opposites, Appearance and Reality, is not quite so fundamental metaphysically as the other two pairs.

In the first place the division between appearance and reality does not cover the whole of experience. It only concerns the objective content, and omits the subjective form of the immediate occasion in question. In the second place, its importance is negligible except in the functionings of the higher phases of experience, when the mental functionings have achieved a peculiar complexity of synthesis with the physical functionings. But in these higher phases, the contrast Appearance and Reality dominates those factors of experience which are discriminated in consciousness with peculiar distinctness. Thus the foundation of metaphysics should be sought in the understanding of the subject-object structure of experience, and in the respective rôles of the physical and mental functionings.

Unfortunately the superior dominance in consciousness of the contrast 'Appearance and Reality' has led metaphysicians from the Greeks onwards to make their start from the more superficial characteristic. This error has warped modern philosophy to a greater extent than ancient or mediaeval philosophy. The warping has taken the form of a consistent reliance upon sensationalist perception as the basis of all experiential activity. It has had the effect of decisively separating 'mind' from 'nature', a modern separation which found its first exemplification in Cartesian dualism. But it must be remembered that this modern development was only the consistent carrying out of principles already present in the older European philosophy. It required two thousand years for the full implication of those principles to dawn upon men's minds in the seventeenth and the eighteenth centuries after Christ.

SECTION II. The distinction between 'appearance and reality' is grounded upon the process of self-formation of each actual occasion. The objective content of the initial phase of reception is the real antecedent world, as given for that occasion. This is the 'reality' from which that creative advance starts. It is the basic fact of the new occasion, with its concordances and discordances awaiting coördination in the new creature. There is nothing there apart from the real agency of the actual past, exercising its function of objective immortality. This is reality, at that moment, for that occasion. Here the term 'reality' is used in the sense of the opposite to 'appearance'.

The intermediate phase of self-formation is a ferment of qualitative valuation. These qualitative feelings are either derived directly from qualities illustrated in the primary phase, or are indirectly derived by their relevance to them. These conceptual feelings pass into novel relations to each other, felt with a novel emphasis of subjective form. The ferment of valuation is integrated with the physical prehensions of the physical pole. Thus the initial objective content is still there. But it is overlaid by, and intermixed with, the novel hybrid prehensions derived from integration with the conceptual ferment. In the higher types of actual occasions, propositional feelings are now dominant. This enlarged objective content obtains a coördination adapting it to the enjoyments and purposes fulfilling the subjective aim of the new occasion.

The mental pole has derived its objective content alike by abstraction from the physical pole and by the immanence of the basic Eros which endows with agency all ideal possibilities. The content of the objective universe has passed from the function of a basis for a new individuality to that of an instrument for purposes. The individual process is now feeling its own completion:—Cogito, ergo sum. And in Descartes' phraseology, 'cogitatio' is more than mere intellectual understanding.

This difference between the objective content of the initial phase of the physical pole and the objective content of the final phase, after the integration of physical and mental poles, constitutes 'appearance' for that occasion. In other words, 'appearance' is the effect of the activity of the mental pole, whereby the qualities and coördinations of the given physical world undergo transformation. It results from the fusion of the ideal with the actual:—The light that never was, on sea or land.

Section III. There can be no general metaphysic principles which determine how in any occasion appearance differs from the reality out of which it originates. The divergencies between reality and appearance depend on the type of social order dominating the environment of the occasion in question. All our information on this topic, direct and inferential, concerns this general epoch of the Universe and, more particularly, animal life on the surface of the Earth.

In respect to the occasions which compose the societies of inorganic bodies or of the so-called empty spaces, there is no reason to believe that in any important way the mental activities depart from functionings which are strictly conformal to those inherent in the objective datum of the first phase. Thus no novelty is introduced. The perspective elimination is effected according to the 'laws of nature' inherent in the epoch. This composition of activities constitutes the laws of physics. There is no effective 'appearance'.

But the case is very different for the high-grade occasions which are components in the animal life on the Earth's surface. Each animal body is an organ of sensation. It is a living society which may include in itself a dominant 'personal' society of occasions. This 'personal' society is composed of occasions enjoying the individual experiences of the animals. It is the soul of man. The whole body is organized, so that a general coördination of mentality is finally poured into the successive occasions of this personal society. Thus in the constitutions of these occasions, appearance is sufficiently coördinated to be effective. Also consciousness arises in the subjective forms in these experiences of the higher animals. It arises peculiarly in connection with the mental functions, and has to do primarily with their product. Now appearance is one product of mentality. Thus in our conscious perceptions appearance is dominant. It possesses a clear distinctness, which is absent from our vague massive feeling of derivation from our actual world. Appearance has shed the note of derivation. It lives in our consciousness as the world presented to us for our enjoyment and our purposes. It is the world in the guise of a subject-matter for an imposed activity. The occasion has gathered the creativity of the Universe into its own completeness, abstracted from the real objective content which is the source of its own derivation.

This status of 'appearance' in the constitution of experience is the reason for the disastrous metaphysical doctrine of physical matter passively illustrating qualities, and devoid of self-enjoyment. As soon as clarity and distinctness are made the test of metaphysical importance, an entire misapprehension of the metaphysical status of appearance is involved.

SECTION IV. When the higher functionings of mentality are socially stabilized in an organism, appearance merges into reality. To take the most conspicuous example, consider the personal succession of experiences in the life of a human being. The present occasion in this personal life inherits with peculiar dominance the antecedent experiences in this succession. But these antecedent experiences include the 'appearances' as in those occasions. These antecedent appearances are part of the real functioning of the real actual world as it stands in the primary phase of the immediately present occasion. It is a real fact of nature that the world has appeared thus from the standpoint of these antecedent occasions of the personal life. And more generally dropping the special case of personality, the objective reality of the past, as it now functions in the present, in its day was appearance. They may be strengthened in emphasis, embroidered upon, and otherwise modified by the novel appearances of the new occasion. In this way, there is an intimate, inextricable fusion of appearance with reality, and of accomplished fact with anticipation. In truth, we have been describing the exact situation which human experience presents for philosophic analysis.

We are apt to think of this fusion from the point of view

of the higher grades of human beings. But it is a fusion proceeding throughout nature. It is the essential mode in which novelty enters into the functionings of the world.

SECTION V. It is a mistake to suppose that, at the level of human intellect, the rôle of mental functionings is to add subtlety to the content of experience. The exact opposite is the case. Mentality is an agent of simplification; and for this reason appearance is an incredibly simplified edition of reality. There should be no paradox in this statement. A moment's introspection assures one of the feebleness of human intellectual operations, and of the dim massive complexity of our feelings of derivation. The point for discussion is how in animal experience this simplification is effected.

The best example of this process of simplification is afforded by the perception of a social nexus as a unity, characterized by qualities derived from its individual members and their interconnections. With some elimination, the defining characteristic of the nexus is directly perceived to be qualifying that nexus as a unity. It often happens that in this perception of the nexus as thus qualified there is a wavering between the ascription of the quality to the group as one, and to its individual components as many. Thus, the orchestra is loud as one entity, and also in virtue of the perceived loudness of the individual members with their musical instruments. The transference of the characteristic from the individuals to the group as one can be explained by the mental operations. There is the conceptual entertainment of the qualities illustrated by the individual actualities. The qualities shared by many individuals are fused into one dominating impression. This dominating prehension is integrated with the nexus, or with some portion of it, perceived as a unity illustrating that quality. The association

of a nexus as one with a quality will, for the experient subject, be in general a mode of exemplification which differs
from the mode in which the respective individuals illustrate
it. The discipline of a regiment inheres in the regiment
in a different mode from its inherence in the individual soldiers. This difference of mode of illustration may be more
or less evident. But it is there. It gives another reason for
the aspect of the passive inherence of quality in substance.
The composite group illustrates its qualities passively. The
activity belongs to the individual actualities. This whole
question of the transference of quality from the many individuals to the nexus as one is discussed at length in *Process
and Reality,* Part III, Chapter III, Section IV, where it is
termed 'Transmutation'. Obviously the transmuted percept
belongs to Appearance. But as it occurs in animal experience, it belongs to appearance merged with reality. For it is
inherited from the past. It is thus a fact of nature that the
world so appears. It is a structural relationship of animate
nature on the Earth's surface. In all Appearance there is an
element of Transmutation.

SECTION VI. For animal life on Earth by far the most
important example of Transmutation is afforded by Sense-
Perception. No doctrine of sense-perception can neglect the
teaching of physiology. The decisive factor in sense-perception is the functioning of the brain, and the functioning
of the brain is conditioned by the antecedent functionings
of the other parts of the animal body. Given requisite
bodily functionings, the sense-perception results. The activities of nature external to the animal body are irrelevant as
to their details, so long as they have the general character
of supporting the existence of the total animal organism.
The human body is the self-sufficient organ of human sense-
perception.

There are external events, such as the transmission of light or the movements of material bodies which respectively are the normal modes of exciting sense-percepts of particular types. But in the first place these external events are only the normal modes. A diet of drugs will do equally well, though its issue in perception is not so definitely to be predicted. Thus no one type of external event is necessarily associated with one type of sense-percept. Hardly any percept is strictly normal. Gross illusions are plentiful, and some element of illusion almost universal. An ordinary looking-glass produces illusive percepts in almost every room.

Secondly, confining ourselves to the normal modes of excitation, the only important factor in the external event is how it affects the functionings of the surface of the body. How the light enters the eye, and a normal healthy state of the body, are the only important factors in normal visual sensation. The light may have come from a nebula distant by a thousand light-years, or it may have its origin in an electric lamp two feet off and have suffered a complex arrangement of reflections and refractions. Nothing matters except how it enters the eye, as to its composition, its intensity, and its geometric ordering. The body is supremely indifferent as to the past history of its exciting agents, and requires no certificate of character. The peculiar bodily excitement is all that matters.

The conclusion is that the direct information to be derived from sense-perception wholly concerns the functionings of the animal body. The sense of unity with the body does in fact dominate our sense-experiences. But the bodily organization is such as finally to promote a wholesale transmutation of sensa, inherited from antecedent bodily functionings, into characteristics of regions with well-marked geometrical relations to the geometrical structures of these functionings. In this transmutation the experient occasion in question belongs to the personal succession of occasions which is the soul of the animal. The bodily functionings and the nexus relevant to them by geometrical relationship are immanent in the experient occasion. The qualitative inheritance from the individual occasions implicated in these functionings is transmuted into the characteristics of regions conspicuously indicated by their geometrical connections. This doctrine is plainly indicated in the analysis of optical vision, where the image occupies the region indicated by geometrical relations within the eyes. It is more obscurely evident in the case of other species of sensa.

It is to be remembered also that along the personal succession of the soul's experiences, there is an inheritance of sense-perception from the antecedent members of the personal succession. Also incipient sense-percepta may be forming themselves in the nerve-routes, or in the neighbouring regions of the brain. But the final synthesis, with its production of appearance, is reserved for the occasions belonging to the personal soul.

SECTION VII. The question of the proper description of the species of qualities termed 'sensa' is important. Unfortunately the learned tradition of philosophy has missed their main characteristic, which is their enormous emotional significance. The vicious notion has been introduced of mere receptive entertainment, which for no obvious reason by reflection acquires an affective tone. The very opposite is the true explanation. The true doctrine of sense-perception is that the qualitative characters of affective tones inherent in the bodily functionings are transmuted into the characters of regions. These regions are then perceived as associated with those character-qualities, but also these same qualities are shared by the subjective forms of the prehensions. This is the reason of the definite æsthetic attitude imposed by sense-perception. The pattern of sensa characterizing the object—that is, those sensa in that pattern of contrast—enters also into the subjective form of the prehension. Thus art is possible. For not only can the objects be prescribed, but also the corresponding affective tones of their prehensions. This is the æsthetic experience so far as it is based upon sense-perception.

SECTION VIII. Another point to be noticed is that in sense-perception a region in the contemporary world is the substratum supporting the sensa. It is the region straight-away in such-and-such a direction. But this geometrical relation of being 'straight-away in such-and-such a direction' is defined by the operations of the brain. It has nothing to do with any physical transmission from the substrate region to the brain. To judge from some descriptions of perception in terms of modern scientific theories, it might be concluded that we perceive along the track of a ray of light. There is not the slightest warrant for such a notion. The track of light in the world external to the animal body is irrelevant. The coloured region is perceived straight-away in such-and-such a direction. This is the fundamental notion of 'straightness'.

It therefore becomes necessary for the self-consistency of this doctrine to enquire whether the dominant structure of geometrical relations includes a determination of straightness. The theory requires that a prehension of a nexus within the brain as exhibiting straightness in the mutual relations of its parts should thereby determine the prolongation of those relations into regions beyond the brain. In simpler language, a segment of a straight line as prehended within the brain should necessarily determine its prolongation externally to the body, irrespective of the particular characters of the external events. The possibility of 'Transmutation' involving the 'Projection' of sensa is then secured.

I have discussed this question elsewhere,[9] and have given a definition of straight lines—and, more generally, of flatness—which satisfies the requirements. The necessity of basing straightness upon measurement, and measurement upon particular happenings is thereby avoided. The notions of straightness and of congruence, and thence of distance, can be derived from those underlying a uniform systematic non-metrical geometry.

It may be noticed in passing that, if straightness depends upon measurement, there can be no perception of straightness in the unmeasured. The notion of 'straight in front' must then be meaningless.

SECTION IX. In this way, the inheritance from the past is precipitated upon the present. It becomes sense-perception, which is the 'appearance' of the present.

The 'mutual immanence' of contemporary occasions to each other is allied to the immanence of the future in the present, though it presents some features of its own. This immanence exhibits a symmetrical relation of causal independence. In human experience, the prehensions of the contemporary world exhibit themselves as sense-perceptions, effected by means of the bodily organs of sensation. The subjective forms of these sense-perceptions involve conscious discrimination, with varying degrees of clarity and distinctness. Indeed sense-perceptions can exhibit themselves as clear and distinct in consciousness to a degree unrivalled by any other type of prehension. The result is that all at-

---

[9] Cf. *Process and Reality*, Part IV, Chapters III, IV, and V. The required definition is given in Chapter III, and the theory of the projection of sensa is discussed in Chapters IV and V.

tempts at an exact systematic doctrine of the nature of things seeks its most obvious verification in the conformity of its theory with sense-perception. The unfortunate effect has been, that all direct observation has been identified with sense-perception. This assumption has been criticized in Chapter XI.

But sense-perception, as conceived in the isolation of its ideal purity, never enters into human experience. It is always accompanied by so-called 'interpretation'. This 'interpretation' does not seem to be necessarily the product of any elaborate train of intellectual cogitation. We find ourselves 'accepting' [10] a world of substantial objects, directly presented for our experience. Our habits, our states of mind, our modes of behaviour, all presuppose this 'interpretation'. In fact the concept of mere sensa is the product of high-grade thinking. It required Plato to frame the myth of the Shadows in the Cave, and it required Hume to construct the doctrine of pure sensationalist perception. Yet even animals share in some 'interpretation'. There is every evidence that animals enjoy a sensationalist experience. Dogs smell, eagles see, and noises attract the attention of most of the higher animals. Also their consequent modes of behaviour suggest their immediate assumption of a substantial world around them. In fact the hypothesis of a mere sensationalist perception does not account for our direct observation of the contemporary world. There is some other factor present, which is equally primitive with our perception of sensa. This factor is provided by the immanence of the past in the immediate occasion whose percipience is under discussion. The

[10] Cf. 'Perception', by H. H. Price, especially Chapter VI, 'Perceptual Assurance, Perceptual Acceptance'. Published by Methuen, London, 1932. Price in his valuable work gives to sense-perception a more fundamental rôle in experience than my doctrine allows to it. Cf. also Santayana's doctrine of 'Animal Faith'.

immanence of the past in this percipient occasion cannot be fully understood apart from due attention to the doctrine of the immanence of the future in the past. Thus the past as an objective constituent in the experience of the percipient occasion carries its own prehension of the future beyond itself. This prehension survives objectively in the primary phase of the percipient. Accordingly there is an indirect prehension of contemporary occasion, *via* the efficient causation, from which they arise. For the immediate future of the immediate past constitutes the set of contemporary occasions for the percipient. Also these prehensions of immediate past and of immediate future operate dominantly in their experience of their respective subjects. Thus the prehension of contemporary occasions is the prehension of those occasions in so far as they are conditioned by the occasions in the immediate past of the prehending subject. Thus the present is perceivable in so far as it is conditioned by the efficient causation from the past of the perceiver. The great dominant relationships, fundamental for the epochal order of nature, thereby stand out with overwhelming distinctness. These are the general, all-pervasive, obligations of perspective. Such relationships are what we term the spatial relationships as perceivable from the standpoint of the observer.

But the particular occasions of the contemporary world, each with its own individual spontaneity, are veiled from the observer. In this respect, the contemporary world in the experience of the percipient shares the characteristics of the future. The relevant environment, which is the immediate past of the human body, is peculiarly sensitive to its geometrical experiences and to the synthesis of its qualitative prehensions with these experiences of geometrical relations. In this way, there is a basis in fact for the association of de-

rivates from significant regions in the past with the geo-
metrical representatives of those regions in the present. [Cf.
Process and Reality, Part III, Chap. III, Section IV, and Part
IV, Chs. IV and V].

The conclusion is that the contemporary world is not perceived in virtue of its own proper activity, but in virtue of
activities derived from the past, the past which conditions
it and which also conditions the contemporary percipient.
These activities are primarily in the past of the human body,
and more remotely in the past of the environment within
which the body is functioning. This environment includes
those occasions dominantly conditioning the perceived contemporary regions. This theory of the perception of contemporaries allows for our habitual belief that we perceive
the contemporary world with a general qualitative relevance
to the essences of the occasions making up its various
regions; and also with a bias of qualitative distortion due to
the functioning of the animal body of the percipient.

One distortion stands out immediately. Each actual occasion is in truth a process of activity. But the contemporary
regions are mainly perceived in terms of their passive perspective relationship to the percipient and to each other.
They are thus perceived merely as passive recipients of the
qualities with which in sense-perception they are associated.
Hence the false notion of a substratum with vacuously inherent qualities. Here the term 'vacuous' means 'devoid of
any individual enjoyment arising from the mere fact of
realization in that context'. In other words, the substratum
with its complex of inherent qualities is wrongly conceived
as bare realization, devoid of self-enjoyment, that is to say,
devoid of intrinsic worth. In this way, the exclusive reliance
on sense-perception promotes a false metaphysics. This error
is the result of high-grade intellectuality. The instinctive

interpretations which govern human life and animal life presuppose a contemporary world throbbing with energetic values. It requires considerable ability to make the disastrous abstraction of our bare sense-perceptions from the massive insistency of our total experiences. Of course, whatever we can do in the way of abstraction is for some purposes useful —provided that we know what we are about.

CHAPTER XV

PHILOSOPHIC METHOD

SECTION I. In this final chapter of Part III my aim is a discussion of some methods which can usefully be employed in the pursuit of speculative philosophy. In illustration, and as a subsidiary aim, I shall refer to some doctrines of my own,[1] and to some comments upon them. In this chapter the transient aspect of nature will be mainly emphasized.

So far as concerns methodology, the general issue of the discussion will be that theory dictates method, and that any particular method is only applicable to theories of one correlate species. An analogous conclusion holds for the technical terms. This close relation of theory to method partly arises from the fact that the relevance of evidence depends on the theory which is dominating the discussion. This fact is the reason why dominant theories are also termed 'working hypotheses'.

An example is afforded when we interrogate experience for direct evidence of the interconnectedness of things. If we hold with Hume, that the sole data originating reflective experience are impressions of sensation, and also if we also admit with him the obvious fact that no one such impression by its own individual nature discloses any information as to another such impression, then on that hypothesis the direct evidence for interconnectedness vanishes. Again, if

[1] Cf. *Process and Reality,* subsequently cited under the abbreviation *P. R.* Also, *Science and The Modern World,* cited as *S. M. W.*

we hold the Cartesian doctrine of substantial souls with many adventures of experience, and of substantial material bodies, then on that hypothesis the relations between two occasions of experience qualifying one soul are no evidence as to the connectedness of two such occasions respectively qualifying two different souls, and are no evidence as the connectedness of a soul and a material body, and are no evidence as to the connectedness of two occasions of agitation of one material body, or of two such occasions respectively belonging to different material bodies. But if we hold, as for example in *Process and Reality,* that all final individual actualities have the metaphysical character of occasions of experience, then on that hypothesis the direct evidence as to the connectedness of one's immediate present occasion of experience with one's immediately past occasions, can be validly used to suggest categories applying to the connectedness of all occasions in nature. A great deal of confused philosophical thought has its origin in obliviousness to the fact that the relevance of evidence is dictated by theory. For you cannot prove a theory by evidence which that theory dismisses as irrelevant. This is also the reason that in any science which has failed to produce any theory with a sufficient scope of application, progress is necessarily very slow. It is impossible to know what to look for, and how to connect the sporadic observations. Philosophical discussion in the absence of a theory has no criterion of the validity of evidence. For example, Hume assumes that his doctrine of association holds for all types of impressions of sensation and of ideas of them indiscriminately. This assumption is part of his theory. In divorce from the theory, a separate appeal to experience is required for each type of impression, for example, tastes, sounds, sights, etc., and likewise, not only for the association of tastes *inter se* and of sounds *inter se,* but for the association of tastes with sounds, and so on for every possible type, and for every possible conjunction of types.

To sum up this preface, every method is a happy simplification. But only truths of a congenial type can be investigated by any one method, or stated in the terms dictated by the method. For every simplification is an over-simplification. Thus the criticism of a theory does not start from the question, True or false? It consists in noting its scope of useful application and its failure beyond that scope. It is an unguarded statement of a partial truth. Some of its terms embody a general notion with a mistaken specialization, and others of its terms are too general and require discrimination of their possibilities of specialization.

Section II. Philosophy is a difficult subject, from the days of Plato to the present time haunted by subtle perplexities. The existence of such perplexities arising from the common obviousness of speech is the reason why the topic exists. Thus the very purpose of philosophy is to delve below the apparent clarity of common speech. In this connection, it is only necessary to refer to Socrates. Another illustration is to be found in the *Sophist,* where Plato states that 'not-being' is a form of 'being'. This statement is at once an extreme instance of the breakdown of language, and the enunciation of a profound metaphysical truth which lies at the foundation of this discussion.

Section III. Speculative Philosophy can be defined [2] as the endeavour to frame a coherent, logical, necessary system of general ideas in terms of which every element of our experience can be interpreted. Here 'interpretation' means that each element shall have the character of a particular instance of the general scheme.

[2] Cf. *P. R.* Pt. I, Ch. I, Sect. I.

Thus speculative philosophy embodies the method of the 'working hypothesis'. The purpose of this working hypothesis for philosophy is to coördinate the current expressions of human experience, in common speech, in social institutions, in actions, in the principles of the various special sciences, elucidating harmony and exposing discrepancies. No systematic thought has made progress apart from some adequately general working hypothesis, adapted to its special topic. Such an hypothesis directs observation, and decides upon the mutual relevance of various types of evidence. In short, it prescribes method. To venture upon productive thought without such an explicit theory is to abandon oneself to the doctrines derived from one's grandfather.

In the preliminary stages of knowledge a haphazard criterion is all that is possible. Progress is then very slow, and most of the effort is wasted. Even an inadequate working hypothesis with some conformation to fact is better than nothing. It coördinates procedure.

The advance of any reasonably developed science is twofold. There is the advance of detailed knowledge within the method prescribed by the reigning working hypothesis; and there is the rectification of the working hypothesis dictated by the inadequacies of the current orthodoxy.

Sometimes it is necessary for a science to entertain concurrently two—or more—working hypotheses, each with its own success and its own failure. Such hypotheses are contradictory as stated; and science awaits their conciliation by the production of a working hypothesis with a wider sweep. When a new working hypothesis is proposed, it must be criticized from its own point of view. For example, it is futile to object to the Newtonian dynamics that, on the Aristotelian system, the loose things on the earth's surface must be left behind by the earth's motion.

Philosophy has been afflicted by the dogmatic fallacy, which is the belief that the principles of its working hypotheses are clear, obvious, and irreformable. Then, as a reaction from this fallacy, it has swayed to the other extreme which is the fallacy of discarding method. Philosophers boast that they uphold no system. They are then a prey to the delusive clarities of detached expressions which it is the very purpose of their science to surmount. Another type of reaction is to assume, often tacitly, that if there can be any intellectual analysis it must proceed according to some one discarded dogmatic method, and thence to deduce that intellect is intrinsically tied to erroneous fictions. This type is illustrated by the anti-intellectualism of Nietzsche and Bergson, and tinges American Pragmatism.

SECTION IV. A method is a way of dealing with data, with evidence. What are the evidences to which philosophy appeals?

It is customary to contrast the objective approach of the ancient Greeks with the subjective approach of the moderns, initiated by Descartes, and further emphasized by Locke and Hume.

But, whether we be ancient or modern, we can only deal with things, in some sense, experienced. The Greeks dealt with things that they thought they experienced, and Hume merely asked, What do we experience? This is exactly the question which Plato and Aristotle thought that they were answering.

To speak of anything, is to speak of something which, by reason of that very speech, is in some way a component in that act of experience. In some sense or other, it is thereby known to exist. This is what Plato pointed out when he wrote, Not-being is itself a sort of being.

Speech consists of noises, or visible shapes, which elicit

an experience of things other than themselves. In so far as vocables fail to elicit a stable coördination of sound-character, or shape-character, to meaning, those vocables fail to function as speech. And in so far as some meaning is not in some sense directly experienced, there is no meaning conveyed. To point at nothing is not to point.

To speak of the same thing twice is to demonstrate that the being of that thing is independent of either singular act of speech, unless we believe that the two acts presuppose each other or are both presupposed by the thing spoken of. If we cannot speak of the same thing twice, knowledge vanishes taking philosophy with it. Thus, since speech can be repeated, things spoken of have a determined being in abstraction from the occasion of experience which includes that act of speech.

The difference between ancients and moderns is that the ancients asked what have we experienced, and the moderns asked what can we experience. But in both cases, they asked about things transcending the act of experience which is the occasion of asking.

SECTION V. The translation of Hume's question from 'What *do* we experience' to 'What *can* we experience' makes all the difference, though in his 'Treatise' Hume makes the transition, time and again, without explicit comment. For modern epistemology the latter form of the question—with its substitution of *can* for *do*—is accompanied by the implicit presupposition of a method, namely that of placing ourselves in an introspective attitude of attention so as to determine the *given* components of experience in abstraction from our private way of subjective reaction, by reflexion, conjecture, emotion, and purpose.

In this attitude of strained attention, there can be no doubt as to the answer. The data are the patterns of sensa provided by the sense organs. This is the sensationalist doctrine of Locke and Hume. Later, Kant has interpreted the patterns as forms introduced by the mode of reception provided by the recipient. Here Kant introduces the Leibnizian notion of the self-development of the experiencing subject. Thus for Kant the data are somewhat narrower than for Hume: they are the sensa devoid of their patterns. Hume's general analysis of the consequences of this doctrine stands unshaken. So also does his final reflection, that the philosophic doctrine fails to justify the practice of daily life. The justification of this procedure of modern epistemology is twofold, and both of its branches are based upon mistakes. The mistakes go back to the Greek philosophers. What is modern, is the exclusive reliance upon them.

SECTION VI. The first error is the assumption of a few definite avenues of communication with the external world, the five sense-organs. This leads to the pre-supposition that the search for the data is to be narrowed to the question, what data are directly provided by the activity of the sense-organs —preferably the eyes. This doctrine of sense-organs has a vague, general truth, very important for practical affairs. In particular all exact scientific observation is derived from such data. The scientific categories of thought are obtained elsewhere.

But the living organ of experience is the living body as a whole. Every instability of any part of it—be it chemical, physical, or molar—imposes an activity of readjustment throughout the whole organism. In the course of such physical activities human experience has its origin. The plausible interpretation of such experience is that it is one of the natural activities involved in the functioning of such a high-grade organism. The actualities of nature must be so interpreted as to be explanatory of this fact. This is one *desideratum* to be aimed at in a philosophic scheme.

Such experience seems to be more particularly related to

the activities of the brain. But how far an exact doctrine can
be based upon this presumption lies beyond our powers of
observation. We cannot determine with what molecules the
brain begins and the rest of the body ends. Further, we
cannot tell with what molecules the body ends and the
external world begins. The truth is that the brain is continuous with the body, and the body is continuous with the
rest of the natural world. Human experience is an act of
self-origination including the whole of nature, limited to
the perspective of a focal region,[3] located within the body,
but not necessarily persisting in any fixed coördination with
a definite part of the brain.

SECTION VII. The second error is the presupposition that
the sole way of examining experience is by acts of conscious
introspective analysis. Such a doctrine of the exclusive
primacy of introspection is already discredited in psychology.
Each occasion of experience has its own individual pattern.
Each occasion lifts some components into primacy and re-
treats others into a background enriching the total enjoyment. The attitude of introspection shares this characteristic
with all other experiential occasions. It lifts the clear-cut
data of sensation into primacy, and cloaks the vague com-
pulsions and derivations which form the main stuff of experience. In particular it rules out that intimate sense of
derivation from the body, which is the reason for our instinctive identification of our bodies with ourselves.

In order to discover some of the major categories under
which we can classify the infinitely various components of
experience, we must appeal to evidence relating to every
variety of occasion. Nothing can be omitted, experience
drunk and experience sober, experience sleeping and experience waking, experience drowsy and experience wide-awake,

[3] Cf. *P. R.* Pt. II, Ch. III, especially Sects. IV-XI, and Pt. IV, Chs. IV and V.

experience self-conscious and experience self-forgetful, experience intellectual and experience physical, experience religious and experience sceptical, experience anxious and experience care-free, experience anticipatory and experience retrospective, experience happy and experience grieving, experience dominated by emotion and experience under self-restraint, experience in the light and experience in the dark, experience normal and experience abnormal.

SECTION VIII. We have now reached the heart of our topic. What is the store-house of that crude evidence on which philosophy should base its discussion, and in what terms should its discussion be expressed?

The main sources of evidence respecting this width of human experience are language, social institutions, and action, including thereby the fusion of the three which is language interpreting action and social institutions.

Language delivers its evidence in three chapters, one on the meanings of words, another on the meanings enshrined in grammatical forms, and the third on meanings beyond individual words and beyond grammatical forms, meanings miraculously revealed in great literature.

Language is incomplete and fragmentary, and merely registers a stage in the average advance beyond ape-mentality. But all men enjoy flashes of insight beyond meanings already stabilized in etymology and grammar. Hence the rôle of literature, the rôle of the special sciences, and the rôle of philosophy:—in their various ways engaged in finding linguistic expressions for meanings as yet unexpressed.

As a special example, consider the line and a half of poetry in which Euripides [4] compresses the main philosophical problems which have tortured European thought from his day to the present:—"Zeus, whether thou are Compulsion of

[4] *Trojan Women*, 886-7.

Nature or Intelligence of Mankind, to thee I prayed." Consider the ideas involved, 'Zeus', 'necessity [compulsion] of nature', 'intelligence of mankind', 'prayer'. These lines have survived the ages with a modern appeal vivid as when first they thrilled an Athenian audience. The biographer [5] of a modern statesman cites them to express the solemnity of the spectacle of life passing into religious emotion.

Yet Hume would be able to find no 'impression of sensation' from which to derive 'Zeus', or 'compulsion', or 'intelligence', or the would-be 'persuasiveness' which we term 'prayer'. John Morley himself selected the quotation in spite of his own positivistic bias which should trivialize these meanings. Also, perhaps even for their original author, the lines represent a triumph of dramatic intuition over temperamental scepticism.

The common practice, interpreted by the common language of mankind, tells the same tale. A statesman, or a president of a business corporation, assumes the 'compulsion of recent events' [ἀνάγκη φύσεως] as laying down inexorable conditions for the future. He frames a 'policy' upon this assumption and advises that it be 'acted on', thereby also assuming that the imposed conditions leave room for the effectiveness of 'choice' and 'intelligence' [νοῦς]. He assumes alternatives in contrast to the immediate fact. He conceives an ideal, to be attained or to be missed. He conceives such ideals as effective in proportion as they are entertained. He praises and he blames by reason of this belief.

In the world, there are elements of order and disorder, which thereby presuppose an essential interconnectedness of things. For disorder shares with order the common characteristic that they imply many things interconnected.

[5] Cf. John Morley's *Life of Gladstone*, Ch. X.

Each experient enjoys a perspective apprehension of the world, and equally is an element in the world by reason of this very prehension, which anchors him to a world transcending his own experience. For, it belongs to the nature of this perspective derivation, that the world thus disclosed proclaims its own transcendence of that disclosure. To every shield, there is another side, hidden.

Thus an appeal to literature, to common language, to common practice, at once carries us away from the narrow basis for epistemology provided by the sense-data disclosed in direct introspection. The world within experience is identical with the world beyond experience, the occasion of experience is within the world and the world is within the occasion. The categories have to elucidate this paradox of the connectedness of things:—the many things, the one world without and within.

SECTION IX. European philosophy is founded upon Plato's dialogues, which in their methods are mainly an endeavour to elicit philosophic categories from a dialectic discussion of the meanings of language taken in combination with shrewd observation of the actions of man and of the forces of nature.

But in one dialogue, the *Sophist,* Plato explicitly considers the methods of philosophy. One of his conclusions is to point out the limitations of common speech. Mere dialectic, uncriticized, is a fallacious instrument, the mark of the *Sophist.* For example, Plato insists that not-being is itself a form of being. Thus in philosophy linguistic discussion is a tool, but should never be a master. Language is imperfect both in its words and in its forms. Thus we discover two main errors to which philosophic method is liable, one is the uncritical trust in the adequacy of language, and the other is the uncritical trust in the strained attitude of introspection as the basis for epistemology.

But since the life-time of Plato nearly two and a half thousand years have intervened, including the continuous activity of European philosophic thought, pagan, Christian, secular. It is widely held that a stable, well-known philosophic vocabulary has been elaborated, and that in philosophic discussion any straying beyond its limits introduces neologisms, unnecessary and therefore to be regretted.

This alleged fact requires examination. In the first place, if the allegation be true, it is very remarkable. It decisively places philosophy apart from the more special sciences. Modern mathematics, most secure and authoritative of sciences, is largely written in verbal and symbolic phrases which would have been unintelligible eighty years ago. In modern physics the old words, where they are still used, convey different meanings, and the new words are abundant. But it is futile to make a catalogue of the sciences accompanied by this refrain. The conclusion is obvious to the most cursory inspection.

SECTION X. Undoubtedly, philosophy is dominated by its past literature to a greater extent than any other science. And rightly so. But the claim that it has acquired a set of technical terms sufficient for its purposes, and exhaustive of its meanings, is entirely unfounded. Indeed its literature is so vast, and the variations of its schools of thought so large, that there is abundant evidence of most excusable ignorance respecting verbal usages.

A recent instance illustrates the vagueness of philosophical terminology. Logic is, by far, that branch of philosophy best systematized with the aid of a stable technical language. Consider the terms Judgment and Proposition. I am not writing a preface to Logic, so I will confine myself to the assertion that there is considerable variation in the usages of these terms among logicians.

Also we may well ask whether there are not subtle variations of meaning stretching far beyond the competence of the two-term vocabulary,—Judgment, Proposition. For example, Mr. Joseph[6] has been examining Mr. W. E. Johnson's use of the term Proposition in his well-known Logical Treatise. Mr. Joseph finds twenty distinct meanings. It is to be remembered that we are here referring to two of the most acute of modern logicians. Whether Mr. Joseph has rightly interpreted Mr. Johnson's phrases is not to the point. If Mr. Joseph has found twenty distinct, though allied, meanings closely connected with the term Proposition, there are twenty such meanings, even though for the moment their divergencies may seem unimportant to Mr. Johnson or to Mr. Joseph. Importance depends on purpose and on point of view. So at any moment twenty new terms may be required by some advance in the subtlety of logical theory. Again, if Mr. Johnson has employed twenty distinct meanings, it is because they were relevant to his argument, even though his argument may require further completion by reason of their unnoted distinction.

It is safe to affirm that this situation can be repeated over every technical term in philosophy.

SECTION XI. Another illustration, in which my use of the words[7] Prehension, Feeling, Satisfaction, is partly concerned, can be drawn from the terms expressive of the connectedness of things. For this topic, the reigning philosophical term is the word Relation. There are various controversies about relations which need not be explicitly referred to. But there is one discussion which illustrates our immediate topic.

It is generally held that relations are universals, so that A

---

[6] Cf. *Mind*, Vols. 36, 37, New Series.
[7] Cf. *S. M. W.*, Ch. IV and *passim* and *P. R.* Part I, Ch. II and *passim*.

can have the same relation to B as C has to D. For example 'loving', 'believing', 'between', 'greater than', are relations. There can be no objection to this doctrine. For it is a mere definition. Universals which require two or more particulars for their illustration need some term to indicate them, and Relation is the word chosen.

But with this meaning to the term, a relation cannot signify the actual connectedness of the actual individual things which constitute the actual course of history. For example, New York lies between Boston and Philadelphia. But the connectedness of the three towns is a real particular fact on the earth's surface involving a particular part of the eastern seaboard of the United States. It is not the universal 'between'. It is a complex actual fact which, among other things, exemplifies the abstract universal 'betweenness'.

This consideration is the basis of Bradley's objection that relations do not relate. Three towns and an abstract universal are not three connected towns. A doctrine of connectedness is wanted. Bradley [8] writes 'Is there, in the end, such a thing as a relation which is merely *between* terms? Or, on the other hand, does not a relation imply an underlying unity and an inclusive whole?'

Bradley's 'inclusive whole' is the connectedness of which we are in search. Throughout this chapter [*loc. cit.*] Bradley uses the term Feeling to express the primary activity at the basis of experience. It is experience itself in its origin and with the minimum of analysis. The analysis of Feeling can never disclose anything lying beyond the essence of the occasion of experience. Hence Bradley terms it 'non-relational'. There are of course grave differences between my

[8] Cf. *Essays on Truth and Reality,* Ch. VI, *On our Knowledge of Immediate Experience, Appendix,* p. 193.

The page references are to the Oxford edition of 1914. Also cf. *Appendix to Ch. VI, passim,* and Supplementary Note to the same.

own doctrine and that of Bradley. This was a reason [9] for expounding my point of view in some independence of Bradley, with due acknowledgement. Surely the proper method of choosing technical terms is to adopt terms from some outstanding exposition of an analogous doctrine. It throws an interesting light on the belief in a well-understood technical phraseology reigning in philosophy, that an accomplished philosopher censured in print, my use of the word Feeling as being in a sense never before employed in philosophy.

I may add that William James also employs the word in much the same sense in his Psychology. For example in the first chapter he writes, "Sensation is the feeling of first things". And in the second chapter he writes, "In general, this higher consciousness about things is called Perception, the mere inarticulate feeling of their presence is Sensation, so far as we have it at all. To some degree we seem able to lapse into this inarticulate feeling at moments when our attention is entirely dispersed." It is interesting to make a few citations from Bradley, illustrating my general adherence to his doctrine of Feeling, as expressed in his Chapter. "In my general feeling at any moment there is more than the objects before me, and no perception of objects will exhaust the sense of a living emotion." [10]

In accordance with this doctrine of Bradley's, I analyze a feeling [or prehension] into the 'datum', which is Bradley's 'object before me', into the 'subjective form' which is Bradley's 'living emotion', and into the 'subject' which is Bradley's 'me'. My reason for using the term 'subjective form' is that I stretch its meaning beyond 'emotion'. For example consciousness, if it be present, is an element in the subjective form. This is, of course, a grave divergence from

[9] Cf. *P. R. passim.*   [10] Bradley, p. 159.

Bradley. Subjective form is the character assumed by the subject by reason of some prehended datum.

But on the whole I conform to Bradley's conception of the function of subjective form. For example, "These puzzles are insoluble unless that which I feel, and which is not an object before me, is present and active. This felt element is used and it must be used in the constitution of that object which satisfies me".[11]

From my point of view there is an ambiguity in this statement, but I adhere to either alternative meaning.

The component of feeling 'which is not an object before me' is the subjective form. If Bradley is stating that the subjective forms of feelings determine the process of integration, I entirely agree. The result, as Bradley states, is the 'satisfaction' which is the final feeling terminating the unrest of the creative process.

Bradley, however, may mean by his phrase "that which I feel, and which is not an object before me" what I term a "negative prehension". Such a prehension is active *via* its contribution of its subjective form to the creative process, but it dismisses its 'object' from the possibility of entering into the datum of the final satisfaction. This final complex datum will be what Bradley calls "that object that satisfies me". Again I agree.

The doctrine of the 'living emotion' which necessarily clothes each concrete exhibition of the subject-object situation is far older than Bradley. We find its germ in Plato, who insists that the whole character is conformed to the adequate knowledge. He implicitly refuses to abstract the 'living emotion' from the bare intellectual perception, and thereby identifies virtue with knowledge. The advance in

[11] P. 161.

psychology has added to our conscious discrimination, but it has not altered the fact that inevitably perception is clothed with emotion.

The historical importance of the doctrine is stated by George Foot Moore: [12]—"Civilization develops only where considerable numbers of men work together for common ends. Such unity is brought about, not so much by community of bare ideas as by community of the feelings by which ideas are 'emotionalized' and become beliefs and motives."

The conventionalized abstractions prevalent in epistemological theory are very far from the concrete facts of experience. The word 'feeling' has the merit of preserving this double significance of subjective form and of the apprehension of an object. It avoids the *disjecta membra* provided by abstraction.[13]

SECTION XII. Thus an occasion of human experience is one illustration of the required doctrine of connectedness.

Bradley's authority can be quoted in support. He writes: [14] "At every moment my stage of experience, whatever else it is, is a whole of which I am immediately aware. It is an experienced non-relational unity of many in one." Here Bradley by 'non-relational' apparently means that experience is not a relation of an experient to something external to it, but is itself the 'inclusive whole' which is the required connectedness of 'many in one'.

In this I thoroughly agree, holding that the connectedness

[12] In the *Prefatory Note* to *Emotion as the Basis of Civilization*, by J. H. Denison, New York, 1928 (Scribner's): a work of importance.

[13] The genetic description of the process of 'emotionalization' is considered in my *'Symbolism, Its Meaning and Effect'* and also in P. R. Pt. II, Ch. VIII, and throughout Pt. III.

[14] *Loc. cit.*, p. 175.

of things is nothing else than the togetherness of things in occasions of experience. Of course, such occasions are only rarely occasions of human experience.

Curiously enough Hume also agrees. For his only togetherness of the stream of impressions of sensation, which in his doctrine are distinct existences at distinct times, lies in the 'gentle force' of association which must lie wholly within an occasion of experience. This is also one aspect of Kant's doctrine, that the occasions of experience provide the forms of connectedness.

Of course there are important differences between all these doctrines. But they agree in their general principle—to look on occasions of experience as the ground of connectedness.

SECTION XIII. Also Leibniz can find no other connectedness between reals except that lying wholly within the individual experiences of the monads, including the Supreme Monad. He employed the terms 'perception' and 'apperception' for the lower and higher ways in which one monad can take account of another, namely for ways of awareness. But these terms are too closely allied to the notion of consciousness which in my doctrine is not a necessary accompaniment. Also they are all entangled in the notion of representative perception which I reject. But there is the term [15] 'apprehension' with the meaning of 'thorough understanding'. Accordingly, on the Leibnizian model, I use the term 'prehension' for the general way in which the occasion of experience can include, as part of its own essence, any other entity, whether another occasion of experience or an entity of another type. This term is devoid of suggestion either of consciousness or of representative perception. Feelings are the positive type of prehensions. In positive pre-

[15] This term is used by L. T. Hobhouse, *Theory of Knowledge*, Chs. I and II.

hensions the 'datum' is preserved as part of the final complex object which 'satisfies' the process of self-formation and thereby completes the occasion.

This nomenclature has been made up to conform to the condition, that, as a theory develops, its technical phraseology should grow out of the usages of the great masters who laid its foundations. The immediate verbal usages at any moment prevalent in any school of philosophy are but a small selection from the total vocabulary of the philosophic tradition. This is rightly the case having regard to the variations of doctrine.

The current usage can express the doctrine of the reigning school of thought and of certain accredited variations from it. The demand that an alternative doctrine with other roots in the historic tradition should confine itself to this selection of terms amounts to the dogmatic claim that certain preliminary assumptions should never be revised. Only those schools of thought are to be allowed which can be expressed in the sacred terms. What can reasonably be asked, is that each doctrine should ground its vocabulary on its own proper tradition. If this precaution has been taken, an outcry as to neologisms is a measure of unconscious dogmatism.

SECTION XIV. The main method of philosophy in dealing with its evidence is that of descriptive generalization. Social institutions exemplify a welter of characteristics. No fact is merely such-and-such. It exemplifies many characters at once, all rooted in the specialities of its epoch. Philosophic generalization seizes on those characters of abiding importance, dismissing the trivial and the evanescent. There is an ascent from a particular fact, or from a species, to the genus exemplified.

It is to be noted that the converse procedure is impossible. There can be no descent from a mere genus to a particular fact, or to a species. For facts and species are the product of the mingling of genera. No genus in its own essence indicates the other genera with which it is compatible. For example, the notion of a backbone does not indicate the notions of suckling the young or of swimming in water. Thus no contemplation of the genus vertebrate, taken by itself, can suggest mammals or fishes, even as abstract possibilities. Neither the species nor the instance are to be discovered by the genus alone, since both include forms not 'given' by the genus. A species is a potential mingling of genera, and an individual instance involves, among other things, an actual mingling of many species. A syllogism is a scheme for demonstration of ways of mingling.

Thus the business of Logic is not the analysis of generalities but their mingling.[16]

Philosophy is the ascent to the generalities with the view of understanding their possibilities of combination. The discovery of new generalities thus adds to the fruitfulness of those already known. It lifts into view new possibilities of combination.

SECTION XV. Even the dim apprehension of some great principle is apt to clothe itself with tremendous emotional force. The welter of particular actions arising out of such complex feelings with their core of deep intuition are in primitive times often brutish and nasty. Finally civilized language provides a whole group of words, each embodying the general idea under its own specialization. If we desire to reach the generality common to these various specializations, we must gather together the whole group of words with the hope of discerning their common element. This is a necessary procedure for the purpose of philosophical generalization. The premature use of one familiar word

[16] Cf. Plato's *Sophist*, 253.

inevitably limits the required generalization by importing the familiar special connotation of that word.

For example,[17] let the working hypothesis be that the ultimate realities are the events in their process of origination. Then each event, viewed in its separate individuality, is a passage between two ideal termini, namely, its components in their ideal disjunctive diversity passing into these same components in their concrete togetherness. There are two current doctrines as to this process. One is that of the external Creator, eliciting this final togetherness out of nothing. The other doctrine is that it is a metaphysical principle belonging to the nature of things, that there is nothing in the Universe other than instances of this passage and components of these instances. Let this latter doctrine be adopted. Then the word Creativity expresses the notion that each event is a process issuing in novelty. Also if guarded in the phrases Immanent Creativity, or Self-Creativity, it avoids the implication of a transcendent Creator. But the mere word Creativity suggests Creator, so that the whole doctrine acquires an air of paradox, or of pantheism. Still it does convey the origination of novelty. The word Concrescence is a derivative from the familiar latin verb, meaning 'growing together'. It also has the advantage that the participle 'concrete' is familiarly used for the notion of complete physical reality. Thus Concrescence is useful to convey the notion of many things acquiring complete complex unity. But it fails to suggest the creative novelty involved. For example, it omits the notion of the individual character arising in the concrescence of the aboriginal data. The event is not suggested as 'emotionalized', that is, as with its 'subjective form'.

Again the term 'together' is one of the most misused terms

[17] Cf. P. R. *passim*, where the second of the doctrines stated below is developed.

in philosophy. It is a generic term illustrated by an endless variety of species. Thus its use as though it conveyed one definite meaning in diverse illustrations is entirely sophistical. Every meaning of 'together' is to be found in various stages of analysis of occasions of experience. No things are 'together' except in experience; and no things *are,* in any sense of 'are', except as components in experience or as immediacies of process which are occasions in self-creation.

SECTION XVI. Thus to arrive at the philosophic generalization which is the notion of a final actuality conceived in the guise of a generalization of an act of experience, an apparent redundancy of terms is required. The words correct each other. We require [18] 'together', 'creativity', 'concrescence', 'prehension', 'feeling', 'subjective form', 'data', 'actuality', 'becoming', 'process'.

SECTION XVII. At this stage of the generalization a new train of thought arises. Events become and perish. In their becoming they are immediate and then vanish into the past. They are gone; they have perished; they are no more and have passed into not-being. Plato terms [19] them things that are 'always becoming and never really are'. But before he wrote this phrase, Plato had made his great metaphysical generalization, a discovery which forms the basis of the present discussion. He wrote in the *Sophist,* not-being is itself a form of being. He only applied this doctrine to his eternal forms. He should have applied the same doctrine to the things that perish. He would then have illustrated another aspect of the method of philosophic generalization. When a general idea has been obtained, it should not be arbitrarily limited to the topic of its origination.

In framing a philosophic scheme, each metaphysical notion should be given the widest extension of which it

[18] Cf. *P. R. passim,* also *S. M. W.*   [19] Cf. *Timaeus.*

seems capable. It is only in this way that the true adjustment of ideas can be explored. More important even than
Occam's doctrine of parsimony—if it be not another aspect
of the same—is this doctrine that the scope of a metaphysical
principle should not be limited otherwise than by the
necessity of its meaning.

Thus we should balance Aristotle's—or, more rightly,
Plato's—doctrine of becoming by a doctrine of perishing.
When they perish, occasions pass from the immediacy of
being into the not-being of immediacy. But that does not
mean that they are nothing. They remain 'stubborn fact':—

Pereunt et imputantur.

The common expressions of mankind fashion the past for
us in three aspects,—Causation, Memory, and our active
transformation of our immediate past experience into the
basis of our present modification of it. Thus 'perishing' is
the assumption of a rôle in a transcendent future. The not-
being of occasions is their 'objective immortality'. A pure
physical prehension is how an occasion in its immediacy of
being absorbs another occasion which has passed into the objective immortality of its not-being. It is how the past lives
in the present. It is causation. It is memory. It is perception
of derivation. It is emotional conformation to a given situation, an emotional continuity of past with present. It is a
basic element from which springs the self-creation of each
temporal occasion. Thus perishing is the initiation of becoming. How the past perishes is how the future becomes.

PART IV

CIVILIZATION

CHAPTER XVI

TRUTH

SECTION I. Truth and Beauty are the great regulative properties in virtue of which Appearance justifies itself to the immediate decision of the experient subject. The justification determines its status in the immediate occasion. The subjective form of the prehension can include immediate emphasis or attenuation, and it can include purpose of prolongation into the future or purpose of exclusion. Truth and Beauty are the ultimate grounds for emphasis and for prolongation. Of course the present can be sacrificed to the future, so that Truth or Beauty in the future can be the reason for the immediate attenuation of either.

SECTION II. Truth is a qualification which applies to Appearance alone. Reality is just itself, and it is nonsense to ask whether it be true or false. Truth is the conformation of Appearance to Reality. This conformation may be more or less, also direct or indirect. Thus Truth is a generic quality with a variety of degrees and modes. In the Law-Courts, the wrong species of Truth may amount to perjury. For example, a portrait may be so faithful as to deceive the eye. Its very truthfulness then amounts to deception. A reflexion in a mirror is at once a truthful appearance and a deceptive appearance. The smile of a hypocrite is deceptive, and that of a philanthropist may be truthful. But both of them were truly smiling.

SECTION III. The notion of Truth can be generalized, so

as to avoid any explicit reference to Appearance. Two objects may be such that (1) neither may be a component of the other, and (2) their composite natures may include a common factor, although in the full sense of the term their 'essences' are different. The two objects can then be said to have a truth-relation to each other. The examination of one of them can disclose some factor belonging to the essence of the other. In other words, an abstraction can be made and some elements of the complete pattern can be omitted. The partial pattern thus obtained will be said to be abstracted from the original. A truth-relation will be said to connect the objective contents of two prehensions when one and the same identical partial pattern can be abstracted from both of them. They each exhibit this same partial pattern, though their omitted elements involve the differences which belong to their diverse individualities. Plato uses the term 'participation' [μέθεξις] to express the relation of a composite fact to some partial pattern which it illustrates. Only he limits the notion of the partial pattern to some purely abstract pattern of qualitative elements, to the exclusion of the notion of concrete particular realities as components in a composite reality. This limitation is misleading. Thus we will speak of a pattern as possibly including concrete particulars among its patterned elements. With this enlargement of meaning, we can say that two objective contents are united in a truth-relation when they severally participate in the same pattern. Either illustrates what in part the other is. Thus they interpret each other. But if we ask what is meant by 'truth', we can only answer that there is a truth-relation when two composite facts participate in the same pattern. Then knowledge about one of the facts involves knowledge about the other, so far as the truth-relation extends.

The truth-relation as realized in experience always involves some element of Appearance. For the separate prehensions of the two composite facts have been integrated so that the two objects stand in the unity of a contrast with each other. There is an intuition of a limited identity of pattern involved in the contrast of the diverse essences. In virtue of this identity there is a transference of subjective form from the feeling of one object to that of the other. What is appropriate to one is appropriate to the other. The intuitive recognition of 'that is so' is the subjective form including in itself justification of its own transference from the object on one side of the contrast to the object on the other side.

In this way one object as a real fact obtains a re-adjustment of the relative values of its factors by reason of its analogies to another object. In other words, it becomes a real fact tinged with Appearance. By itself, its factors would not be felt in those proportions. To know the truth partially is to distort the Universe. For example, the savage who can only count up to ten enormously exaggerates the importance of the small numbers, and so do we whose imaginations fail when we come to millions. It is an erroneous moral platitude, that it is necessarily good to know the truth. The minor truth may beget the major evil. And this major evil may take the form of the major error. Henri Poincaré points out that instruments of precision, used unseasonably, may hinder the advance of science. For example, if Newton's imagination had been dominated by the errors in Kepler's Laws as disclosed by modern observation, the world might still be waiting for the Law of Gravitation. The Truth must be seasonable.

SECTION III. The two conspicuous examples of the truth relation in human experience are afforded by propositions and by sense-perception. A proposition is the abstract possibility of some specified nexus of actualities realizing some eternal object, which may either be simple, or may be a complex pattern of simpler objects. The realization may (1) concern the complete nexus with its component occasions in assigned functions, or (2) it may concern the individual realization of the eternal object by some or all, of the component occasions, or (3) it may concern the joint realization by some unspecified subordinate nexus. All of these alternatives merely concern the possibility of propositions of the various types, so important for the purposes of Formal Logic.

But for the present discussion we need simply consider the broad fact that a proposition is the abstract possibility of an assigned nexus illustrating an assigned pattern.

No verbal sentence merely enunciates a proposition. It always includes some incitement for the production of an assigned psychological attitude in the prehension of the proposition indicated. In other words, it endeavours to fix the subjective form which clothes the feeling of the proposition as a datum. There may be an incitement to believe, or to doubt, or to enjoy, or to obey. This incitement is conveyed partly by the grammatical mood and tense of the verb, partly by the whole suggestion of the sentence, partly by the whole content of the book, partly by the material circumstances of the book, including its cover, partly by the names of the author and of the publisher. In the discussion of the nature of a proposition, a great deal of confusion has been introduced by confusing this psychological incitement with the proposition itself.

A proposition is a notion about actualities, a suggestion, a theory, a supposition about things. Its entertainment in experience subserves many purposes. It is an extreme case of Appearance. For actualities which are the logical subjects are conceived in the guise of illustrating the predicate. The unconscious entertainment of propositions is a stage in the transition from the Reality of the initial phase of experience to the Appearance of the final phase. In the lowest types of actualities in whose processes propositions hardly arise, there is practically no Appearance differentiating the final and initial phases.

It is more important that a proposition be interesting than that it be true. This statement is almost a tautology. For the energy of operation of a proposition in an occasion of experience is its interest, and is its importance. But of course a true proposition is more apt to be interesting than a false one. Also action in accordance with the emotional lure of a proposition is more apt to be successful if the proposition be true. And apart from action, the contemplation of truth has an interest of its own. But, after all this explanation and qualification, it remains true that the importance of a proposition lies in its interest. Nothing illustrates better the danger of specialist sciences than the confusion due to handing over propositions for theoretical consideration by logicians, exclusively. The truth of a proposition lies in its truth-relation to the nexus which is its logical subject. A proposition is true when the nexus does in reality exemplify the pattern which is the predicate of the proposition. Thus in the analysis of the various component factors involved the proposition, if true, seems to be identical with the nexus. For there are the same actual occasions and the same eternal objects involved. But in all analysis there is one supreme factor which is apt to be omitted, namely, the mode of togetherness. The nexus includes the eternal object in the mode of realization. Whereas in the true proposition the togetherness of the nexus and the eternal object belongs to the mode of abstract possibility. The eternal object is then united to the nexus as a mere 'predicate'. Thus a nexus and a proposition belong to different categories of being. Their identification is mere nonsense. It is the nonsense of the same sort as the fashionable identification of physical fact with formulæ of pure mathematics.

Propositions, like everything else except experience in its own immediacy, only exist as entertained in experience. It is the peculiar function of the mental pole that the objective content of its prehensions only exists in the mode of possibility. But matter of fact essentially involves a mental pole. Thus in the analysis of an actual occasion, we necessarily find components belonging to the mode of possibility. The most conspicuous example of truth and falsehood arises in the comparison of existences in the mode of possibility with existences in the mode of actuality.

SECTION IV. For animals on this Earth, sense-perception is the culmination of Appearance. The sensa derived from bodily activities in the past are precipitated upon the regions in the contemporary world. The note of hypothesis, the note of mere suggested possibility is eliminated. The regions appear to the percipient as in their own right associated with the sensa. The Appearance now is, that the sensa qualify the regions.

The question then arises, Do the sensa in fact qualify the regions? The answer depends on what is meant by 'in fact', and what is meant by 'qualification'. It is here that the notion of truth and falsehood applies to sense-perception. But in the realm of truth there are many mansions; and we have to analyse the types of truth and of falsehood which sense-perception is capable of.

In the first place, the primary status of the sensa as qualifications of affective tone must be kept in mind. They are

primarily inherited as such qualifications and then by 'transmutation' are objectively perceived as qualifications of regions. The immense æsthetic importance of sensa is due to
this status of sensa. For the sensum as a factor in the datum
of a prehension imposes itself as a qualification of the affective tone which is the subjective form of that prehension.
Thus a pattern of affective tone is conformally produced by
a pattern of sensa as datum. Now when a region appears as
red in sense-perception, the question arises whether red is
qualifying in any dominant manner the affective tones of
the actualities which in fact make up the region.

If so, there is in this sense a truth-relation between the
reality of the region and its appearance for the contemporary percipient. For example, if the light has undergone reflexions in a mirror, the appearance of the region behind
the mirror affords no ground for conjecture as to the affective tones of its component actualities.

This notion of the sensa as qualifications of affective tone
is a paradox for philosophy, though it is fairly obvious to
common sense. A red-irritation is prevalent among nerve-
racked people and among bulls. The affective tone of perception of a green woodland in spring can only be defined
by the delicate shades of the green. It is a strong æsthetic
emotion with the qualification of green in spring-time. The
intellect fastens on smell as a datum: the animal experiences
it as a qualification of his subjective feelings. Our developed
consciousness fastens on the sensum as datum: our basic
animal experience entertains it as a type of subjective feeling. The experience starts as that smelly feeling, and is
developed by mentality into the feeling of that smell.

We can also observe qualifications of moods hovering on
the verge of becoming sensa, in fact functioning as sensa
for the infant, and being dismissed from that category by

the developed intellect of the grown-up person. For example, the emotional moods of the mother nursing the infant, moods of love, or gaiety, or depression, or irritation, are directly perceived on the mother's face by the infant, and are responded to. It certainly is in the highest degree improbable that the subtle trains of thought by which our epistemologists obtain their knowledge should have occurred to speechless infants, or to dogs and horses. Direct perceptions of such moods in these cases must enter on equal terms with the other sensa. But in respect to the perception of such moods, the animal body functions vary differently from its functionings in the conveyance of sensa. Hence for the educated intellect there is a distinction of type.

But in any case the infant feels its mother's cheerfulness as a datum, and feels it conformally, with that affective tone. The datum is derived from the past, the immediate past. It is precipitated upon that present region occupied by the nexus of occasions which constitute the complex fact of the mother's existence, body and soul. For the infant, the Appearance includes the qualification of cheerfulness. And in this respect it may have—it often does have—to the contemporary real mother a truth-relation in the fullest sense of the term 'truth'.

SECTION V. The relation of sense-perception to contemporary occasions can also exemplify another type of truth-relation between Appearance and Reality.

The sense-perception may result from the normal functioning of the healthy animal body. The consequent inheritance from the antecedent occasions of the personal soul may likewise share in this healthy normality. Also the particular body and soul in question may share in that conformation of their reactions to those main external activities of fluent energy which is normally required for the preservation of that species of animal. Given these conditions of normality, the resulting appearance will be that proper to that species of animal under circumstances of that type. This is a fact of nature, and the Appearance expresses the issue of a Law of Nature, belonging to that cosmic epoch and to those more special conditions within that epoch. This is a truth-relation between Appearance and Reality of a more indirect character than the first sort of truth-relation. It is wider, vaguer, and more diffuse in its reference. We have perceived what well-conditioned individuals of our own type would perceive under those circumstances.

SECTION VI. Within any type of truth-relation a distinction arises. The Reality functions in the past, the Appearance is perceived in the present. On a moonless night, the faintly luminous stretch of the sky which is the Milky Way is an Appearance of the contemporary world, namely, it is a great region within the 'Receptacle' of that world as it appears. But the Reality whose functioning issues in that Appearance, is a flux of light-energy travelling through the utmost depths of space and, to our imaginations, through illimitable time.

Beyond that Milky Way as it stands in sight, at a finite ill-defined distance, a barrier separating us from the contemporary space beyond:—Does that remote activity of the transference of light-energy still persist as a contemporary fact? Perhaps the occasions whose interconnections constitute that distant region have changed the ordering of their goings-on. Stars flare out in a few days, and in a few years, their light has died. The Appearance of the contemporary regions has its truth-relations to the past, and its truth-relations to contemporary Reality. These latter truth-relations can only be estimated by an imaginative leap, which has as its basis for justification the truth-relations to the past and our experience of the stability of the types of order involved.

Perhaps in the mutual immanence of occasions, although the antecedence and the consequence,—the past, the present and the future—still hold equally for physical and mental poles, yet the relations of the mental poles to each other are not subject to the same laws of perspective as are those of the physical poles. Measureable time and measureable space are then irrelevant to their mutual connections. Thus in respect to some types of Appearance there may be an element of immediacy in its relations to the mental side of the contemporary world. Other types of Appearance, such as the located sensa in sense-perception, may depend on the time and space which express the perspective arising in the mutual immanence of the physical poles.

If such be the case, some types of Appearance will have a more direct relation than others to contemporary Reality.

SECTION VII. There is a third type of truth-relation which is even vaguer and more indirect than the second type considered above. It may be termed the type of 'symbolic truth'. This species of truth may be included under the second type, as an extreme instance of it. But on the whole, it is clearer to consider it as a distinct species.

The relation of Appearance to Reality, when there is symbolic truth, is that for certain sets of percipients the prehension of the Appearance leads to the prehension of the Reality, such that the subjective forms of the two prehensions are conformal. There is however no direct causal relation between the Appearance and the Reality; so that in no direct sense is the Appearance the cause of the Reality, or the Reality the cause of the Appearance. A set of adventitious circumstances has brought about this connection between those Appearances and those Realities as prehended in the

experiences of those percipients. In their own natures the
Appearances throw no light upon the Realities, nor do the
Realities upon the Appearances, except in the experiences of
a set of peculiarly conditioned percipients. Languages and
their meanings are examples of this third type of truth.
There is an indirect truth-relation of the sounds or of the
visual marks on paper to the propositions conveyed. We are
confining the discussion to the relation of written or spoken
sentences to propositions. There is a right and a wrong use
of any particular language among the group of people who
are properly conditioned. Also, having regard to the
æsthetics of literature, language not only conveys objective
meaning, but also involves a conveyance of subjective form.

   Music, ceremonial clothing, ceremonial smells, and ceremonial rhythmic visual appearances, also have symbolic
truth, or symbolic falsehood. In these latter instances, the
conveyance of objective meaning is at a minimum, while
the conveyance of suitable subjective form is at its height.
Music provides an example when it interprets some strong
sentiment, patriotic, martial, or religious, by providing the
emotion which the votaries dumbly feel ought to be attached
to the apprehension of national life, or of the clash of nations, or of the activities of God. Music elicits some confused feeling into distinct apprehension. It performs this
service, or dis-service, by introducing an emotional clothing which changes the dim objective reality into a clear
Appearance matching the subjective form provided for its
prehension.

   There is then the vague truth-relation, *via* community
of subjective form, between the music and the resulting
Appearance. There is also the truth-relation between the
Appearance and the Reality—the Reality of National Life,
or of Strife between nations, or of the Essence of God. This

complex fusion of truth-relations, with their falsehoods intermixed, constitutes the indirect interpretative power of Art to express the truth about the nature of things. Of course a somewhat gross, almost vulgar, instance has been given, for the sake of easy explanation. But the delicate inner truth of Art is mostly of this sort.

SECTION VIII. This discussion suggests an illustrative digression on the origins of socially diffused habits of behaviour and of habits of interpretation, among human beings. An idea arises from the antecedent establishment of modes of human functioning which are germane to it. In the infancy of its incarnation in human history, it lurks in the penumbra of consciousness, undiscriminated and unexpressed. For the historian in later ages it discloses itself by the dim growth of the sense of importance attached to those functionings of the tribe which dimly elicit its discrimination. But soon an inversion takes place. These modes of functioning are interpreted by some restless intellects of the tribe. The behaviour patterns then, in addition to their own intrinsic value for tribal life, take on the rôle of an apparatus of expression. They become linked to an intellectual construction. The behaviour patterns, with their entwined emotions, evoke the apprehension of the construction. Conversely, the entertainment of the construction constitutes an urge towards the modes of behaviour. In this way, the ceremonies with their output of emotion become the mode of expression for the ideas; and the ideas become an interpretation of the ceremonies. This is the account of the primitive origination of the linkage of an idea to an apparatus of expression.

The linkage between an idea and its expression has been described above as being 'interpretation'. Some analysis of this concept of 'interpretation' has now to be made. Two behaviour patterns mutually interpret each other, only when some common factor of experience is realized in the enactment of either pattern. The common factor constitutes the reason for the transition from one pattern to the other pattern. Each pattern interprets the other as expressive of that common factor. Here a behaviour-pattern is merely another phrase for a mode of experience. Thus, in this sense, the entertainment of a myth is one behaviour-pattern, and a tribal dance, or a Court ceremonial, is another behaviour pattern.

SECTION IX. But after all, it is the blunt truth that we want. The final contentment of our aims requires something more than vulgar substitutes, or subtle evasions, however delicate. The indirections of truth can never satisfy us. Our purposes seek their main justification in sheer matter-of-fact. All the rest is addition, however important, to this foundation. Apart from blunt truth, our lives sink decadently amid the perfume of hints and suggestions.

The blunt truth that we require is the conformal correspondence of clear and distinct Appearance to Reality. In human experience, clear and distinct Appearance is primarily sense-perception. The blunt truth required for sense-perception is the truth of the first type, already partially discussed in Section IV of this Chapter. In that section the doctrine was developed that the prehension of a sensum, as an apparent object qualifying a region, involved for that prehension a subjective form also involving that sensum as a factor. We enjoy the green foliage of the spring greenly: we enjoy the sunset with an emotional pattern including among its elements the colours and the contrasts of the vision. It is this that makes Art possible: it is this that procures the glory of perceived nature. For if the subjective form of reception be not conformal to the objective sensa, then the values of the percept would be at the mercy of the chance make-up of the other components in that experience. For example, in the intuition of a multiplicity of three or four objects, the mere number imposes no subjective form. It is merely a condition regulating some pattern of effective components. In abstraction from those components, mere triplicity can dictate no subjective form for its prehension. But green can. And there lies the difference between the sensa and the abstract mathematical forms.

The steady values derived from sense-perception, which are there even when disregarded and even when jarring with other emotions, exist because the sensa themselves enter into the subjective forms of their physical prehensions.

SECTION X. The point to be decided is whether the green meadow in spring-time, as it appears to us, in any direct way conforms to the happenings within the region of the meadow, and more particularly within the regions of the blades of grass. Have we any grounds for the belief that in some way things really are in those regions as our senses perceive those regions? In the first place, such conformation evidently cannot arise from the necessities of nature. The delusive perceptions prove that. Double vision, and images due to reflexion and refraction of light, show that the appearance of regions may be quite irrelevant to the happenings within regions. Appearances are finally controlled by the functionings of the animal body. These functionings and the happenings within the contemporary regions are both derived from a common past, highly relevant to both. It is thereby pertinent to ask, whether the animal body and the external regions are not attuned together, so that under normal circumstances, the appearances conform to natures within the regions.

The attainment of such conformation would belong to

the perfection of nature in respect to the higher types of its animal life. There is no necessity about it. Evidently there is failure, interference, and only partial adjustment. But we have to ask whether nature does not contain within itself a tendency to be in tune, an Eros urging towards perfection. This question cannot be discussed without passing beyond the narrow grounds of the truth-relation.

CHAPTER XVII

BEAUTY

SECTION I. Beauty is the mutual adaptation of the several factors in an occasion of experience. Thus in its primary sense Beauty is a quality which finds its exemplification in actual occasions: or put conversely, it is a quality in which such occasions can severally participate. There are gradations in Beauty and in types of Beauty.

"Adaptation" implies an end. Thus Beauty is only defined when the aim of the 'adaptation' has been analysed. This aim is twofold. It is in the first place, the absence of mutual inhibition among the various prehensions, so that the intensities of subjective form, which naturally and properly—or in one word, conformally—arise from the objective contents of the various prehensions, do not inhibit each other. When this aim is secured, there is the minor form of beauty, the absence of painful clash, the absence of vulgarity. In the second place, there is the major form of Beauty. This form presupposes the first form, and adds to it the condition that the conjunction in one synthesis of the various prehensions introduces new contrasts of objective content with objective content. These contrasts introduce new conformal intensities of feelings natural to each of them, and by so doing raise the intensities of conformal feeling in the primitive component feelings. Thus the parts contribute to the massive feeling of the whole, and the whole contributes to the intensity of feeling of the parts. Thus the subjective forms of these prehensions are severally and jointly interwoven in patterned contrasts. In other words, the perfection of Beauty is defined as being the perfection of Harmony; and the perfection of Harmony is defined in terms of the perfection of Subjective Form in detail and in final synthesis. Also the perfection of Subjective Form is defined in terms of 'Strength'. In the sense here meant, Strength has two factors, namely, variety of detail with effective contrast, which is Massiveness, and Intensity Proper which is comparative magnitude without reference to qualitative variety. But the maximum of intensity proper is finally dependent upon massiveness.

Section II. In order to understand this definition of Beauty, it is necessary to keep in mind three doctrines which belong to the metaphysical system in terms of which the World is being interpreted in these chapters. These three doctrines respectively have regard to the mutual relations (a) between the objective content of a prehension and the subjective form of that prehension, and (b) between the subjective forms of various prehensions in the same occasion, and (c) between the subjective form of a prehension and the spontaneity involved in the subjective aim of the prehending occasion. These doctrines are interconnected; but each of them introduces a principle which is not made explicit by the other two. They will now be successively explained:—

(a) It is held that every qualitative factor in the Universe is primarily a qualification of subjective form, so that the infinite variety of qualities involves the possibility of an infinite variety of subjective forms exemplifying those qualities. This does not mean that the subjective forms exemplifying various qualities are all equally prominent in human consciousness. Consciousness is a variable uncertain element which flickers uncertainly on the surface of experience. But it is part of the doctrine that the qualitative content of the object prehended enters into the qualities exemplified in the subjective form of that prehension. This is the general principle underlying (1) the doctrine of conformal [1] feelings, constituting the primary phase of the occasion, and (2) the doctrine of the qualitative valuations forming the activities of the mental pole, and (3) the doctrine of the valuations involved in the Primordial Nature of God, here also termed the Eros of the Universe. It follows that the subjective form of a prehension is partly dictated by the qualitative element in the objective content of that prehension. There is in fact initial conformation. It has been repeatedly stated above that this is what makes Art possible. Also the factor of compulsive determinism in the Universe depends on this principle.

This doctrine of conformation only holds for the qualitative side of the content of the objective datum. It follows that two exceptions arise to the more general statement that subjective form conforms to the objective datum. Both exceptions arise when abstraction has reached its extreme limit. The extremity of abstraction from all qualitative elements reduces pattern to bare mathematical form—for example, triplicity or the abstract relationship of sets of numbers, such as the squareness of the number four. Such forms by their very natures cannot qualify subjective form. For example, there is not a square-ness of emotion. Thus, except in an indirect fashion—such as the qualitative feelings of smoothness of a sphere, of spikeyness of a square, of amplitude of a volume—, the doctrine of conformation does not apply to mathematical pattern. Here pure mathematics in its strictest modern sense is in question.

[1] Cf. Part III, above, and *Process and Reality, passim,* as indexed.

Again the notion of an actual occasion—that is, of individual actuality—can be entertained in abstraction from any qualitative or mathematical components which in any sense are realized in its essence, either as objective data, or as subjective forms, or as relations between prehensions. A particular actuality can also be abstracted from the mode of its initial indication, so that in a later phase of experience it is entertained [2] as a bare 'It'. Only the qualitative components of an actuality in the datum can pass into the subjective form. The only actuality implicated in the subjective form is the immediate occasion in process of self-formation. The subjective form is that immediate subject in that state of subjective feeling. In the sense in which an actuality can be indicated as a bare *It* for objective prehension—in that sense it does not enter into the subjective form of the prehension.

(b) The second doctrine expresses the unity of the immediate occasion in process of formation. The subjective forms are merely contributions to the one fact which is the subjective feeling of the one occasion. There is a certain distribution among the various prehensions, by reason of the fact that each part of the total objective datum dictates its conformal qualitative reproduction in the subjective form. In so far as identical qualities occur in diverse objective data, then the efficiency of that quality in the subjective form must be dictated by a process of integration, and also by compatibility with the other qualitative feelings. Thus the distribution of subjective form among the separate prehensions refers primarily to the conformal origins of subjective form derived from the various components of the total objective datum.

(c) The third doctrine expresses the final autonomy of

[2] Cf. *The Concept of Nature,* Chapter I, and *Process and Reality,* Part II, Section III, Chapter IX, and Part III, Chapter IV.

the process. This process of the synthesis of subjective forms derived conformally is not settled by the antecedent fact of the data. For these data in their own separate natures do not carry any regulative principle for their synthesis. The regulative principle is derived from the novel unity which is imposed on them by the novel creature in process of constitution. Thus the immediate occasion from the spontaneity of its own essence must supply the missing determination for the synthesis of subjective form. Thus the future of the Universe, though conditioned by the immanence of its past, awaits for its complete determination the spontaneity of the novel individual occasions as in their season they come into being.

SECTION III. A distinction must now be made between two meanings of the term Beauty. There is the primary meaning which has been given in Section I of this chapter. This is Beauty realized in actual occasions which are the completely real things in the Universe. But in the analysis of an occasion, some parts of its objective content may be termed Beautiful by reason of their conformal contribution to the perfection of the subjective form of the complete occasion. This secondary sense of the term Beauty is more accurately to be considered as a definition of the term 'Beautiful'. The Beauty realized in an occasion depends both on the objective content from which that occasion originates and also on the spontaneity of the occasion. The objective content is 'beautiful' by reason of the Beauty that would be realized in that occasion by a fortunate exercise of its spontaneity. In the same way any part of the objective content is 'beautiful' in a still more indirect sense, capable of slight variations in meaning. It may be beautiful by reason of the Beauty that would be realized by a fortunate association with other data combined with a fortunate exercise of spontaneity by the occasion prehending it. But such supreme fortune is an ideal, not for this world. By the term 'beautiful' we usually mean the presupposition of the sort of objective environment which in that general social setting may be presupposed, and the sort of spontaneity which may be hoped for from the percipient occasions in question. We may be thinking of artists, or of cultivated men of the modern world, or of the ruck of mankind in a given city at a given time. But in all its senses, 'beautiful' means the inherent capability for the promotion of Beauty when functioning as a datum in a percipient occasion. When 'Beauty' is ascribed to any component in a datum, it is in this secondary sense.

SECTION IV. In the initial definition of Beauty, the notion of 'perfection' was tacitly introduced. The 'perfection' of subjective form means the absence from it of component feelings which mutually inhibit each other so that neither rises to the strength proper to it. But there are two meanings to 'inhibition' which must be carefully distinguished, since only one of them involves a derogation from perfection. Complete inhibition is an example of the finiteness of subjective form. It does not derogate from 'perfection'. There is then 'perfection' in its kind—that is to say, in its type of finiteness with such-and-such exclusions. But then the completely inhibited component subjective feeling is not properly a component of that subjective form. It is merely what would have been a component under other conditions. This sense of inhibition will be termed 'anæsthesia'.

The other meaning of inhibition—the meaning which derogates from perfection—involves the true active presence of both component feelings. In this case there is a third feeling of mutual destructiveness, so that one or other—or both—of the component feelings fails to attain the strength properly belonging to the prehension of the datum from which it arises. This is the feeling of evil in the most general sense, namely physical pain or mental evil, such as sorrow, horror, dislike. This type of inhibition will be termed 'æsthetic destruction'. Æsthetic destruction is a positive component in subjective form, and is inconsistent with perfection. The subjective experience of æsthetic destruction will be termed a 'discordant feeling'. Such a feeling is a factor in the subjective form of the percipient occasion. The more intense the discordant feeling, the further the retreat from perfection. A complex datum is 'objectively discordant' when among the type of percipients in question it will normally produce discordant feelings.

It follows from this discussion that in the definition of Beauty a distinction has been overlooked. The subjective feelings which are of the type of an emotional experience of æsthetic destruction must be excepted—or rather, as we shall find, belong to a class requiring special treatment. 'Perfection', properly so called, requires the exclusion of feelings of this class. On further consideration we shall find that always there are imperfect occasions better than occasions which realize some given type of perfection. There are in fact higher and lower perfections, and an imperfection aiming at a higher type stands above lower perfections. The most material and the most sensuous enjoyments are yet types of Beauty. Progress is founded upon the experience of discordant feelings. The social value of liberty lies in its production of discords. There are perfections beyond perfections. All realization is finite, and there is no perfection which is the infinitude of all perfections. Perfections of diverse types are among themselves discordant. Thus the contribution to Beauty which can be supplied by Discord —in itself destructive and evil—is the positive feeling of a

quick shift of aim from the tameness of outworn perfection
to some other ideal with its freshness still upon it. Thus the
value of Discord is a tribute to the merits of Imperfection.

SECTION V. A consideration of ancient Greek civilization
illustrates the value of discordance. The race was awakened
into progress by a great ideal of perfection. This ideal was
an immense advance upon the ideals which the surrounding
civilizations had produced. It was effective and realized in a
civilization which attained its proper beauty in human lives
to an extent not surpassed before or since. Its art, its theoretic
sciences, its modes of life, its literature, its philosophic
schools, its religious rituals, all conspired to express every
aspect of this wonderful ideal. Perfection was attained, and
with the attainment inspiration withered. With repetition
in successive generations, freshness gradually vanished.
Learning and learned taste replaced the ardour of adventure.
Hellenism was replaced by the Hellenistic epoch in which
genius was stifled by repetition. We can imagine the fate of
the Mediterranean civilization if it had been spared the ir-
ruptions of Barbarians and the rise of two new religions,
Christianity and Mahometanism:—For two thousand years
the Greek art-forms lifelessly repeated: The Greek schools
of philosophy, Stoic, Epicurean, Aristotelian, Neo-Platonic,
arguing with barren formulæ: Conventional histories: A
stabilized Government with the sanctity of ancient cere-
mony, supported by habitual pieties: Literature without
depth: Science elaborating details by deductions from unquestioned premises: Delicacies of feeling without robust-
ness of adventure.

This is no fancy picture. Despite all storms, something of
this sort did happen to the Byzantine Empire for a thousand
years; and despite the inroad of a new religion, Buddhism,
and despite Tartar invasions, something of this sort did hap-

pen to the vast Chinese Empire for a thousand years. The Chinese and the Greeks both achieved certain perfections of civilization—each worthy of admiration. But even perfection will not bear the tedium of indefinite repetition. To sustain a civilization with the intensity of its first ardour requires more than learning. Adventure is essential, namely, the search for new perfections.

SECTION VI. There is nothing to be astonished at in this conclusion. Spontaneity, originality of decision, belongs to the essence of each actual occasion. It is the supreme expression of individuality: its conformal subjective form is the freedom of enjoyment derived from the enjoyment of freedom. Freshness, zest, and the extra keenness of intensity arise from it. In a personal succession of occasions the upward path towards an ideal of perfection, with the end in sight, gives a thrill keener than any prolonged halt in a stage of attainment with the major variations completely tried out. Thus the wise advice is, Not to rest too completely in any continued realization of the same perfection of type. Each occasion in a society of occasions, and more particularly each occasion in a personal society, seeks this zest by finding some contrast between the Appearance resulting from the operations of the mental pole and the inherited Realities of the physical pole. When spontaneity is at its lowest, in practice negligible, the final trace of its operation is found in alternations backwards and forwards between alternative modes. This is the reason for the predominant importance of wave-transmission in physical nature.

But—considering occasions at their highest, with effective exercise of mental originality—the preservation of zest, after the attainment of a stage of perfection, first requires the exploration of all variations which do not introduce discordances into the type of perfection attained. The variation of styles and of decorative detail in mediaeval Gothic architecture may serve as an illustration. But such variations are easily exhausted. Bolder adventure is needed—the adventure of ideas, and the adventure of practice conforming itself to ideas. The best service that ideas can render is gradually to lift into the mental poles the ideal of another type of perfection which becomes a program for reform. An illustration of this is the service of Christianity by its introduction of new ideals for the social life of mankind. In other words, the ideal of a new society derived from a new defining characteristic is introduced.

SECTION VII. The doctrine has been stated that the experience of destruction is in itself evil; in fact that it constitutes the meaning of evil. We find now that this enunciation is much too simple-minded. Qualifications have to be introduced, though they leave unshaken the fundamental position that 'destruction as a dominant fact in the experience' is the correct definition of evil.

The intermingling of Beauty and Evil arises from the conjoint operation of three metaphysical principles:—(1) That all actualization is finite; (2) That finitude involves the exclusion of alternative possibility; (3) That mental functioning introduces into realization subjective forms conformal to relevant alternatives excluded from the completeness of physical realization.

The result is that the concerns of the actual world are deflected from harmony of feeling by the divergent tonalities introduced from the mental poles. The new occasion, even apart from its own spontaneous mentality, is thus confronted by basic disharmony in the actual world from which it springs. This is fortunate. For otherwise actuality would consist in a cycle of repetition, realizing only a finite group of possibilities. This was the narrow, stuffy doctrine of some ancient thinkers.

In an individual experience there are three ways of dealing with this disharmony of the world as given for initial prehension. Two of these ways have been discussed under the general term 'inhibition'. One way is termed 'Anæsthesia', and is the way of mere negative prehension. The other way is by positive realization with the positive feeling of discordance. In this case, the elimination of the sheer incompatibility is accompanied by a positive feeling of acute disruption of affective tone. This experience is the prehension of a qualitative datum which also imposes itself conformally on the subjective form. The third way depends on another principle, that a readjustment of the relative intensives of incompatible feelings can in some cases reduce them to compatibilities. This possibility arises when the clash in affective tones is a clash of intensities, and is not a sheer logical incompatibility of qualities. Thus two systems of prehensions may each be internally harmonious; but the two systems in the unity of one experience may be discordant, when the two intensities of their subjective forms are comparable in magnitude. There may be a discordance in feeling *this* as much as *that,* or in feeling *that* as much as *this.* But if one be kept at a lower intensity in the penumbra of feeling, it may act as a background to the other, providing a sense of massiveness and variety. This is the habitual state of human experience, a vast undiscriminated, or dimly discriminated background, of low intensity, and a clear foreground. This third way of eliminating discordance may be termed the method of 'reduction to a background'. Alternatively, it can equally well be termed the method of 'raising to a foreground'. For the avoidance of anæsthesia may come by the percipient occasion so functioning as to increase the intensity of subjective tone belonging to the prehension of one of the two systems.

Yet a fourth way now discloses itself, and this way is the explanation of the second and third ways for all occasions of experience where mentality has been developed into its higher activities. The second and the third ways, when they are not in truth this fourth way, are examples of the low type of mental functionings termed [3] 'physical purposes'. This fourth way is by spontaneity of the occasion so directing its mental functionings as to introduce a third system of prehensions, relevant to both the inharmonious systems. This novel system is such as radically to alter the distribution of intensities throughout the two given systems, and to change the importance of both in the final intensive experience of the occasion. This way is in fact the introduction of Appearance, and its use to preserve the massive qualitative variety of Reality from simplification by negative prehensions.

Appearance preserves this variety by concentrating on itself the intensities properly derived from Reality in the background. It is a procedure of simplification. For example, in Appearance the one Region supersedes the many individual occasions which compose it. Also qualities widely spread throughout the occasions in Reality are in Appearance inherent either in Regions occupied by these occasions, or in Regions having some definite association with such Regions. The Reality is in the background as explanatory of the procedures by which its rich variety has been saved. Also the variety of affective tone is now transferred to Appearance, with that amount of transformation which saves its compatibility. There is massive feeling transferred to Appearance, either of Harmony, or of Discords, or of Vul-

[3] Cf. *Process and Reality*, Part III, Ch. V, Sections VII, VIII.

garity, or of utter Commonplaceness. Appearance raises
into a distinctness of feeling, factors which can be generalized for salvation from the welter of Fact. In this way, it
emphasizes for individual experience widespread qualities
of feeling. Massiveness of subjective form is somewhat at
variance with the intensity of individual feelings. The variety of individual intensities thwart each other by their
diversities of objects. Appearance combines massiveness
with intensity by unifying the diversities of objects. It sim-
plifies the objects and precipitates upon the simplification
the qualitative contents of the given world. It saves intensities and massiveness at the cost of eliciting vivid experiences
of affective tones, good and bad. It makes possible the
height of Beauty and height of Evil; because it saves both
from a tame elimination or a tame scaling down.

SECTION VIII. We can now consider more closely the
grounds of Harmony and the grounds for the positive feeling of its destruction. It must be remembered that just
as there is a positive integral feeling of Harmony lost, so
there is a positive integral feeling of Harmony attained.
There is not only the fact of details in experience allowing
each other: beyond that there is the positive feeling of the
whole as Harmonious. Analogously there is the positive
feeling of the whole as discordant. Either feeling as the
case may be. The Harmony is felt as such, and so is the
Discord. Now Harmony is more than logical compatibility,
and Discord is more than logical incompatibility. Logicians
are not called in to advise artists. The key to the explanation is the understanding of the prehension of individuality.
This is the feeling of each objective factor as an individual
'It' with its own significance. The emotional significance
of an object as 'It', divorced from its qualitative aspects
at the moment presented, is one of the strongest forces

in human nature. It is at the base of family affection, and of the love of particular possessions. This trait is not a peculiarity of mankind alone. A dog smells in order to find out if the person in question is that *It* to which its affections cling. The room, or stable, may be full of odours, many of them for a dog sweeter. But he is not smelling for the pleasure of that smell, but to discover that *It* who claims his whole affection. An analogous substitute may deceive, but when discovered never does as well. The analogy may claim affection. But the original *It* commands a poignancy of feeling. This type of interest is at the base of much in archæology—an inscribed stone, executed at the command of and under the very eyes of Sennacherib. A really admirable replica by a modern workman lacks interest, except for certain purposes of scholarship. The worship of relics touches upon the pathology of such concerns.

Undoubtedly the emotional value of particular individuality arises from the generalization of emotions, so as to get rid of their mere sensory elements. Such generalized emotional qualities are love, admiration, the feeling of exquisiteness, the feeling of worth, hate, horror, the general feeling of association, that is of particular objects entwined with one's own existence. The successive immanence of occasion after occasion in the life of the soul will in the present occasion of that life include the cumulation of the successive prehensions of some particular object. In the various prehensions of it new qualities secure prominence, original qualities are present with some difference. There is thus a gradual elimination of the more special types of quality, which vary and fluctuate, from conformal effectiveness in the tone of the final prehensions. Generalized aromas take their place—the basic feelings of lifelong devotion, of lifelong repulsion, or of æsthetic excellence. Thus the indication of that *It,* partly by its status in the pattern of experience and partly by its immediate exhibition of minor qualities, produces a strong sharp-cut emotional tone of dominating significance. The significance is not merely for the general complex of subjective form in the immediate percipient. It is also reflected back onto the original objective *It.* Thus the *It* which is indicated by minor details of a status and quality is finally prehended in Appearance as *It* with its permanent character.

For epistemology of the sensationalist school, this final prehension is construed as an interpretation of original sense-impressions. But in this final prehension there is no logical train, inductive or deductive. The percipient directly integrates antecedent real functionings of that object in antecedent occasions of the soul's life. The so-called 'interpretation' is the conflation of real history, and is not a top-dressing of conjecture. The notion of purely qualitative sense-impressions as the origin of experience has no warrant in direct intuition.

For the understanding of Harmony and Discord it is essential to remember that strength of experience, in massiveness and in intensity, depends upon the substratum of detail being composed of significant individuals. Appearance has been constituted fortunately when it has simplified the welter of occasions, individually insignificant, into a few significant individual things. It has 'interpreted' the world in terms of factors received from the world—so that each factor of interpretation can be substantiated by direct intuition—if only consciousness can analyse so far. Such is fortunate experience. It derives its strength from the concurrence of significant individual objects, and its own existence adds to the significance of those objects. This is the enjoyment of Harmony, and a factor in this enjoyment is the intuition that the future, where its objective immortality lies, is increasing the grounds for Harmony. Destruction is absent.

But there can be intense experience without Harmony. In this event, there is Destruction of the significant characters of individual objects. When the direct feeling of such Destruction dominates the whole, there is the immediate feeling of evil, and the anticipation of destructive or weakened data for the future. Harmony is bound up with the preservation of the individual significance of detail, and Discord consists in its destruction. In Discord there is always a frustration. But even Discord may be preferable to a feeling of slow relapse into general anæsthesia, or into tameness which is its prelude. Perfection at a low level ranks below Imperfection with higher aim.

A mere qualitative Harmony within an experience comparatively barren of objects of high significance is a debased type of Harmony, tame, vague, deficient in outline and intention. It is one property of a beautiful system of objects that as entertained in a succession of occasions adapted for its enjoyment, it quickly builds up a system of apparent objects with vigorous characters. The sculptures on the famous porch of the Cathedral at Chartres at once assume individual importance with definite character while performing their office as details in the whole. There is not a mere pattern of qualitative beauty. There are those statues, each with its individual beauty, and all lending themselves to the beauty of the whole. Enduring Individuality in the details is the backbone of strong experience.

Art at its highest exemplifies the metaphysical doctrine of the interweaving of absoluteness upon relativity. In the work of art the relativity becomes the harmony of the composition, and the absoluteness is the claim for separate individuality advanced by component factors. We also understand how Appearance leads to the Aristotelian doctrine of a substantial, enduring *It* with essential character. The point of view expresses important truth. Hence its obviousness. The æsthetic importance of this apparent individuality lies in its claim to attention. In so far as Appearance has a truth-relation to Reality such enduring individuality indicates a real society important for its control of the future. The claim to æsthetic attention thus represents the indirect importance of anticipation and purpose as factors in the immediate enjoyment of the immediate percipient. The danger of a street-crossing is for the pedestrian a regulative factor in the æsthetic values of the apparent scene. The concept of completely passive contemplation in abstraction from action and purpose is a fallacious extreme. It omits the final regulative factor in the æsthetic complex. But of course there are large diversities of action and large diversities of purpose. The final point is that the foundation of Reality upon which Appearance rests can never be neglected in the evaluation of Appearance.

CHAPTER XVIII

TRUTH AND BEAUTY

SECTION I. It appears from the discussion in the two previous chapters of this Part that Beauty is a wider, and more fundamental, notion than Truth. Of course both terms have been used here in a very generalized sense. Narrower usages are not marked off from the wider meanings, here employed, by anything except habitual presupposition respecting importance and triviality. Beauty is the internal conformation of the various items of experience with each other, for the production of maximum effectiveness. Beauty thus concerns the inter-relations of the various components of Reality, and also the inter-relations of the various components of Appearance, and also the relations of Appearance to Reality. Thus any part of experience can be beautiful. The teleology of the Universe is directed to the production of Beauty. Thus any system of things which in any wide sense is beautiful is to that extent justified in its existence. It may however fail in another sense, by inhibiting more Beauty than it creates. Thus the system, though in a sense beautiful, is on the whole evil in that environment. But Truth has a narrower meaning in two ways. First, Truth, in any important sense, merely concerns the relations of Appearance to Reality. It is the conformation of Appearance to Reality. But in the second place the notion of 'conformation' in the case of Truth is narrower than that in the case of Beauty. For the truth-relation requires that the two relata have some factor in common.

In itself, and apart from other factors, there seems to be no special importance about the truth-relation. There is the bare fact of a certain limited relationship of identity. There is nothing in such a fact which will necessarily dictate any corresponding type of subjective form within the percipient occasion. Still less is there any reason why such influence as a truth-relation does have upon subjective form should be in the direction of the promotion of Beauty. In other words, a truth-relation is not necessarily beautiful. It may not even be neutral. It may be evil. Thus Beauty is left as the one aim which by its very nature is self-justifying. The Discord in the Universe arises from the fact that modes of Beauty are various, and not of necessity compatible. And yet some admixture of Discord is a necessary factor in the transition from mode to mode. The objective life of the past and the future in the present is an inevitable element of disturbance. Discord may take the form of freshness or hope, or it may be horror or pain. In the higher types of mentality the note of displacement impresses its qualitative character upon subjective form with peculiar keenness:—welcome or antagonism. Wide purpose is in its own nature beautiful by reason of its contribution to the massiveness of experience. It increases the dimensions of the experient subject, adds to its ambit. Then the destruction of immediate realizations for the sake of purpose is, on the face of it, a sacrifice to Harmony.

SECTION II. Notwithstanding the possible unseasonableness of the truth-relation, the general importance of Truth for the promotion of Beauty is overwhelming. After all has been said, yet the truth-relation remains the simple, direct mode of realizing Harmony. Other ways are indirect. and indirectness is at the mercy of the environment. There is a blunt force about Truth, which in the subjective form of its prehension is akin to cleanliness—namely, the removal of dirt, which is unwanted irrelevance. The sense of directness which it carries with it, sustains the upstanding individualities so necessary for the beauty of a complex. Falsehood is corrosive.

Truth is various in its extent, its modes, and its relevance. But an apparent object, beautiful beyond the hope of antecedent imagination, as it functions in experience is realizing some hidden, penetrating Truth with a keenness beyond compare. The type of Truth required for the final stretch of Beauty is a discovery and not a recapitulation. The Truth that for such extremity of Beauty is wanted is that truth-relation whereby Appearance summons up new resources of feeling from the depths of Reality. It is a Truth of feeling, and not a Truth of verbalization. The relata in Reality must lie below the stale presuppositions of verbal thought. The Truth of supreme Beauty lies beyond the dictionary meanings of words.

When Appearance has to Reality, in some important direct sense, a truth-relation, there is a security about the Beauty attained, that is to say, a pledge for the future.

From these functions of Truth in the service of Beauty, the realization of Truth becomes in itself an element promoting Beauty of feeling. Consciousness, with its dim intuitions, welcomes a factor so generally on the right side, so habitually necessary. The element of anticipation under the influence of Truth is in a deep sense satisfied, and thus adds a factor to the immediate Harmony. Thus Truth, in itself and apart from special reasons to the contrary, becomes self-justifying. It is accompanied by a sense of rightness in the deepest Harmony. But Truth derives this self-justify-

ing power from its services in the promotion of Beauty.
Apart from Beauty, Truth is neither good, nor bad.

SECTION III. Art is purposeful adaptation of Appearance
to Reality. Now 'purposeful adaptation' implies an end, to
be obtained with more or less success. This end, which is the
purpose of art, is two-fold,—namely Truth and Beauty. The
perfection of art has only one end, which is Truthful Beauty.
But some measure of success has been reached, when either
Truth or Beauty is gained. In the absence of Truth, Beauty
is on a lower level, with a defect of massiveness. In the
absence of Beauty, Truth sinks to triviality. Truth matters
because of Beauty.

The relation of 'appearance' to 'reality' is such that in the
final phase of experience ['satisfaction' or 'anticipation'] the
reality of the primary phase is prehended with subjective
form as though it participated in the qualitative characters
of 'appearance'. When in fact the reality does so participate,
the relation is truthful. When it does not so participate, the
relation is falsifying.

Beauty, so far as concerns its exemplification in Appearance alone, does not necessarily involve the attainment of
truth. Appearance is beautiful when the qualitative objects
which compose it are interwoven in patterned contrasts, so
that the prehensions of the whole of its parts produces the
fullest harmony of mutual support. By this it is meant, that
in so far as the qualitative characters of the whole and the
parts pass into the subjective forms of their prehensions, the
whole heightens the feelings for the parts, and the parts
heighten the feelings for the whole, and for each other.
This is harmony of feeling; and with harmony of feeling
its objective content is beautiful.

It is evident that when appearance has obtained truth

in addition to beauty, harmony in a wider sense has been produced. For in this sense, it also involves the relation of appearance to reality. Thus, when the adaptation of appearance to reality has obtained truthful Beauty, there is a perfection of art. That is to say, if there be art: for the result may be the slow outcome of nature. Such an outcome may be due to some wide universal purpose. But it will not be due to quick purposeful adaptation originated by finite creatures, the sort of adaptation usually termed art.

Goodness is the third member of the trinity which traditionally has been assigned as the complex aim of art—namely, Truth, Beauty, and Goodness. With the point of view here adopted, Goodness must be denied a place among the aims of art. For Goodness is a qualification belonging to the constitution of reality, which in any of its individual actualizations is better or worse. Good and evil lie in depths and distances below and beyond appearance. They solely concern inter-relations within the real world. The real world is good when it is beautiful. Art has essentially to do with perfections attainable by purposeful adaptation of appearance. With a larger view and a deeper analysis, some instance of the perfection of art may diminish the good otherwise inherent in some specific situation as it passes into its objective actuality for the future. Unseasonable art is analogous to an unseasonable joke, namely, good in its place, but out of place a positive evil. It is a curious fact that lovers of art who are most insistent on the doctrine of 'art for art's sake' are apt to be indignant at the banning of art for the sake of other interests. The charge of immorality is not refuted by pointing to the perfection of art. Of course it is true that the defence of morals is the battle-cry which best rallies stupidity against change. Perhaps countless ages ago respectable amœbæ refused to migrate from ocean to dry land—refusing in defence of morals. One incidental service of art to society lies in its adventurousness.

SECTION IV. It is a tribute to the strength of the sheer craving for freshness, that change, whose justification lies in aim at the distant ideal, should be promoted by Art which is the adaptation of immediate Appearance for immediate Beauty. Art neglects the safety of the future for the gain of the present. In so doing it is apt to render its Beauty thin. But after all, there must be some immediate harvest. The good of the Universe cannot lie in indefinite postponement. The Day of Judgment is an important notion: but that Day is always with us. Thus Art takes care of the immediate fruition, here and now; and in so doing is apt to lose some depth by reason of the immediate fruition at which it is aiming. Its business is to render the Day of Judgment a success, now. The effect of the present on the future is the business of morals. And yet the separation is not so easy. For the inevitable anticipation adds to the present a qualitative element which profoundly affects its whole qualitative harmony.

There is a paradox concerning morals to be added to the one concerning art. Morals consists in the aim at the ideal, and at its lowest it concerns the prevention of relapse to lower levels. Thus stagnation is the deadly foe of morality. Yet in human society the champions of morality are on the whole the fierce opponents of new ideals. Mankind has been afflicted with low-toned moralists, objecting to expulsion from some Garden of Eden. And in a way they are right. For after all we can aim at nothing except from the standpoint of a well-assimilated system of customs—that is, of *mores*. The fortunate changes are made 'Hand in hand, with wand'ring steps and slow'.

SECTION V. The factor in experience that renders Art possible is consciousness.[1] Of course consciousness, like everything else, is in a sense indefinable. It is just itself and must be experienced. But, also like other things, it is the emergent quality illustrated in the essence of a conjunction of circumstances. It is a qualitative aspect of that conjunction. We can ask therefore for an analysis of the details whose conjunction in experience issues in consciousness.

Consciousness is that quality which emerges into the objective content as the result of the conjunction of a fact and a supposition about that fact. It passes conformally from the complex object to the subjective form of the prehension. It is the quality inherent in the contrast between Actuality and Ideality, that is, between the products of the physical pole and the mental pole in experience. When that contrast is a feeble element in experience, then consciousness is there merely in germ, as a latent capacity. So far as the contrast is well-defined and prominent, the occasion includes a developed consciousness. That portion of experience irradiated by consciousness is only a selection. Thus consciousness is a mode of attention. It provides the extreme of selective emphasis. The spontaneity of an occasion finds its chief outlets, first in the direction of consciousness, and secondly in production of ideas to pass into the area of conscious attention. Thus consciousness, spontaneity, and art are closely interconnected. But that art which arises within clear consciousness is only a specialization of the more widely distributed art within dim consciousness or within the unconscious activities of experience.

Consciousness is the weapon which strengthens the artificiality of an occasion of experience. It raises the impor-

[1] Cf. *P. R.,* Part II, Chapter VII, Section II, and Part III, Chapter II, Section IV, and Chapters IV and V.

tance of the final Appearance relatively to that of the initial Reality. Thus it is Appearance which in consciousness is clear and distinct, and it is Reality which lies dimly in the background with its details hardly to be distinguished in consciousness. What leaps into conscious attention is a mass of presuppositions about Reality rather than the intuitions of Reality itself. It is here that the liability to error arises. The deliverances of clear and distinct consciousness require criticism by reference to elements in experience which are neither clear nor distinct. On the contrary, they are dim, massive, and important. These dim elements provide for art that final background of tone apart from which its effects fade. The type of Truth which human art seeks lies in the eliciting of this background to haunt the object presented for clear consciousness.

SECTION VI. The merit of Art in its service to civilization lies in its artificiality and its finiteness. It exhibits for consciousness a finite fragment of human effort achieving its own perfection within its own limits. Thus the mere toil for the slavish purpose of prolonging life for more toil or for mere bodily gratification, is transformed into the conscious realization of a self-contained end, timeless within time. The work of Art is a fragment of nature with the mark on it of a finite creative effort, so that it stands alone, an individual thing detailed from the vague infinity of its background. Thus Art heightens the sense of humanity. It gives an elation of feeling which is supernatural. A sunset is glorious, but it dwarfs humanity and belongs to the general flow of nature. A million sunsets will not spur on men towards civilization. It requires Art to evoke into consciousness the finite perfections which lie ready for human achievement.

Consciousness itself is the product of art in its lowliest

form. For it results from the influx of ideality into its contrast with reality, with the purpose of reshaping the latter into a finite, select appearance. But consciousness having emerged from Art at once produces the new specialized art of the conscious animals—in particular human art. In a sense art is a morbid overgrowth of functions which lie deep in nature. It is the essence of art to be artificial. But it is its perfection to return to nature, remaining art. In short art is the education of nature. Thus, in its broadest sense, art is civilization. For civilization is nothing other than the unremitting aim at the major perfections of harmony.

SECTION VII. The human body is an instrument for the production of art in the life of the human soul. It concentrates upon those elements in human experience selected for conscious perception intensities of subjective form derived from components dismissed into shadow. It thereby enhances the value of that appearance which is the subject-matter for art. In this way the work of art is a message from the Unseen. It unlooses depths of feeling from behind the frontier where precision of consciousness fails. The starting-point for the highly developed human art is thus to be sought amid the cravings generated by the physiological functionings of the body. The origin of art lies in the craving for re-enaction. In some mode of repetition we need by our personal actions, or perceptions, to dramatize the past and the future, so as to re-live the emotional life of ourselves, and of our ancestors. There is a biological law—which however must not be pressed too far—that in some vague sense the embryo in the womb reproduces in its life-history features of ancestors in remote geologic epochs. Thus art has its origin in ceremonial [2] evolutions from which issue play, religious ritual, tribal ceremonial, dance, pictures

[2] Cf. *Religion in the Making*, Ch. I, Section III.

on caves, poetic literature, prose, music. In this list each member in its simpler forms enshrines some effort to reproduce a vivid experience flashed out among the necessities of daily life. But the secret of art lies in its freedom. The emotion and some elements of the experience itself are lived again divorced from their necessity. The strain is over, but the joy of intense feeling remains. Originally the intensity arose from some dire necessity; but in art it has outlived the compulsion which was its origin. If Odysseus among the shades could hear Homer chanting his Odyssey, he then re-enacted with free enjoyment the perils of his wanderings.

The arts of civilization now spring from many origins, physical and purely imaginative. But they are all sublimations, and sublimations of sublimations, of the simple craving to enjoy freely the vividness of life which first arises in moments of necessity. With a slight shift of the focus of our attention, Art can be described as a psychopathic reaction of the race to the stresses of its existence. From that point of view, Odysseus as he listened to Homer was evading the Furies. This psychopathic function of Art is lost when the conviction of Truth is absent. It is here that the concept of Art as the pursuit of Beauty is shallow. Art has a curative function in human experience when it reveals as in a flash intimate, absolute Truth regarding the Nature of Things. This service of Art is even hindered by trivial truths of detail. Such petty conformations place in the foreground the superficialities of sense-experience. Art performing this great service belongs to the essence of civilization. By the growth of such Art the adventure of mentality gains upon the physical basis of existence.

Science and Art are the consciously determined pursuit of Truth and of Beauty. In them the finite consciousness of mankind is appropriating as its own the infinite fecundity of nature. In this movement of the human spirit types of institutions and types of professions are evolved. Churches and Rituals, Monasteries with their dedicated lives, Universities with their search for knowledge, Medicine, Law, methods of Trade—they all represent that aim at civilization, whereby the conscious experience of mankind preserves for its use the sources of Harmony.

CHAPTER XIX

ADVENTURE

SECTION I. The notion of civilization is very baffling. We all know what it means. It suggests a certain ideal for life on this earth, and this ideal concerns both the individual human being and also societies of men. A man can be civilized, and a whole society can be civilized; although the senses are somewhat different in the two cases.

Yet civilization is one of those general notions that are very difficult to define. We pronounce upon particular instances. We can say *this* is civilized, or *that* is savage. Yet somehow the general notion is elusive. Thus we proceed by examples. During the last six centuries, the culture of Europe has guided itself by example. The Greeks and Romans at their best period have been taken as the standard of civilization. We have aimed at reproducing the excellencies of these societies—preferably the society of Athens in its prime.

These standards have served the Western races well. But the procedure has its disadvantages. It is backward looking, and it is limited to one type of social excellence. Today the world is passing into a new stage of its existence. New knowledge, and new technologies have altered the proportions of things. The particular example of an ancient society sets too static an ideal, and neglects the whole range of opportunity. It is really not sufficient to direct attention to the best that has been said and done in the ancient world. The result is static, repressive, and promotes a decadent habit of mind.

Also I suggest that the Greeks themselves were not backward looking, or static. Compared to their neighbours, they were singularly unhistorical. They were speculative, adventurous, eager for novelty. The most un-Greek thing that we can do, is to copy the Greeks. For emphatically they were not copyists.

Another danger in forming our notions of civilization is to concentrate exclusively upon passive, critical qualities concerned chiefly with the Fine Arts. Such qualities are an important element in a civilized society. But civilization is more than the appreciation of the Fine Arts. We must not tie it down to museums and studios.

I put forward as a general definition of civilization, that a civilized society is exhibiting the five qualities of Truth, Beauty, Adventure, Art, Peace.

Here by the last quality of Peace, I am not referring to political relations. I mean a quality of mind steady in its reliance that fine action is treasured in the nature of things.

It is impossible in the short space of five chapters to discuss all the various questions which are suggested by these notions. In this chapter I will concentrate upon a few points in philosophy and history which throw light upon the various functions of these elements in civilization.

SECTION II. From the three preceding chapters and with this short explanation as to Peace, let us assume for the moment that Truth, Beauty, and Peace are sufficiently obvious as to their meanings. We will now concentrate upon Adventure and Art as necessary elements in civilization. It is in respect to these two factors that prevalent concepts of civilization are weakest.

The foundation of all understanding of sociological

theory—that is to say, of all understanding of human life—
is that no static maintenance of perfection is possible. This
axiom is rooted in the nature of things. Advance or Decadence are the only choices offered to mankind. The pure
conservative is fighting against the essence of the universe.
This doctrine requires justification. It is implicitly denied
in the learned tradition derived from ancient thought.

The doctrine is founded upon three metaphysical principles. One principle is that the very essence of real actuality—that is, of the completely real—is *process*. Thus each
actual thing is only to be understood in terms of its becoming and perishing. There is no halt in which the actuality
is just its static self, accidentally played upon by qualifications derived from the shift of circumstances. The converse
is the truth.

The static notion, here rejected, is derived by two different
paths from ancient thought. Plato in the earlier period of
his thought, deceived by the beauty of mathematics intelligible in unchanging perfection, conceived of a super-world
of ideas, forever perfect and forever interwoven. In his
latest phase he sometimes repudiates the notion, though he
never consistently banishes it from his thought. His later
Dialogues circle round seven notions, namely—The Ideas,
The Physical Elements, The Psyche, The Eros, The Harmony, The Mathematical Relations, The Receptacle. I mention them because I hold that all philosophy is in fact an
endeavour to obtain a coherent system out of some modification of these notions. They largely explain themselves as to
their general meanings, apart from any precise coördination.
The Psyche is, of course, the Soul; the Eros is the urge
towards the realization of ideal perfection. The Receptacle
is expressly stated by Plato to be a difficult notion; so that we
may safely put aside easy explanations of it. I explain it to

myself as the conception of the essential unity of the Universe conceived as an actuality, and yet in abstraction from the 'life and motion' in which all actualities must partake. If we omit the Psyche and the Eros, we should obtain a static world. The 'life and motion', which are essentials in Plato's later thought, are derived from the operation of these two factors. But Plato left no system of metaphysics.

Thus in the modern development of these seven metaphysical notions, we should start from the notion of actuality as in its essence a process. This process involves a physical side which is the perishing of the past as it transforms itself into a new creation. It also involves a mental side which is the Soul entertaining ideas.

The Soul thereby by synthesis creates a new fact which is the Appearance woven out of the old and the new—a compound of reception and anticipation, which in its turn passes into the future. The final synthesis of these three complexes is the end to which its indwelling Eros urges the soul. Its good resides in the realization of a strength of many feelings fortifying each other as they meet in the novel unity. Its evil lies in the clash of vivid feelings, denying to each other their proper expansion. Its triviality lies in the anæsthesia by which evil is avoided. In this way through sheer omission, fewer, fainter feelings constitute the final Appearance. Evil is the half-way house between perfection and triviality. It is the violence of strength against strength.

Aristotle introduced the static fallacy by another concept which has infected all subsequent philosophy. He conceived of primary substances as the static foundations which received the impress of qualification. In the case of human experience, a modern version of the same notion is Locke's metaphor of the mind as an 'empty cabinet' receiving the impress of ideas. Thus for Locke the reality does not reside in the process but in the static recipient of process. According to the versions of Aristotle and Locke, one primary substance cannot be a component in the nature of another primary substance. Thus the interconnections of primary substances must be devoid of the substantial reality of the primary substances themselves. With this doctrine, the conjunction of actualities has, in various shapes, been a problem throughout modern philosophy—both for metaphysics and for epistemology. The taint of Aristotelian Logic has thrown the whole emphasis of metaphysical thought upon substantives and adjectives, to the neglect of prepositions and conjunctions. This Aristotelian doctrine is in this book summarily denied. The process is itself the actuality, and requires no antecedent static cabinet. Also the processes of the past, in their perishing, are themselves energizing as the complex origin of each novel occasion. The past is the reality at the base of each new actuality. The process is its absorption into a new unity with ideals and with anticipation, by the operation of the creative Eros.

SECTION III. I now pass to the second metaphysical principle. It is the doctrine that every occasion of actuality is in its own nature finite. There is no totality which is the harmony of all perfections. Whatever is realized in any one occasion of experience necessarily excludes the unbounded welter of contrary possibilities. There are always 'others', which might have been and are not. This finiteness is not the result of evil, or of imperfection. It results from the fact that there are possibilities of harmony which either produce evil in joint realization, or are incapable of such conjunction. This doctrine is a commonplace in the fine arts. It also is— or should be—a commonplace of political philosophy. History can only be understood by seeing it as the theatre of diverse groups of idealists respectively urging ideals incom-

patible for conjoint realization. You cannot form any historical judgment of right or wrong by considering each
group separately. The evil lies in the attempted conjunction.

This principle of intrinsic incompatibility has an important bearing upon our conception of the nature of God. The
concept of impossibility such that God himself cannot surmount it, has been for centuries quite familiar to theologians.
Indeed, apart from it there would be difficulty in conceiving
any determinate divine nature. But curiously enough, so
far as I know, this notion of incompatibility has never been
applied to ideals in the Divine realization. We must conceive the Divine Eros as the active entertainment of all
ideals, with the urge to their finite realization, each in its
due season. Thus a process must be inherent in God's
nature, whereby his infinity is acquiring realization.

It is unnecessary to pursue theology further. But the point
stands out that the conceptual entertainment of incompatibilities is possible, and so is their conceptual comparison.
Also there is the synthesis of conceptual entertainment with
physical realization. The idea conceptually entertained may
be identical with the idea exemplified in the physical fact;
or it may be different, compatible or incompatible. This
synthesis of the ideal with the real is just what happens in
each finite occasion.

Thus in every civilization at its culmination we should
find a large measure of realization of a certain type of perfection. This type will be complex and will admit of variation of detail, this way or that. The culmination can maintain itself at its height so long as fresh experimentation
within the type is possible. But when these minor variations
are exhausted, one of two things must happen. Perhaps the
society in question lacks imaginative force. Staleness then
sets in. Repetition produces a gradual lowering of vivid

appreciation. Convention dominates. A learned orthodoxy suppresses adventure.

The last flicker of originality is exhibited by the survival of satire. Satire does not necessarily imply a decadent society, though it flourishes upon the outworn features in the social system. It was characteristic that at the close of the silver age of Roman culture, shortly after the deaths of the younger Pliny and of Tacitus, the satirist Lucian was born. Again, at the close of the silver age of the Renaissance culture, during the eighteenth century, Voltaire and Edward Gibbon perfected satire in their various styles. Satire was natural to the age as it neared the American Revolution, the French Revolution, and the Industrial Revolution. Again a new epoch arose, the first phase of modern industrialism. It flourished with consistent growth for a hundred and fifty years. Its central period has been termed the Victorian Epoch. Within that period, the European races created new methods of industry; they peopled North America; they developed trade with the old civilizations of Asia; they gave new directions to literature and to art; they re-fashioned their forms of government. The nineteenth century was an epoch of civilized advance—humanitarian, scientific, industrial, literary, political. But at length it wore itself out. The crash of the Great War marked its end, and marked the decisive turn of human life into some new direction as yet not fully understood. But the close of the epoch has been marked by the rise of satire—Lytton Strachey in England, Sinclair Lewis in the United States of America. Satire is the last flicker of originality in a passing epoch as it faces the onroad of staleness and boredom. Freshness has gone: bitterness remains. The prolongation of outworn forms of life means a slow decadence in which there is repetition without any fruit in the reaping of value. There may be high survival power. For decadence, undisturbed by originality or by external forces, is a slow process. But the values of life are slowly ebbing. There remains the show of civilization, without any of its realities.

There is an alternative to this slow decline. A race may exhaust a form of civilization without having exhausted its own creative springs of originality. In that case, a quick period of transition may set in, which may or may not be accompanied by dislocations involving widespread unhappiness. Such periods are Europe at the close of the Middle Ages, Europe during the comparatively long Reformation Period, Europe at the end of the eighteenth century. Also let us hope that our present epoch is to be viewed as a period of change to a new direction of civilization, involving in its dislocations a minimum of human misery. And yet surely the misery of the Great War was sufficient for any change of epoch.

These quick transitions to new types of civilization are only possible when thought has run ahead of realization. The vigour of the race has then pushed forward into the adventure of imagination, so as to anticipate the physical adventures of exploration. The world dreams of things to come, and then in due season arouses itself to their realization. Indeed all physical adventure which is entered upon of set purpose involves an adventure of thought regarding things as yet unrealized. Before Columbus set sail for America, he had dreamt of the far East, and of the round world, and of the trackless ocean. Adventure rarely reaches its predetermined end. Columbus never reached China. But he discovered America.

Sometimes adventure is acting within limits. It can then calculate its end, and reach it. Such adventures are the ripples of change within one type of civilization, by which an epoch of given type preserves its freshness. But, given the vigour of adventure, sooner or later the leap of imagination reaches beyond the safe limits of the epoch, and beyond the safe limits of learned rules of taste. It then produces the dislocations and confusions marking the advent of new ideals for civilized effort.

A race preserves its vigour so long as it harbours a real contrast between what has been and what may be; and so long as it is nerved by the vigour to adventure beyond the safeties of the past. Without adventure civilization is in full decay.

It is for this reason that the definition of culture as the knowledge of the best that has been said and done, is so dangerous by reason of its omission. It omits the great fact that in their day the great achievements of the past were the adventures of the past. Only the adventurous can understand the greatness of the past. In its day, the literature of the past was an adventure. Æschylus, Sophocles, Euripides were adventurers in the world of thought. To read their plays without any sense of new ways of understanding the world and of savouring its emotions is to miss the vividness which constitutes their whole value. But adventures are to the adventurous. Thus a passive knowledge of the past loses the whole value of its message. A living civilization requires learning; but it lies beyond it.

SECTION IV. The third metaphysical principle may be termed the principle of Individuality. It concerns the doctrine of Harmony; and its omission is, I think, the greatest gap in traditional discussions of that doctrine. Indeed, in recent times, with the predominance of the sensationalist doctrine of perception, modern views of the Harmony characterizing a great experience have reached their lowest point. This sensationalist doctrine concentrates attention upon a

mere qualitative harmony within an experience comparatively barren of objects of high significance. The complex
to which the term Harmony is applicable is conceived as a
mere spatio-temporal pattern of sensa. The Harmony to be
derived from such a complex belongs to a debased type—
tame, vague, deficient in outline and intention. At the best,
it can only excite by a sense of strangeness. At the worst, it
fades into insignificance. It lacks any strong, exciting element
capable of stirring the depths of feeling. Sense-perception,
despite its prominence in consciousness, belongs to the superficialities of experience. It is here that the Aristotelian doctrine of primary substances has done some of its worst harm.
For according to this doctrine no individual primary substance can enter into the complex of objects observed in any
occasion of experience. The qualifications of the soul are
thus confined to universals. According to the metaphysical
system that I suggest to you, this Aristotelian doctrine is a
complete mistake. The individual, real facts of the past lie
at the base of our immediate experience in the present. They
are the reality from which the occasion springs, the reality
from which it derives its source of emotion, from which it
inherits its purposes, to which it directs its passions. At the
base of experience there is a welter of feeling, derived from
individual realities or directed towards them. Thus for
strength of experience we require to discriminate the component factors, each as an individual 'It' with its own
significance.

Our lives are dominated by enduring things, each experienced as a unity of many occasions bound together by the
force of inheritance. Each such individual endurance collects into its unity the shifting qualities of its many occasions. Perhaps it is the thing we love, or perhaps it is the
thing we hate. There is a bare It—a real fact of the past,

stretching into the present, which concentrates upon itself the wealth of emotion derived from its many occasions. Such enduring individualities, as factors in experience, control a wealth of feeling, an amplitude of purpose, and a regulative power to subdue into background the residue of things belonging to the immensity of the past. Surely, this is what Descartes must have meant by the *realitas objectiva* which, according to his doctrine, clings more or less to our perceptions.

A complex experience which includes conscious attention to such enduring individualities at once unlooses a wealth of feeling far beyond anything derived from patterns of sensa, merely as such. The great Harmony is the harmony of enduring individualities, connected in the unity of a background. It is for this reason that the notion of freedom haunts the higher civilizations. For freedom, in any one of its many senses, is the claim for vigorous self-assertion.

In considering the process which constitutes the existence of an occasion of experience, the perception of the enduring individuals must belong to the final Appearance wherein the occasion terminates. For in the primary phase, the past is initiating the process in virtue of the energizing of its diverse individual occasions. This is the Reality from which the new occasion springs. The process is urged onward by operation of the mental pole providing conceptual subject-matter for synthesis with the Reality. There finally emerges the Appearance, which is the transformed Reality after synthesis with the conceptual valuations. The Appearance is a simplification by a process of emphasis and combination. Thus the enduring individuals, with their wealth of emotional significance, appear in the foreground. In the background there lie a mass of undistinguished occasions providing the environment with its vague emotional tone. In

a general sense, the Appearance is a work of Art, elicited
from the primary Reality. In so far as the Appearance emphasizes connections and qualities of connections which in
fact reside in the Reality, then the Appearance is truthful in
its relation to Reality. But the Appearance may have effected
connections, and have introduced qualities, which have no
counterpart in Reality. In that case, the occasion of experience contains in itself a falsehood, namely the disconnection
of its Appearance from its Reality. In any case, the Appearance is a simplification of Reality, reducing it to a foreground of enduring individuals and to a background of
undiscriminated occasions. Sense-perception belongs to Appearance. It is interpreted as indicating enduring individuals,
truthfully or otherwise.

Thus, the basis of a strong, penetrating experience of Harmony is an Appearance with a foreground of enduring individuals carrying with them a force of subjective tone, and
with a background providing the requisite connection. Undoubtedly, the Harmony is finally a Harmony of qualitative
feelings. But the introduction of the enduring individuals
evokes from the Reality a force of already harmonized feelings which no surface show of sensa can produce. It is not a
question of intellectual interpretation. There is a real conflation of fundamental feeling.

Thus civilization in its aim at fineness of feeling should so
arrange its social relations, and the relations of its members
to their natural environment, as to evoke into the experiences of its members Appearances dominated by the harmonies of forceful enduring things. In other words, Art
should aim at the production of individuality in the component details of its compositions. It cannot trust to a mere
composition of qualities. In that case, it becomes tame and
vapid. It must create, so that in the experience of the be-

holder there appear Individuals as it were immortal by their appeal to the deep recesses of feeling. For this reason, it is hardly a paradox to say, that a great civilization interfused with Art presents the world to its members clothed with the Appearance of immortality. The Individuals it presents for Appearance belong equally to all time.

This is exactly what we find in great Art. The very details of its compositions live supremely in their own right. They make their own claim to individuality, and yet contribute to the whole. Each such detail receives an access of grandeur from the whole, and yet manifests an individuality claiming attention in its own right.

As an example, the sculpture and the tracery in a Gothic cathedral—Chartres for instance—subserve the harmony. They lead the eye upward to the vaulting above, and they lead the eye onward horizontally to the supreme symbolism of the altar. They claim attention by their beauty of detail. Yet they shun attention by guiding the eye to grasp the sig, nificance of the whole. Yet the sculpture and the tracery could not perform this service apart from their supreme individuality, evoking a wealth of feeling in their own right. Each detail claims a permanent existence for its own sake, and then surrenders it for the sake of the whole composition.

Again, the value of discord arises from this importance of the forceful individuality of the details. The discord enhances the whole, when it serves to substantiate the individuality of the parts. It brings into emphatic feeling their claim to existence in their own right. It rescues the whole from the tameness of a merely qualitative harmony.

Also the importance of truth now emerges. Truth of belief is important, both in itself and in its consequences. But above all, there emerges the importance of the truthful relation of Appearance to Reality. A grave defect in truth limits the extent to which any force of feeling can be summoned from the recesses of Reality. The falsehood thus lacks the magic by which a beauty beyond the power of speech to express can be called into being, as if by the wand of an enchanter. It is for these reasons that the civilization of a society requires the virtues of Truth, Beauty, Adventure and **Art.**

CHAPTER XX

PEACE

SECTION I. Our discussions have concerned themselves with specializations in History, of seven Platonic generalities, namely, The Ideas, The Physical Elements, The Psyche, The Eros, The Harmony, The Mathematical Relations, The Receptacle. The historical references have been selected and grouped with the purpose of illustrating the energizing of specializations of these seven general notions among the peoples of Western Europe, driving them towards their civilization.

Finally, in this fourth and last Part of the book, those essential qualities, whose joint realization in social life constitutes civilization, are being considered. Four such qualities have, so far, been examined:—Truth, Beauty, Adventure, Art.

SECTION II. Something is still lacking. It is difficult to state it in terms that are wide enough. Also, where clearly distinguished and exposed in all its bearings, it assumes an air of exaggeration. Habitually it is lurking on the edge of consciousness, a modifying agency. It clings to our notion of the Platonic 'Harmony', as a sort of atmosphere. It is somewhat at variance with the notion of the 'Eros'. Also the Platonic 'Ideas' and 'Mathematical Relations' seem to kill it by their absence of 'life and motion'. Apart from it, the pursuit of 'Truth, Beauty, Adventure, Art' can be ruthless, hard, cruel; and thus, as the history of the Italian Renaissance illustrates, lacking in some essential quality of civilization. The notions of 'tenderness' and of 'love' are too narrow, important though they be. We require the concept of some more general quality, from which 'tenderness' emerges as a specialization. We are in a way seeking for the notion of a Harmony of Harmonies, which shall bind together the other four qualities, so as to exclude from our notion of civilization the restless egotism with which they have often in fact been pursued. 'Impersonality' is too dead a notion, and 'Tenderness' too narrow. I choose the term 'Peace' for that Harmony of Harmonies which calms destructive turbulence and completes civilization. Thus a society is to be termed civilized whose members participate in the five qualities—Truth, Beauty, Adventure, Art, Peace.

SECTION III. The Peace that is here meant is not the negative conception of anæsthesia. It is a positive feeling which crowns the 'life and motion' of the soul. It is hard to define and difficult to speak of. It is not a hope for the future, nor is it an interest in present details. It is a broadening of feeling due to the emergence of some deep metaphysical insight, unverbalized and yet momentous in its coördination of values. Its first effect is the removal of the stress of acquisitive feeling arising from the soul's preoccupation with itself. Thus Peace carries with it a surpassing of personality. There is an inversion of relative values. It is primarily a trust in the efficacy of Beauty. It is a sense that fineness of achievement is as it were a key unlocking treasures that the narrow nature of things would keep remote. There is thus involved a grasp of infinitude, an appeal beyond boundaries. Its emotional effect is the subsidence of turbulence which inhibits. More accurately, it preserves the springs of energy, and at the same time masters them for the avoidance of paralyzing distractions. The trust in the self-justification of Beauty introduces faith, where reason fails to reveal the details.

The experience of Peace is largely beyond the control of purpose. It comes as a gift. The deliberate aim at Peace very easily passes into its bastard substitute, Anæsthesia. In other words, in the place of a quality of 'life and motion', there is substituted their destruction. Thus Peace is the removal of inhibition and not its introduction. It results in a wider sweep of conscious interest. It enlarges the field of attention. Thus Peace is self-control at its widest,—at the width where the 'self' has been lost, and interest has been transferred to coördinations wider than personality. Here the real motive interests of the spirit are meant, and not the superficial play of discursive ideas. Peace is helped by such superficial width, and also promotes it. In fact it is largely for this reason that Peace is so essential for civilization. It is the barrier against narrowness. One of its fruits is that passion whose existence Hume denied, the love of mankind as such.

SECTION IV. The meaning of Peace is most clearly understood by considering it in its relation to the tragic issues which are essential in the nature of things. Peace is the understanding of tragedy, and at the same time its preservation.

We have seen that there can be no real halt of civilization in the indefinite repetition of a perfected ideal. Staleness sets in. And this fatigue is nothing other than the creeping growth of anæsthesia, whereby that social group is gradually sinking towards nothingness. The defining characteristics are losing their importance. There may be no pain or conscious loss. There is merely a slow paralysis of surprise. And apart from surprise, intensity of feeling collapses.

Decay, Transition, Loss, Displacement belong to the

essence of the Creative Advance. The new direction of aim is initiated by Spontaneity, an element of confusion. The enduring Societies with their rise, culmination, and decay, are devices to combine the necessities of Harmony and Freshness. There is the deep underlying Harmony of Nature, as it were a fluid, flexible support; and on its surface the ripples of social efforts, harmonizing and clashing in their aims at ways of satisfaction. The lower types of physical objects can have a vast endurance of inorganic life. The higher types, involving animal life and the dominance of a personality primarily mental, preserve their zest by the quick succession of stages from birth, culmination, to death. As soon as high consciousness is reached, the enjoyment of existence is entwined with pain, frustration, loss, tragedy. Amid the passing of so much beauty, so much heroism, so much daring, Peace is then the intuition of permanence. It keeps vivid the sensitiveness to the tragedy; and it sees the tragedy as a living agent persuading the world to aim at fineness beyond the faded level of surrounding fact. Each tragedy is the disclosure of an ideal:—What might have been, and was not: What can be. The tragedy was not in vain. This survival power in motive force, by reason of appeal to reserves of Beauty, marks the difference between the tragic evil and the gross evil. The inner feeling belonging to this grasp of the service of tragedy is Peace—the purification of the emotions.

SECTION V. The deepest definition of Youth is, Life as yet untouched by tragedy. And the finest flower of youth is to know the lesson in advance of the experience, undimmed. The question here for discussion is how the intuition of Peace asserts itself apart from its disclosure in tragedy. Evidently observation of the earlier stages of personal life will afford the clearest evidence.

Youth is distinguished for its whole-hearted absorption in personal enjoyments and personal discomforts. Quick pleasure and quick pain, quick laughter and quick tears, quick absence of care, and quick diffidence, quick courage and quick fear, are conjointly characters of youth. In other words, immediate absorption in its own occupations. On this side, Youth is too chequered to be termed a happy period. It is vivid rather than happy. The memories of youth are better to live through, than is youth itself. For except in extreme cases, memory is apt to count the sunny hours. Youth is not peaceful in any ordinary sense of that term. In youth despair is overwhelming. There is then no tomorrow, no memory of disasters survived.

The short-sightedness of youth matches the scantiness of its experience. The issues of its action are beyond its ken, perhaps with literature supplying a delusory sense of knowledge. Thus generosity and cruelty are equally natural, by reason of the fact that their full effects lie beyond conscious anticipation.

All this is the veriest commonplace in the characterization of Youth. Nor does the modern wealth of social literature in any fundamental way alter the case. The reason for its statement here is to note that these features of character belong to all animals at all ages, including human beings at every stage of their lives. The differences only lie in relative proportions. Also the success of language in conveying information is vastly over-rated, especially in learned circles. Not only is language highly elliptical, but also nothing can supply the defect of first-hand experience of types cognate to the things explicitly mentioned. The general truth of Hume's doctrine as to the necessity of first-hand impressions is inexorable.

There is another side. Youth is peculiarly susceptible to

appeals for beauty of conduct. It understands motives which
presuppose the irrelevance of its own person. Such motives
are understood as contributing to the magnification of its
own interests. Its very search for personal experience thus
elicits impersonality, self-forgetfulness. Youth forgets itself
in its own ardour. Of course, not always. For it can fall in
love. But the test of the better nature, so happily plentiful, is that love passes from selfishness to devotion. The
higher forms of love break down the narrow self-regarding
motives.

When youth has once grasped where Beauty dwells—
with a real knowledge and not as a mere matter of literary
phraseology in some poetic, scriptural, or psychological version—when youth has once grasped, its self-surrender is
absolute. The vision may pass. It may traverse consciousness in a flash. Some natures may never permit it to emerge
into attention. But Youth is peculiarly liable to the vision
of that Peace, which is the harmony of the soul's activities
with ideal aims that lie beyond any personal satisfaction.

SECTION VI. The vigour of civilized societies is preserved
by the wide-spread sense that high aims are worth-while.
Vigorous societies harbour a certain extravagance of objectives, so that men wander beyond the safe provision of personal gratifications. All strong interests easily become impersonal, the love of a good job well done. There is a sense
of harmony about such an accomplishment, the Peace
brought by something worth-while. Such personal gratification arises from aim beyond personality.

The converse tendency is at least equally noticeable; the
egotistic desire for fame—'that last infirmity'—is an inversion of the social impulse, and yet presupposes it. The tendency shows itself in the trivialities of child-life, as well as
in the career of some conqueror before whom mankind

trembled. In the widest sense, it is the craving for sympathy. It involves the feeling that each act of experience is a central reality, claiming all things as its own. The world has then no justification except as a satisfaction of such claims. But the point is that the desire for admiring attention becomes futile except in the presence of an audience fit to render it. The pathology of feeling, so often exemplified, consists in the destruction of the audience for the sake of the fame. There is also, of course, the sheer love of command, finally devoid of high purpose. The complexity of human motive, the entwinement of its threads, is infinite. The point, which is here relevant, is that the zest of human adventure presupposes for its material a scheme of things with a worth beyond any single occasion. However perverted, there is required for zest that craving to stand conspicuous in this scheme of things as well as the purely personal pleasure in the exercise of faculties. It is the final contentment aimed at by the soul in its retreat to egoism, as distinct from anæsthesia. In this, it is beyond human analysis to detect exactly where the perversion begins to taint the intuition of Peace. Milton's phrase states the whole conclusion —'That last infirmity of noble mind'.

Fame is a cold, hard notion. Another half-way house between the extreme ecstasy of Peace and the extreme of selfish desire, is the love of particular individual things. Such love is the completion almost necessary for finite reality, and all reality is in some way finite. In the extreme of love, such as mother's love, all personal desire is transferred to the thing loved, as a desire for its perfection. Personal life has here evidently passed beyond itself, but with explicit, definite limitation to particular realities. It is partly based upon the importance of the individuality of details for the æsthetic value of objective appearance. This has been dis-

cussed before.[1] This aspect of personal love is simply a cling-
ing to a condition for selfish happiness. There is no transcendence of personality.

But some closeness of status, such as the relation of parent
to child or the relation of marriage, can produce the love
of self-devotion where the potentialities of the loved object
are felt passionately as a claim that it find itself in a friendly
Universe. Such love is really an intense feeling as to how
the harmony of the world should be realized in particular
objects. It is the feeling as to what would happen if right
could triumph in a beautiful world, with discord routed.
It is the passionate desire for the beautiful result, in this
instance. Such love is distracting, nerve-racking. But, unless darkened by utter despair, it involves deep feeling of an
aim in the Universe, winning such triumph as is possible to
it. It is the sense of Eros, hovering between Peace as the
crown of Youth and Peace as the issue of Tragedy.

SECTION VII. The general health of social life is taken care
of by formularized moral precepts, and formularized religious beliefs and religious institutions. All of these explicitly
express the doctrine that the perfection of life resides in aims
beyond the individual person in question.

It is a doctrine of great generality, capable of a large
variety of specialization, not all of them mutually consistent.
For example, consider the patriotism of the Roman farmers,
in the full vigour of the Republic. Certainly Regulus did not
return to Carthage, with the certainty of torture and death,
cherishing any mystic notions of another life—either a
Christian Heaven or a Buddhist Nirvana. He was a practical
man, and his ideal aim was the Roman Republic flourishing
in this world. But this aim transcended his individual personality; for this aim he entirely sacrificed every gratification

---

[1] Cf. Ch. XVII, Sect. VIII, and Ch. XIX, Sect. IV.

bounded by such limits. For him there was something in the world which could not be expressed as sheer personal gratification—and yet in thus sacrificing himself, his personal existence rose to its full height. He may have been mistaken in his estimate of the worth of the Roman Republic. The point is that with that belief, he achieved magnificence by the sacrifice of himself.

In this estimate, Regulus has not in any way proved himself to be exceptional. His conduct showed heroism that is unusual. But his estimate of the worth of such conduct has evoked widest assent. The Roman farmers agreed; and generation after generation, amid all the changes of history, have agreed by the instinctive pulse of emotion as the tale is handed down.

Moral codes have suffered from the exaggerated claims made for them. The dogmatic fallacy has here done its worst. Each such code has been put out by a God on a mountain top, or by a Saint in a cave, or by a divine Despot on a throne, or, at the lowest, by ancestors with a wisdom beyond later question. In any case, each code is incapable of improvement; and unfortunately in details they fail to agree either with each other or with our existing moral intuitions. The result is that the world is shocked, or amused, by the sight of saintly old people hindering in the name of morality the removal of obvious brutalities from a legal system. Some *Acta Sanctorum* go ill with civilization.

The details of these codes are relative to the social circumstances of the immediate environment—life at a certain date on 'the fertile fringe' of the Arabian desert, life on the lower slopes of the Himalayan Mountains, life on the plains of China, or on the plains of India, life on the delta of some great river. Again the meaning of the critical terms is shifting and ambiguous, for example, the notions of ownership,

family, marriage, murder, God. Conduct which in one environment and at one stage produces its measure of harmonious satisfaction, in other surroundings at another stage
is destructively degrading. Each society has its own type of
perfection, and puts up with certain blots, at that stage inevitable. Thus the notion that there are certain regulative
notions, sufficiently precise to prescribe details of conduct,
for all reasonable beings on Earth, in every planet, and in
every star-system, is at once to be put aside. That is the
notion of the one type of perfection at which the Universe
aims. All realization of the Good is finite, and necessarily
excludes certain other types.

But what these codes do witness to, and what their interpretation by seers of various races throughout history does
witness to, is the aim at a social perfection. Such a realized
fact is conceived as an abiding perfection in the nature of
things, a treasure for all ages. It is not a romance of thought,
it is a fact of Nature. For example, in one sense the Roman
Republic declined and fell; in another sense, it stands a
stubborn fact in the Universe. To perish is to assume a new
function in the process of generation. Devotion to the Republic magnified the type of personal satisfactions for those
who conformed their purposes to its maintenance. Such conformation of purpose to ideal beyond personal limitations is
the conception of that Peace with which the wise man can
face his fate, master of his soul.

SECTION VIII. The wide scope of the notion of 'society'
requires attention. Transcendence begins with the leap from
the actuality of the immediate occasion to the notion of
personal existence, which is a society of occasions. In terms
of human life, the soul is a society. Care for the future of
personal existence, regret or pride in its past, are alike feelings which leap beyond the bounds of the sheer actuality

of the present. It is in the nature of the present that it should thus transcend itself by reason of the immanence in it of the 'other'. But there is no necessity as to the scale of emphasis that this fact of nature should receive. It belongs to the civilization of consciousness, to magnify the large sweep of harmony.

Beyond the soul, there are other societies, and societies of societies. There is the animal body ministering to the soul: there are families, groups of families, nations, species, groups involving different species associated in the joint enterprise of keeping alive. These various societies, each in its measure, claim loyalties and loves. In human history the various responses to these claims disclose the essential transcendence of each individual actuality beyond itself. The stubborn reality of the absolute self-attainment of each individual is bound up with a relativity which it issues from and issues into. The analysis of the various strands of relativity is the analysis of the social structure of the Universe, as in this epoch.

Although particular codes of morality reflect, more or less imperfectly, the special circumstances of social structure concerned, it is natural to seek for some highly general principles underlying all such codes. Such generalities should reflect the very notions of the harmonizing of harmonies, and of particular individual actualities as the sole authentic reality. These are the principles of the generality of harmony, and of the importance of the individual. The first means 'order', and the second means 'love'. Between the two there is a suggestion of opposition. For 'order' is impersonal; and love, above all things, is personal. The antithesis is solved by rating types of order in relative importance according to their success in magnifying the individual actualities, that is to say, in promoting strength of experience.

Also in rating the individual on the double basis, partly on the intrinsic strength of its own experience, and partly on its influence in the promotion of a high-grade type of order. These two grounds in part coalesce. For a weak individual exerts a weak influence. The essence of Peace is that the individual whose strength of experience is founded upon this ultimate intuition, thereby is extending the influence of the source of all order.

The moral code is the behaviour-patterns which in the environment for which it is designed will promote the evolution of that environment towards its proper perfection.

SECTION IX. The attainment of Truth belongs to the essence of Peace. By this it is meant, that the intuition constituting the realization of Peace has as its objective that Harmony whose inter-connections involve Truth. A defect in Truth is a limitation to Harmony. There can be no secure efficacy in the Beauty which hides within itself the dislocations of falsehood.

The truth or falsehood of propositions is not directly to the point in this demand for Truth. Since each proposition is yoked to a contradictory proposition, and since of these one must be true and the other false, there are necessarily as many false as there are true propositions. This bare 'truth or falsehood' of propositions is a comparatively superficial factor affecting the discursive interests of the intellect. The essential truth that Peace demands is the conformation of Appearance to Reality. There is the Reality from which the occasion of experience springs—a Reality of inescapable, stubborn fact; and there is the Appearance with which the occasion attains its final individuality—an Appearance including its adjustment of the Universe by simplification, valuation, transmutation, anticipation. A feeling of dislocation of Appearance from Reality is the final destructive force, robbing life of its zest for adventure. It spells the decadence of civilization, by stripping from it the very reason for its existence.

There can be no necessity governing this conformation. Sense-perception, which dominates the appearance of things, in its own nature re-arranges, and thus in a way distorts. Also there can be no mere blunt truth about the Appearance which it provides. In its own nature Sense-perception is an interpretation, and this interpretation may be completely misleading. If there were a necessary conformation of Appearance to Reality, then Morality would vanish. There is no morality about the multiplication table, whose items are necessarily linked. Art would also be a meaningless term. For it presupposes the efficacy of purpose. Art is an issue of Adventure.

The question for discussion is whether there exists any factor in the Universe constituting a general drive towards the conformation of Appearance to Reality. This drive would then constitute a factor in each occasion persuading an aim at such truth as is proper to the special appearance in question. This concept of truth, proper to each special appearance, would mean that the appearance has not built itself up by the inclusion of elements that are foreign to the reality from which it springs. The appearance will then be a generalization and an adaptation of emphasis; but not an importation of qualities and relations without any corresponding exemplification in the reality. This concept of truth is in fact the denial of the doctrine of Appearance which lies on the surface of Kant's *Critique of Pure Reason*. It is a denial of his answer to the question,—How are synthetic *a priori* judgments possible? It is at least the introduction of guarding limitations, which Kant explicitly in that work does not introduce.

SECTION X. The answer to this question must issue from a survey of the factors in terms of which individual experience has been interpreted:—The antecedent World from which each occasion springs, a World of many occasions presenting for the new creature harmonies and discords: the easy road of Anæsthesia by which discordant factors are dismissed into irrelevance: the activity of the mental poles in building conceptual experience into patterns of feeling which rescue discords from loss: the spontaneity of the mental action and its persuasion by a sense of relevance: the selective nature of consciousness and its initial failure to discriminate the deeper sources of feeling: that there is no agency in abstraction from actual occasions, and that existence involves implication in agency: the sense of a unity of many occasions with a value beyond that of any individual occasion; for example, the soul, the complete animal, the social group of animals, the material body, the physical epoch: the aim at immediate individual contentment.

The justification for the suggestion derived from this group of factors must mainly rest upon their direct elucidation of first-hand experience. They are not, and should not be, the result of an argument. For all argument must rest upon premises more fundamental than the conclusions. Discussion of fundamental notions is merely for the purpose of disclosing their coherence, their compatibility, and the specializations which can be derived from their conjunction.

The above set of metaphysical notions rests itself upon the ordinary, average experience of mankind, properly interpreted. But there is a further set for which the appeal lies to occasions and modes of experience which in some degree are exceptional. It must be remembered that the present level of average waking human experience was at one time exceptional among the ancestors of mankind. We are justified therefore in appealing to those modes of experience which in our direct judgment stand above the average level. The gradual emergence of such modes, and their effect on human history, have been among the themes of this book in its appeal to history. We have found the growth of Art: its gradual sublimation into the pursuit of Truth and Beauty: the sublimation of the egoistic aim by its inclusion of the transcendent whole: the youthful zest in the transcendent aim: the sense of tragedy: the sense of evil: the persuasion towards Adventure beyond achieved perfection: the sense of Peace.

SECTION XI. The concept of Civilization, as developed up to this stage, remains inherently incomplete. No logical argument can demonstrate this gap. Such arguments are merely subsidiary helps for the conscious realization of metaphysical intuitions.—*Non in dialectica complacuit Deo salvum facere populum suum.* This saying, quoted by Cardinal Newman,[2] should be the motto of every metaphysician. He is seeking, amid the dim recesses of his ape-like consciousness and beyond the reach of dictionary language, for the premises implicit in all reasoning. The speculative methods of metaphysics are dangerous, easily perverted. So is all Adventure; but Adventure belongs to the essence of civilization.

The incompleteness of the concept relates to the notion of Transcendence, the feeling essential for Adventure, Zest, and Peace. This feeling requires for its understanding that we supplement the notion of the Eros by including it in the concept of an Adventure in the Universe as One. This Adventure embraces all particular occasions but as an actual fact stands beyond any one of them. It is, as it were, the complement to Plato's Receptacle, its exact oppo-

[2] *Grammar of Assent.*

site, yet equally required for the unity of all things. In every
way, it is contrary to the Receptacle. The Receptacle is bare
of all forms: the Unity of Adventure includes the Eros
which is the living urge towards all possibilities, claiming
the goodness of their realization. The Platonic Receptacle is
void, abstract from all individual occasions: The Unity of
Adventure includes among its components all individual
realities, each with the importance of the personal or social
fact to which it belongs. Such individual importance in the
components belongs to the essence of Beauty. In this Supreme Adventure, the Reality which the Adventure trans-
mutes into its Unity of Appearance, requires the real occasions of the advancing world each claiming its due share of
attention. This Appearance, thus enjoyed, is the final Beauty
with which the Universe achieves its justification. This
Beauty has always within it the renewal derived from the
Advance of the Temporal World. It is the immanence of
the Great Fact including this initial Eros and this final
Beauty which constitutes the zest of self-forgetful transcendence belonging to Civilization at its height.

At the heart of the nature of things, there are always the
dream of youth and the harvest of tragedy. The Adventure
of the Universe starts with the dream and reaps tragic
Beauty. This is the secret of the union of Zest with Peace:—
That the suffering attains its end in a Harmony of Harmonies. The immediate experience of this Final Fact, with
its union of Youth and Tragedy, is the sense of Peace. In
this way the World receives its persuasion towards such perfections as are possible for its diverse individual occasions.

INDEX OF PROPER NAMES

INDEX OF TERMS

Absolute Being, 142
Absolute Individuality, 80, 235
Absolute Reality, 227
Absolute Self-Attainment, 227
Absoluteness, 54-56
Abstraction, 187
Actuality, 172, 230, 242, 347, 354
Adventure, vii, 332, 350, 352-381
Æsthetic Destruction, 330
Affective Tone, 226, 315
Agencies, Intellectual, 13
Agency, 253, 254
Agriculture, 139-141
Alexandrian Scholarship, 150, 155
Alexandrian Theologians, 166, 167
American Civil War, 26, 29
Anæsthesia, 329, 334, 355, 367, 368
Anglican Settlement, 205
Animal Body, 263, 275, 376
Anticipation, 248, 249, 340, 343, 344
Appeal to History, 207, 208, 211
Appearance, 309-322, 332-348, 355, 362, 363, 377-381
Appearance and Reality, 268-282
Arabs, 133
Argument, 379
Arian Solution, 216
Aristotle's Logic, 169-171, 356
Art, 277, 320, 321, 344-353, 364-381
Association, 300
Association of Ideas, 234
Atoms, 155, 156, 159, 169, 227
Atomicity, 238
Atomism, 159, 160, 168
Autonomy, 327, 328

Background, 334
Beautiful, 328, 329
Beauty, 12, 153, 154, 190, 309, 324-351, 353, 365-381
Body, 243
Body, Animal, 263, 275, 376
Body, Human, 242, 243, 274, 275, 281, 349
Brain, 290

British Government, The, 23
Brotherhood, 46
Brotherhood of Man, 28, 35, 37
Buddhism, 41
Business Mind, 123-125
Byzantines, 104

Capriciousness, 141
Carthaginians, 30
Catholic Church, 34, 74, 107
Catholic Missionaries, 28, 37
Catholic Theology, 212
Causal Action, 153
Causal Independence, 251, 252, 278
Causation, 237, 251
Certainties of Science, 198
Chance, 157, 158
Chaos, 147
Christian Ethics, 105, 107
Christianity, 18-20, 41, 102, 108, 133
Christians, 69
Civilization, vii, ix, 9, 10, 25, 95, 96, 105-108, 127, 140, 181, 188, 212, 218-220, 348-352, 357-363, 380, 381
Cities, 120-122
Classification, Aristotelian, 120-122, 176, 183, 196
Coercive Forces, 213
Commerce, 83, 88-125
Common Law, 36, 81
Communal Customs, 52
Communication, 171, 172
Compatibility, 188
Competition, 35, 38, 39, 42
Complete Fact, 203
Composition, 197
Compulsion, 6, 71, 87, 89, 106, 108, 213, 218
Conceptual Order, The, 198
Conceptual Prehensions, 250
Concern, 226, 232
Concrescence, 303, 304
Conformal Feeling, 235, 236, 326
Conformal Inheritance, 239

387